DICTIONARY

THEME–BASED

British English Collection

ENGLISH-
THAI

The most useful words
To expand your lexicon and sharpen
your language skills

9000 words

Theme-based dictionary British English-Thai vocabulary - 9000 words
By Andrey Taranov

T&P Books vocabularies are intended for helping you learn, memorize and review foreign words. The dictionary is divided into themes, covering all major spheres of everyday activities, business, science, culture, etc.

The process of learning words using T&P Books' theme-based dictionaries gives you the following advantages:

- Correctly grouped source information predetermines success at subsequent stages of word memorization
- Availability of words derived from the same root allowing memorization of word units (rather than separate words)
- Small units of words facilitate the process of establishing associative links needed for consolidation of vocabulary
- Level of language knowledge can be estimated by the number of learned words

T&P Books Publishing
www.tpbooks.com

This book is also available in E-book formats.
Please visit www.tpbooks.com or the major online bookstores.

THAI VOCABULARY
British English collection

T&P Books vocabularies are intended to help you learn, memorize, and review foreign words. The vocabulary contains over 9000 commonly used words arranged thematically.

- Vocabulary contains the most commonly used words
- Recommended as an addition to any language course
- Meets the needs of beginners and advanced learners of foreign languages
- Convenient for daily use, revision sessions, and self-testing activities
- Allows you to assess your vocabulary

Special features of the vocabulary

- Words are organized according to their meaning, not alphabetically
- Words are presented in three columns to facilitate the reviewing and self-testing processes
- Words in groups are divided into small blocks to facilitate the learning process
- The vocabulary offers a convenient and simple transcription of each foreign word

The vocabulary has 256 topics including:

Basic Concepts, Numbers, Colors, Months, Seasons, Units of Measurement, Clothing & Accessories, Food & Nutrition, Restaurant, Family Members, Relatives, Character, Feelings, Emotions, Diseases, City, Town, Sightseeing, Shopping, Money, House, Home, Office, Working in the Office, Import & Export, Marketing, Job Search, Sports, Education, Computer, Internet, Tools, Nature, Countries, Nationalities and more …

TABLE OF CONTENTS

PRONUNCIATION GUIDE

T&P phonetic alphabet	Thai example	English example

Vowels

[a]	ห้า [hâː] – hâa *	shorter than in 'ask'
[e]	เป็นลม [pen lom] – bpen lom	elm, medal
[i]	วินัย [wi? naj] – wí–nai	shorter than in 'feet'
[o]	โกน [koːn] – gohn	pod, John
[u]	ขุนเคือง [kʰùn kʰɯːaŋ] – khùn kheuang	book
[aa]	ราคา [raː kʰaː] – raa–khaa	calf, palm
[oo]	ภูมิใจ [pʰuːm tɕaj] – phoom jai	pool, room
[ee]	บัญชี [ban tɕʰiː] – ban–chee	feet, meter
[ɯ]	เดือน [dɯːan] – deuan	similar to a longue schwa sound
[ɤ]	เงิน [ŋɤn] – ngern	e in 'the'
[ae]	แปล [plɛː] – bplae	longer than 'bed', 'fell'
[ay]	เลข [lêːk] – lâyk	longer than in bell
[ai]	ไปป์ [paj] – bpai	time, white
[oi]	โพย [pʰoːj] – phoi	oil, boy, point
[ya]	สัญญา [sǎn jaː] – sǎn–yaa	Kenya, piano
[ɤːi]	อบเชย [ʔòp tɕʰɤːj] – òp–choie	combination [ə:i]
[i:a]	หน้าเชียว [nâː sĭːaw] – nâa sieow	year, here

Initial consonant sounds

[b]	บาง [baːŋ] – baang	baby, book
[d]	สีแดง [sĭː dɛːŋ] – sĕe daeng	day, doctor
[f]	มันฝรั่ง [man fà ràŋ] – man fà–ràng	face, food
[h]	เฮลซิงกิ [heːn siŋ kì?] – hayn–sing–gì	home, have
[y]	ยี่สิบ [jîː sìp] – yêe sìp	yes, New York
[g]	กรง [kroŋ] – grorng	game, gold
[kh]	เลขา [le: kʰǎː] – lay–khǎa	work hard
[l]	เล็ก [lék] – lék	lace, people
[m]	เมลอน [me: lɔːn] – may–lorn	magic, milk
[n]	หนัง [nǎŋ] – nǎng	name, normal
[ng]	เงือก [ŋɯːak] – ngêuak	English, ring
[bp]	เป็น [pen] – bpen	pencil, private
[ph]	เผา [pʰǎw] – phào	top hat
[r]	เบอร์รี่ [bɤː rîː] – ber–rêe	rice, radio
[s]	ซอน [sôn] – sôrn	city, boss
[dt]	ดนตรี [don triː] – don–dtree	tourist, trip
[j]	ปั่นจั่น [pân tɕàn] – bpân jàn	cheer

11

T&P phonetic alphabet   **Thai example**   **English example**

[ch]   วิชา [wi? tɕʰa:] – wí–chaa   hitchhiker
[th]   แถว [tʰɛ:w] – thăe   don't have
[w]   เคียว [kʰi:aw] – khieow   vase, winter

Final consonant sounds

[k]   แม่เหล็ก [mɛ: lèk] – mâe lèk   clock, kiss
[m]   เพิ่ม [pʰɤ:m] – phêrm   magic, milk
[n]   เนียน [ni:an] – nian   name, normal
[ng]   เป็นห่วง [pen hù:aŋ] – bpen hùang   English, ring
[p]   ไม่ขยับ [mâj kʰà ja p] – mâi khà–yàp   pencil, private
[t]   ลูกเป็ด [lû:k pèt] – lôok bpèt   tourist, trip

Comments

    Mid tone - [ā] การคูณ [gaan khon]
Low tone - [à] แจกจ่าย [jàek jàai]
Falling tone - [â] ยุติม [dtâem]
High tone - [á] แซ็กโซโฟน [sáek-soh-fohn]
Rising tone - [ǎ] เนินเขา [nern khǎo]

ABBREVIATIONS
used in the dictionary

English abbreviations

ab.	-	about
adj	-	adjective
adv	-	adverb
anim.	-	animate
as adj	-	attributive noun used as adjective
e.g.	-	for example
etc.	-	et cetera
fam.	-	familiar
fem.	-	feminine
form.	-	formal
inanim.	-	inanimate
masc.	-	masculine
math	-	mathematics
mil.	-	military
n	-	noun
pl	-	plural
pron.	-	pronoun
sb	-	somebody
sing.	-	singular
sth	-	something
v aux	-	auxiliary verb
vi	-	intransitive verb
vi, vt	-	intransitive, transitive verb
vt	-	transitive verb

BASIC CONCEPTS

Basic concepts. Part 1

1. Pronouns

you	คุณ	khun
he	เขา	khǎo
she	เธอ	ther
it	มัน	man

we	เรา	rao
you (to a group)	คุณทั้งหลาย	khun tháng lǎai
you (polite, sing.)	คุณ	khun
you (polite, pl)	คุณทั้งหลาย	khun tháng lǎai

| they (masc.) | เขา | khǎo |
| they (fem.) | เธอ | ther |

2. Greetings. Salutations. Farewells

Hello! (fam.)	สวัสดี!	sà-wàt-dee
Hello! (form.)	สวัสดี ครับ/ค่ะ!	sà-wàt-dee khráp/khâ
Good morning!	อรุณสวัสดี!	a-run sà-wàt
Good afternoon!	สวัสดีตอนบ่าย	sà-wàt-dee dtorn-bàai
Good evening!	สวัสดีตอนค่ำ	sà-wàt-dee dtorn-khâm

to say hello	ทักทาย	thák thaai
Hi! (hello)	สวัสดี!	sà-wàt-dee
greeting (n)	คำทักทาย	kham thák thaai
to greet (vt)	ทักทาย	thák thaai
How are you? (form.)	คุณสบายดีไหม?	khun sà-baai dee mǎi
How are you? (fam.)	สบายดีไหม?	sà-baai dee mǎi
What's new?	มีอะไรใหม?	mee à-rai mài

Goodbye!	ลาก่อน!	laa gòrn
Bye!	บาย!	baai
See you soon!	พบกันใหม่	phóp gan mài
Farewell! (to a friend)	ลาก่อน!	laa gòrn
Farewell! (form.)	สวัสดี!	sà-wàt-dee
to say goodbye	บอกลา	bòrk laa
Cheers!	ลาก่อน!	laa gòrn

Thank you! Cheers!	ขอบคุณ!	khòrp khun
Thank you very much!	ขอบคุณมาก!	khòrp khun mâak
My pleasure!	ยินดีช่วย	yin dee chûay
Don't mention it!	ไม่เป็นไร	mâi bpen rai

It was nothing	ไม่เป็นไร	mâi bpen rai
Excuse me! (fam.)	ขอโทษที!	khǒr thôht thee
Excuse me! (form.)	ขอโทษ ครับ/ค่ะ!	khǒr thôht khráp / khâ
to excuse (forgive)	ให้อภัย	hâi a-phai

to apologize (vi)	ขอโทษ	khǒr thôht
My apologies	ขอโทษ	khǒr thôht
I'm sorry!	ขอโทษ!	khǒr thôht
to forgive (vt)	อภัย	a-phai
It's okay! (that's all right)	ไม่เป็นไร!	mâi bpen rai
please (adv)	โปรด	bpròht

Don't forget!	อย่าลืม!	yàa leum
Certainly!	แน่นอน!	nâe norn
Of course not!	ไม่ใช่แน่!	mâi châi nâe
Okay! (I agree)	โอเค!	oh-khay
That's enough!	พอแล้ว	phor láew

3. How to address

Excuse me, ...	ขอโทษ	khǒr thôht
mister, sir	ทาน	thâan
madam	คุณ	khun
miss	คุณ	khun
young man	พ่อหนุ่ม	phôr nùm
young man (little boy)	หนู	nǒo
miss (little girl)	หนู	nǒo

4. Cardinal numbers. Part 1

0 zero	ศูนย์	sǒon
1 one	หนึ่ง	nèung
2 two	สอง	sǒrng
3 three	สาม	sǎam
4 four	สี่	sèe

5 five	ห้า	hâa
6 six	หก	hòk
7 seven	เจ็ด	jèt
8 eight	แปด	bpàet
9 nine	เก้า	gâo

10 ten	สิบ	sìp
11 eleven	สิบเอ็ด	sìp èt
12 twelve	สิบสอง	sìp sǒrng
13 thirteen	สิบสาม	sìp sǎam
14 fourteen	สิบสี่	sìp sèe

15 fifteen	สิบห้า	sìp hâa
16 sixteen	สิบหก	sìp hòk
17 seventeen	สิบเจ็ด	sìp jèt
18 eighteen	สิบแปด	sìp bpàet

19 nineteen	สิบเก้า	sìp gâo
20 twenty	ยี่สิบ	yêe sìp
21 twenty-one	ยี่สิบเอ็ด	yêe sìp èt
22 twenty-two	ยี่สิบสอง	yêe sìp sŏrng
23 twenty-three	ยี่สิบสาม	yêe sìp săam
30 thirty	สามสิบ	săam sìp
31 thirty-one	สามสิบเอ็ด	săam-sìp-èt
32 thirty-two	สามสิบสอง	săam-sìp-sŏrng
33 thirty-three	สามสิบสาม	săam-sìp-săam
40 forty	สี่สิบ	sèe sìp
41 forty-one	สี่สิบเอ็ด	sèe-sìp-èt
42 forty-two	สี่สิบสอง	sèe-sìp-sŏrng
43 forty-three	สี่สิบสาม	sèe-sìp-săam
50 fifty	ห้าสิบ	hâa sìp
51 fifty-one	ห้าสิบเอ็ด	hâa-sìp-èt
52 fifty-two	ห้าสิบสอง	hâa-sìp-sŏrng
53 fifty-three	หาสิบสาม	hâa-sìp-săam
60 sixty	หกสิบ	hòk sìp
61 sixty-one	หกสิบเอ็ด	hòk-sìp-èt
62 sixty-two	หกสิบสอง	hòk-sìp-sŏrng
63 sixty-three	หกสิบสาม	hòk-sìp-săam
70 seventy	เจ็ดสิบ	jèt sìp
71 seventy-one	เจ็ดสิบเอ็ด	jèt-sìp-èt
72 seventy-two	เจ็ดสิบสอง	jèt-sìp-sŏrng
73 seventy-three	เจ็ดสิบสาม	jèt-sìp-săam
80 eighty	แปดสิบ	bpàet sìp
81 eighty-one	แปดสิบเอ็ด	bpàet-sìp-èt
82 eighty-two	แปดสิบสอง	bpàet-sìp-sŏrng
83 eighty-three	แปดสิบสาม	bpàet-sìp-săam
90 ninety	เก้าสิบ	gâo sìp
91 ninety-one	เก้าสิบเอ็ด	gâo-sìp-èt
92 ninety-two	เก้าสิบสอง	gâo-sìp-sŏrng
93 ninety-three	เกาสิบสาม	gâo-sìp-săam

5. Cardinal numbers. Part 2

100 one hundred	หนึ่งร้อย	nèung rói
200 two hundred	สองร้อย	sŏrng rói
300 three hundred	สามร้อย	săam rói
400 four hundred	สี่ร้อย	sèe rói
500 five hundred	หาร้อย	hâa rói
600 six hundred	หกร้อย	hòk rói
700 seven hundred	เจ็ดร้อย	jèt rói
800 eight hundred	แปดร้อย	bpàet rói
900 nine hundred	เการ้อย	gâo rói
1000 one thousand	หนึ่งพัน	nèung phan

2000 two thousand	สองพัน	sŏrng phan
3000 three thousand	สามพัน	săam phan
10000 ten thousand	หนึ่งหมื่น	nèung mèun
one hundred thousand	หนึ่งแสน	nèung săen
million	ล้าน	láan
billion	พันล้าน	phan láan

6. Ordinal numbers

first (adj)	แรก	râek
second (adj)	ที่สอง	thêe sŏrng
third (adj)	ที่สาม	thêe săam
fourth (adj)	ที่สี่	thêe sèe
fifth (adj)	ที่ห้า	thêe hâa
sixth (adj)	ที่หก	thêe hòk
seventh (adj)	ที่เจ็ด	thêe jèt
eighth (adj)	ที่แปด	thêe bpàet
ninth (adj)	ที่เก้า	thêe gâo
tenth (adj)	ที่สิบ	thêe sìp

7. Numbers. Fractions

fraction	เศษส่วน	sàyt sùan
one half	หนึ่งส่วนสอง	nèung sùan sŏrng
one third	หนึ่งส่วนสาม	nèung sùan săam
one quarter	หนึ่งส่วนสี่	nèung sùan sèe
one eighth	หนึ่งส่วนแปด	nèung sùan bpàet
one tenth	หนึ่งส่วนสิบ	nèung sùan sìp
two thirds	สองส่วนสาม	sŏrng sùan săam
three quarters	สามส่วนสี่	săam sùan sèe

8. Numbers. Basic operations

subtraction	การลบ	gaan lóp
to subtract (vi, vt)	ลบ	lóp
division	การหาร	gaan hăan
to divide (vt)	หาร	hăan
addition	การบวก	gaan bùak
to add up (vt)	บวก	bùak
to add (vi)	เพิ่ม	phêrm
multiplication	การคูณ	gaan khon
to multiply (vt)	คูณ	khoon

9. Numbers. Miscellaneous

digit, figure	ตัวเลข	dtua lâyk
number	เลข	lâyk

numeral	ตัวเลข	dtua lâyk
minus sign	เครื่องหมายลบ	khrêuang măai lóp
plus sign	เครื่องหมายบวก	khrêuang măai bùak
formula	สูตร	sòot

calculation	การนับ	gaan náp
to count (vi, vt)	นับ	náp
to count up	นับ	náp
to compare (vt)	เปรียบเทียบ	bprìap thîap

| How much? | เท่าไหร่? | thâo rài |
| How many? | กี่...? | gèe...? |

sum, total	ผลรวม	phŏn ruam
result	ผลลัพธ์	phŏn láp
remainder	ที่เหลือ	thêe lĕua

a few (e.g., ~ years ago)	สองสาม	sŏrng săam
little (I had ~ time)	นิดหน่อย	nít nòi
few (I have ~ friends)	น้อย	nói

the rest	ที่เหลือ	thêe lĕua
one and a half	หนึ่งครึ่ง	nèung khrêung
dozen	โหล	lŏh

in half (adv)	เป็นสองส่วน	bpen sŏrng sùan
equally (evenly)	เท่าเทียมกัน	thâo thiam gan
half	ครึ่ง	khrêung
time (three ~s)	ครั้ง	khráng

10. The most important verbs. Part 1

to advise (vt)	แนะนำ	náe nam
to agree (say yes)	เห็นด้วย	hĕn dûay
to answer (vi, vt)	ตอบ	dtòrp
to apologize (vi)	ขอโทษ	khŏr thôht
to arrive (vi)	มา	maa

to ask (~ oneself)	ถาม	thăam
to ask (~ sb to do sth)	ขอ	khŏr
to be (vi)	เป็น	bpen

to be afraid	กลัว	glua
to be hungry	หิว	hĭw
to be interested in ...	สนใจใน	sŏn jai nai
to be needed	ต้องการ	dtôrng gaan
to be surprised	ประหลาดใจ	bprà-làat jai

to be thirsty	กระหายน้ำ	grà-hăai náam
to begin (vt)	เริ่ม	rêrm
to belong to ...	เป็นของของ...	bpen khŏrng khŏrng...
to boast (vi)	โอ้อวด	ôh ùat
to break (split into pieces)	แตก	dtàek
to call (~ for help)	เรียก	rîak

can (v aux)	สามารถ	săa-mâat
to catch (vt)	จับ	jàp
to change (vt)	เปลี่ยน	bplìan
to choose (select)	เลือก	lêuak
to come down (the stairs)	ลง	long
to compare (vt)	เปรียบเทียบ	bprìap thîap
to complain (vi, vt)	บน	bòn
to confuse (mix up)	สับสน	sàp sŏn
to continue (vt)	ทำต่อไป	tham dtòr bpai
to control (vt)	ควบคุม	khûap khum
to cook (dinner)	ทำอาหาร	tham aa-hăan
to cost (vt)	ราคา	raa-khaa
to count (add up)	นับ	náp
to count on …	พึ่งพา	phêung phaa
to create (vt)	สร้าง	sâang
to cry (weep)	ร้องให้	rórng hâi

11. The most important verbs. Part 2

to deceive (vi, vt)	หลอก	lòrk
to decorate (tree, street)	ประดับ	bprà-dàp
to defend (a country, etc.)	ปกป้อง	bpòk bpông
to demand (request firmly)	เรียกร้อง	rîak rórng
to dig (vt)	ขุด	khùt
to discuss (vt)	หารือ	hăa-reu
to do (vt)	ทำ	tham
to doubt (have doubts)	สงสัย	sŏng-săi
to drop (let fall)	ทิ้งให้ตก	thíng hâi dtòk
to enter (room, house, etc.)	เข้า	khâo
to excuse (forgive)	ให้อภัย	hâi a-phai
to exist (vi)	มีอยู่	mee yòo
to expect (foresee)	คาดหวัง	khâat wăng
to explain (vt)	อธิบาย	à-thí-baai
to fall (vi)	ตก	dtòk
to fancy (vt)	ชอบ	chôrp
to find (vt)	พบ	phóp
to finish (vt)	จบ	jòp
to fly (vi)	บิน	bin
to follow … (come after)	ไปตาม...	bpai dtaam...
to forget (vi, vt)	ลืม	leum
to forgive (vt)	ให้อภัย	hâi a-phai
to give (vt)	ให้	hâi
to give a hint	บอกใบ้	bòrk bâi
to go (on foot)	ไป	bpai
to go for a swim	ไปว่ายน้ำ	bpai wâai náam
to go out (for dinner, etc.)	ออกไป	òrk bpai
to guess (the answer)	คาดเดา	khâat dao

to have (vt)	มี	mee
to have breakfast	ทานอาหารเช้า	thaan aa-hăan cháo
to have dinner	ทานอาหารเย็น	thaan aa-hăan yen
to have lunch	ทานอาหารเที่ยง	thaan aa-hăan thîang
to hear (vt)	ได้ยิน	dâai yin
to help (vt)	ช่วย	chûay
to hide (vt)	ซ่อน	sôrn
to hope (vi, vt)	หวัง	wăng
to hunt (vi, vt)	ล่า	lâa
to hurry (vi)	รีบ	rêep

12. The most important verbs. Part 3

to inform (vt)	แจ้ง	jâeng
to insist (vi, vt)	ยืนยัน	yeun yan
to insult (vt)	ดูถูก	doo thòok
to invite (vt)	เชิญ	chern
to joke (vi)	ลอเล่น	lór lên
to keep (vt)	รักษา	rák-săa
to keep silent, to hush	นิ่งเงียบ	nîng ngîap
to kill (vt)	ฆ่า	khâa
to know (sb)	รู้จัก	róo jàk
to know (sth)	รู้	róo
to laugh (vi)	หัวเราะ	hŭa rór
to liberate (city, etc.)	ปลดปล่อย	bplòt bplòi
to look for … (search)	หา	hăa
to love (sb)	รัก	rák
to make a mistake	ทำผิด	tham phìt
to manage, to run	บริหาร	bor-rí-hăan
to mean (signify)	หมาย	măai
to mention (talk about)	กล่าวถึง	glàao thĕung
to miss (school, etc.)	พลาด	phlâat
to notice (see)	สังเกต	săng-gàyt
to object (vi, vt)	ค้าน	kháan
to observe (see)	สังเกตการณ์	săng-gàyt gaan
to open (vt)	เปิด	bpèrt
to order (meal, etc.)	สั่ง	sàng
to order (mil.)	สั่งการ	sàng gaan
to own (possess)	เป็นเจ้าของ	bpen jâo khŏrng
to participate (vi)	มีส่วนร่วม	mee sùan rûam
to pay (vi, vt)	จ่าย	jàai
to permit (vt)	อนุญาต	a-nú-yâat
to plan (vt)	วางแผน	waang phăen
to play (children)	เล่น	lên
to pray (vi, vt)	ภาวนา	phaa-wá-naa
to prefer (vt)	ชอบ	chôrp
to promise (vt)	สัญญา	săn-yaa

to pronounce (vt)	ออกเสียง	òrk sĭang
to propose (vt)	เสนอ	sà-nĕr
to punish (vt)	ลงโทษ	long thôht

13. The most important verbs. Part 4

to read (vi, vt)	อ่าน	àan
to recommend (vt)	แนะนำ	náe nam
to refuse (vi, vt)	ปฏิเสธ	bpà-dtì-sàyt
to regret (be sorry)	เสียใจ	sĭa jai
to rent (sth from sb)	เช่า	châo

to repeat (say again)	ซ้ำ	sám
to reserve, to book	จอง	jorng
to run (vi)	วิ่ง	wîng
to save (rescue)	กู้	gôo

to say (~ thank you)	บอก	bòrk
to scold (vt)	ดุด่า	dù dàa
to see (vt)	เห็น	hĕn
to sell (vt)	ขาย	khăai

to send (vt)	ส่ง	sòng
to shoot (vi)	ยิง	ying
to shout (vi)	ตะโกน	dtà-gohn
to show (vt)	แสดง	sà-daeng
to sign (document)	ลงนาม	long naam

to sit down (vi)	นั่ง	nâng
to smile (vi)	ยิ้ม	yím
to speak (vi, vt)	พูด	phôot
to steal (money, etc.)	ขโมย	khà-moi
to stop (for pause, etc.)	หยุด	yùt

to stop (please ~ calling me)	หยุด	yùt
to study (vt)	เรียน	rian
to swim (vi)	ว่ายน้ำ	wâai náam
to take (vt)	เอา	ao
to think (vi, vt)	คิด	khít

to threaten (vt)	ขู่	khòo
to touch (with hands)	แตะต้อง	dtàe dtôrng
to translate (vt)	แปล	bplae
to trust (vt)	เชื่อ	chêua
to try (attempt)	พยายาม	phá-yaa-yaam

to turn (e.g., ~ left)	เลี้ยว	líeow
to underestimate (vt)	ดูถูก	doo thòok
to understand (vt)	เขาใจ	khâo jai
to unite (vt)	สมาน	sà-măan
to wait (vt)	รอ	ror

| to want (wish, desire) | ต้องการ | dtôrng gaan |
| to warn (vt) | เตือน | dteuan |

to work (vi)	ทำงาน	tham ngaan
to write (vt)	เขียน	khĭan
to write down	จด	jòt

14. Colours

colour	สี	sĕe
shade (tint)	สีอ่อน	sĕe òrn
hue	สีสัน	sĕe săn
rainbow	สายรุ้ง	săai rúng
white (adj)	สีขาว	sĕe khăao
black (adj)	สีดำ	sĕe dam
grey (adj)	สีเทา	sĕe thao
green (adj)	สีเขียว	sĕe khĭeow
yellow (adj)	สีเหลือง	sĕe lĕuang
red (adj)	สีแดง	sĕe daeng
blue (adj)	สีน้ำเงิน	sĕe nám ngern
light blue (adj)	สีฟ้า	sĕe fáa
pink (adj)	สีชมพู	sĕe chom-poo
orange (adj)	สีส้ม	sĕe sôm
violet (adj)	สีม่วง	sĕe mûang
brown (adj)	สีน้ำตาล	sĕe nám dtaan
golden (adj)	สีทอง	sĕe thorng
silvery (adj)	สีเงิน	sĕe ngern
beige (adj)	สีน้ำตาลอ่อน	sĕe nám dtaan òrn
cream (adj)	สีครีม	sĕe khreem
turquoise (adj)	สีเขียวแกม น้ำเงิน	sĕe khĭeow gaem náam ngern
cherry red (adj)	สีแดงเชอร์รี่	sĕe daeng cher-rêe
lilac (adj)	สีม่วงอ่อน	sĕe mûang-òrn
crimson (adj)	สีแดงเข้ม	sĕe daeng khâym
light (adj)	อ่อน	òrn
dark (adj)	แก่	gàe
bright, vivid (adj)	สด	sòt
coloured (pencils)	สี	sĕe
colour (e.g. ~ film)	สี	sĕe
black-and-white (adj)	ขาวดำ	khăao-dam
plain (one-coloured)	สีเดียว	sĕe dieow
multicoloured (adj)	หลากสี	làak sĕe

15. Questions

Who?	ใคร?	khrai
What?	อะไร?	a-rai
Where? (at, in)	ที่ไหน?	thêe năi

Where (to)?	ที่ไหน?	thêe năi
From where?	จากที่ไหน?	jàak thêe năi
When?	เมื่อไหร่?	mêua rài
Why? (What for?)	ทำไม?	tham-mai
Why? (~ are you crying?)	ทำไม?	tham-mai
What for?	เพื่ออะไร?	phêua a-rai
How? (in what way)	อย่างไร?	yàang rai
What? (What kind of ...?)	อะไร?	a-rai
Which?	ไหน?	năi
To whom?	สำหรับใคร?	săm-ràp khrai
About whom?	เกี่ยวกับใคร?	gìeow gàp khrai
About what?	เกี่ยวกับอะไร?	gìeow gàp a-rai
With whom?	กับใคร?	gàp khrai
How many?	กี่...?	gèe...?
How much?	เท่าไหร่?	thâo rài
Whose?	ของใคร?	khŏrng khrai

16. Prepositions

with (accompanied by)	กับ	gàp
without	ปราศจาก	bpràat-sà-jàak
to (indicating direction)	ไปที่	bpai thêe
about (talking ~ ...)	เกี่ยวกับ	gìeow gàp
before (in time)	ก่อน	gòrn
in front of ...	หน้า	nâa
under (beneath, below)	ใต้	dtâi
above (over)	เหนือ	nĕua
on (atop)	บน	bon
from (off, out of)	จาก	jàak
of (made from)	ทำใช้	tham chái
in (e.g. ~ ten minutes)	ใน	nai
over (across the top of)	ข้าม	khâam

17. Function words. Adverbs. Part 1

Where? (at, in)	ที่ไหน?	thêe năi
here (adv)	ที่นี่	thêe nêe
there (adv)	ที่นั่น	thêe nân
somewhere (to be)	ที่ใดที่หนึ่ง	thêe dai thêe nèung
nowhere (not in any place)	ไม่มีที่ไหน	mâi mee thêe năi
by (near, beside)	ข้าง	khâang
by the window	ข้างหน้าต่าง	khâang nâa dtàang
Where (to)?	ที่ไหน?	thêe năi
here (e.g. come ~!)	ที่นี่	thêe nêe

there (e.g. to go ~)	ที่นั่น	thêe nân
from here (adv)	จากที่นี่	jàak thêe nêe
from there (adv)	จากที่นั่น	jàak thêe nân
close (adv)	ใกล้	glâi
far (adv)	ไกล	glai
near (e.g. ~ Paris)	ใกล้	glâi
nearby (adv)	ใกล้ๆ	glâi glâi
not far (adv)	ไม่ไกล	mâi glai
left (adj)	ซ้าย	sáai
on the left	ทางซ้าย	khâang sáai
to the left	ซ้าย	sáai
right (adj)	ขวา	khwǎa
on the right	ข้างขวา	khâang kwǎa
to the right	ขวา	khwǎa
in front (adv)	ข้างหน้า	khâang nâa
front (as adj)	หน้า	nâa
ahead (the kids ran ~)	หนา	nâa
behind (adv)	ข้างหลัง	khâang lǎng
from behind	จากข้างหลัง	jàak khâang lǎng
back (towards the rear)	หลัง	lǎng
middle	กลาง	glaang
in the middle	ตรงกลาง	dtrorng glaang
at the side	ข้าง	khâang
everywhere (adv)	ทุกที่	thúk thêe
around (in all directions)	รอบ	rôrp
from inside	จากข้างใน	jàak khâang nai
somewhere (to go)	ที่ไหน	thêe nǎi
straight (directly)	ตรงไป	dtrorng bpai
back (e.g. come ~)	กลับ	glàp
from anywhere	จากที่ใด	jàak thêe dai
from somewhere	จากที่ใด	jàak thêe dai
firstly (adv)	ข้อที่หนึ่ง	khôr thêe nèung
secondly (adv)	ข้อที่สอง	khôr thêe sǒrng
thirdly (adv)	ข้อที่สาม	khôr thêe sǎam
suddenly (adv)	ในทันที	nai than thee
at first (in the beginning)	ตอนแรก	dtorn-râek
for the first time	เป็นครั้งแรก	bpen khráng râek
long before …	นานก่อน	naan gòrn
anew (over again)	ใหม่	mài
for good (adv)	ให้จบสิ้น	hâi jòp sîn
never (adv)	ไม่เคย	mâi khoie
again (adv)	อีกครั้งหนึ่ง	èek khráng nèung
now (at present)	ตอนนี้	dtorn-née

often (adv)	บ่อย	bòi
then (adv)	เวลานั้น	way-laa nán
urgently (quickly)	อย่างเร่งด่วน	yàang râyng dùan
usually (adv)	มักจะ	mák jà

by the way, ...	อนึ่ง	à-nèung
possibly	เป็นไปได้	bpen bpai dâai
probably (adv)	อาจจะ	àat jà
maybe (adv)	อาจจะ	àat jà
besides ...	นอกจากนั้น...	nôrk jàak nán...
that's why ...	นั่นเป็นเหตุผลที่...	nân bpen hàyt phǒn thêe...
in spite of ...	แม้ว่า...	máe wâa...
thanks to ...	เนื่องจาก...	nêuang jàak...

what (pron.)	อะไร	a-rai
that (conj.)	ที่	thêe
something	อะไร	a-rai
anything (something)	อะไรก็ตาม	a-rai gôr dtaam
nothing	ไม่มีอะไร	mâi mee a-rai

who (pron.)	ใคร	khrai
someone	บางคน	baang khon
somebody	บางคน	baang khon

nobody	ไม่มีใคร	mâi mee khrai
nowhere (a voyage to ~)	ไม่ไปไหน	mâi bpai nǎi
nobody's	ไม่เป็นของ ของใคร	mâi bpen khǒrng khǒrng khrai
somebody's	ของคนหนึ่ง	khǒrng khon nèung

so (I'm ~ glad)	มาก	mâak
also (as well)	ด้วย	dûay
too (as well)	ด้วย	dûay

18. Function words. Adverbs. Part 2

Why?	ทำไม?	tham-mai
for some reason	เพราะเหตุผลอะไร	phrór hàyt phǒn à-rai
because ...	เพราะว่า...	phrór wâa
for some purpose	ด้วยจุดประสงค์อะไร	dûay jùt bprà-sǒng a-rai

and	และ	láe
or	หรือ	rěu
but	แต	dtàe
for (e.g. ~ me)	สำหรับ	sǎm-ràp

too (excessively)	เกินไป	gern bpai
only (exclusively)	เท่านั้น	thâo nán
exactly (adv)	ตรง	dtrorng
about (more or less)	ประมาณ	bprà-maan

approximately (adv)	ประมาณ	bprà-maan
approximate (adj)	ประมาณ	bprà-maan
almost (adv)	เกือบ	gèuap

25

the rest	ที่เหลือ	thêe lĕua
the other (second)	อีก	èek
other (different)	อื่น	èun
each (adj)	ทุก	thúk
any (no matter which)	ใดๆ	dai dai
many (adj)	หลาย	lăai
much (adv)	มาก	mâak
many people	หลายคน	lăai khon
all (everyone)	ทุกๆ	thúk thúk

in return for ...	ที่จะเปลี่ยนเป็น	thêe jà bplìan bpen
in exchange (adv)	แทน	thaen
by hand (made)	ใช้มือ	chái meu
hardly (negative opinion)	แทบจะไม่	thâep jà mâi

probably (adv)	อาจจะ	àat jà
on purpose (intentionally)	โดยเจตนา	doi jàyt-dtà-naa
by accident (adv)	บังเอิญ	bang-ern

very (adv)	มาก	mâak
for example (adv)	ยกตัวอย่าง	yók dtua yàang
between	ระหว่าง	rá-wàang
among	ทามกลาง	tâam-glaang
so much (such a lot)	มากมาย	mâak maai
especially (adv)	โดยเฉพาะ	doi chà-phór

Basic concepts. Part 2

19. Opposites

English	Thai	Transcription
rich (adj)	รวย	ruay
poor (adj)	จน	jon
ill, sick (adj)	เจ็บป่วย	jèp bpùay
well (not sick)	สบายดี	sà-baai dee
big (adj)	ใหญ่	yài
small (adj)	เล็ก	lék
quickly (adv)	อย่างเร็ว	yàang reo
slowly (adv)	อยางชา	yàang cháa
fast (adj)	เร็ว	reo
slow (adj)	ชา	cháa
glad (adj)	ยินดี	yin dee
sad (adj)	เสียใจ	sǐa jai
together (adv)	ด้วยกัน	dûay gan
separately (adv)	ตางหาก	dtàang hàak
aloud (to read)	ออกเสียง	òrk sǐang
silently (to oneself)	อยางเงียบๆ	yàang ngîap ngîap
tall (adj)	สูง	sǒong
low (adj)	ตา	dtàm
deep (adj)	ลึก	léuk
shallow (adj)	ตื้น	dtêun
yes	ใช่	châi
no	ไม่ใช่	mâi châi
distant (in space)	ไกล	glai
nearby (adj)	ใกล	glâi
far (adv)	ไกล	glai
nearby (adv)	ใกลๆ	glâi glâi
long (adj)	ยาว	yaao
short (adj)	สั้น	sân
good (kindhearted)	ใจดี	jai dee
evil (adj)	เลวราย	leo ráai

| married (adj) | แต่งงานแล้ว | dtàeng ngaan láew |
| single (adj) | เป็นโสด | bpen sòht |

| to forbid (vt) | ห้าม | hâam |
| to permit (vt) | อนุญาต | a-nú-yâat |

| end | จบ | jòp |
| beginning | จุดเริ่มต้น | jùt rêrm-dtôn |

| left (adj) | ซ้าย | sáai |
| right (adj) | ขวา | khwǎa |

| first (adj) | แรก | râek |
| last (adj) | สุดท้าย | sùt tháai |

| crime | อาชญากรรม | àat-yaa-gam |
| punishment | การลงโทษ | gaan long thôht |

| to order (vt) | สั่ง | sàng |
| to obey (vi, vt) | เชื่อฟัง | chêua fang |

| straight (adj) | ตรง | dtrorng |
| curved (adj) | โค้ง | khóhng |

| paradise | สวรรค์ | sà-wǎn |
| hell | นรก | ná-rók |

| to be born | เกิด | gèrt |
| to die (vi) | ตาย | dtaai |

| strong (adj) | แข็งแรง | khǎeng raeng |
| weak (adj) | อ่อนแอ | òrn ae |

| old (adj) | แก่ | gàe |
| young (adj) | หนุ่ม | nùm |

| old (adj) | เก่าแก่ | gào gàe |
| new (adj) | ใหม่ | mài |

| hard (adj) | แข็ง | khǎeng |
| soft (adj) | อ่อน | òrn |

| warm (tepid) | อุ่น | ùn |
| cold (adj) | หนาว | nǎao |

| fat (adj) | อ้วน | ûan |
| thin (adj) | ผอม | phǒrm |

| narrow (adj) | แคบ | khâep |
| wide (adj) | กว้าง | gwâang |

| good (adj) | ดี | dee |
| bad (adj) | ไม่ดี | mâi dee |

| brave (adj) | กล้าหาญ | glâa hǎan |
| cowardly (adj) | ขี้ขลาด | khêe khlàat |

20. Weekdays

Monday	วันจันทร์	wan jan
Tuesday	วันอังคาร	wan ang-khaan
Wednesday	วันพุธ	wan phút
Thursday	วันพฤหัสบดี	wan phá-réu-hàt-sà-bor-dee
Friday	วันศุกร	wan sùk
Saturday	วันเสาร	wan săo
Sunday	วันอาทิตย์	wan aa-thít

today (adv)	วันนี้	wan née
tomorrow (adv)	พรุงนี้	phrûng-née
the day after tomorrow	วันมะรืนนี้	wan má-reun née
yesterday (adv)	เมื่อวานนี้	mêua waan née
the day before yesterday	เมื่อวานซืนนี้	mêua waan-seun née

day	วัน	wan
working day	วันทำงาน	wan tham ngaan
public holiday	วันนักขัตฤกษ์	wan nák-khàt-rêrk
day off	วันหยุด	wan yùt
weekend	วันสุดสัปดาห์	wan sùt sàp-daa

all day long	ทั้งวัน	tháng wan
the next day (adv)	วันรุงขึ้น	wan rûng khêun
two days ago	สองวันกอน	sŏrng wan gòrn
the day before	วันกอนหนานี้	wan gòrn nâa née
daily (adj)	รายวัน	raai wan
every day (adv)	ทุกวัน	thúk wan

week	สัปดาห์	sàp-daa
last week (adv)	สัปดาห์กอน	sàp-daa gòrn
next week (adv)	สัปดาห์หนา	sàp-daa nâa
weekly (adj)	รายสัปดาห์	raai sàp-daa
every week (adv)	ทุกสัปดาห์	thúk sàp-daa
twice a week	สัปดาห์ละสองครั้ง	sàp-daa lá sŏrng khráng
every Tuesday	ทุกวันอังคาร	túk wan ang-khaan

21. Hours. Day and night

morning	เช้า	cháo
in the morning	ตอนเช้า	dtorn cháo
noon, midday	เที่ยงวัน	thîang wan
in the afternoon	ตอนบาย	dtorn bàai

evening	เย็น	yen
in the evening	ตอนเย็น	dtorn yen
night	คืน	kheun
at night	กลางคืน	glaang kheun
midnight	เที่ยงคืน	thîang kheun

second	วินาที	wí-naa-thee
minute	นาที	naa-thee
hour	ชั่วโมง	chûa mohng

half an hour	ครึ่งชั่วโมง	khrêung chûa mohng
a quarter-hour	สิบห้านาที	sìp hâa naa-thee
fifteen minutes	สิบห้านาที	sìp hâa naa-thee
24 hours	24 ชั่วโมง	yêe sìp sèe · chûa mohng

sunrise	พระอาทิตย์ขึ้น	phrá aa-thít khêun
dawn	ใกล้รุ่ง	glâi rûng
early morning	เช้า	cháo
sunset	พระอาทิตย์ตก	phrá aa-thít dtòk

early in the morning	ตอนเช้า	dtorn cháo
this morning	เช้านี้	cháo née
tomorrow morning	พรุ่งนี้เช้า	phrûng-née cháo

this afternoon	บ่ายนี้	bàai née
in the afternoon	ตอนบ่าย	dtorn bàai
tomorrow afternoon	พรุ่งนี้บ่าย	phrûng-née bàai

tonight (this evening)	คืนนี้	kheun née
tomorrow night	คืนพรุ่งนี้	kheun phrûng-née

at 3 o'clock sharp	3 โมงตรง	săam mohng dtrorng
about 4 o'clock	ประมาณ 4 โมง	bprà-maan sèe mohng
by 12 o'clock	ภายใน 12 โมง	phaai nai sìp sŏng mohng

in 20 minutes	อีก 20 นาที	èek yêe sìp naa-thee
in an hour	อีกหนึ่งชั่วโมง	èek nèung chûa mohng
on time (adv)	ทันเวลา	than way-laa

a quarter to ...	อีกสิบห้านาที	èek sìp hâa naa-thee
within an hour	ภายในหนึ่งชั่วโมง	phaai nai nèung chûa mohng
every 15 minutes	ทุก 15 นาที	thúk sìp hâa naa-thee
round the clock	ทั้งวัน	tháng wan

22. Months. Seasons

January	มกราคม	mók-gà-raa khom
February	กุมภาพันธ์	gum-phaa phan
March	มีนาคม	mee-naa khom
April	เมษายน	may-săa-yon
May	พฤษภาคม	phréut-sà-phaa khom
June	มิถุนายน	mí-thù-naa-yon

July	กรกฎาคม	gà-rá-gà-daa-khom
August	สิงหาคม	sĭng hăa khom
September	กันยายน	gan-yaa-yon
October	ตุลาคม	dtù-laa khom
November	พฤศจิกายน	phréut-sà-jì-gaa-yon
December	ธันวาคม	than-waa khom

spring	ฤดูใบไม้ผลิ	réu-doo bai máai phlì
in spring	ฤดูใบไม้ผลิ	réu-doo bai máai phlì
spring (as adj)	ฤดูใบไม้ผลิ	réu-doo bai máai phlì
summer	ฤดูร้อน	réu-doo rórn

in summer	ฤดูร้อน	réu-doo rórn
summer (as adj)	ฤดูร้อน	réu-doo rórn
autumn	ฤดูใบไม้ร่วง	réu-doo bai máai rûang
in autumn	ฤดูใบไม้ร่วง	réu-doo bai máai rûang
autumn (as adj)	ฤดูใบไม้ร่วง	réu-doo bai máai rûang
winter	ฤดูหนาว	réu-doo năao
in winter	ฤดูหนาว	réu-doo năao
winter (as adj)	ฤดูหนาว	réu-doo năao
month	เดือน	deuan
this month	เดือนนี้	deuan née
next month	เดือนหน้า	deuan nâa
last month	เดือนที่แลว	deuan thêe láew
a month ago	หนึ่งเดือนก่อนหน้านี้	nèung deuan gòrn nâa née
in a month (a month later)	อีกหนึ่งเดือน	èek nèung deuan
in 2 months (2 months later)	อีกสองเดือน	èek sŏrng deuan
the whole month	ทั้งเดือน	tháng deuan
all month long	ตลอดทั้งเดือน	dtà-lòrt tháng deuan
monthly (~ magazine)	รายเดือน	raai deuan
monthly (adv)	ทุกเดือน	thúk deuan
every month	ทุกเดือน	thúk deuan
twice a month	เดือนละสองครั้ง	deuan lá sŏrng kráng
year	ปี	bpee
this year	ปีนี้	bpee née
next year	ปีหน้า	bpee nâa
last year	ปีที่แลว	bpee thêe láew
a year ago	หนึ่งปีก่อน	nèung bpee gòrn
in a year	อีกหนึ่งปี	èek nèung bpee
in two years	อีกสองปี	èek sŏng bpee
the whole year	ทั้งปี	tháng bpee
all year long	ตลอดทั้งปี	dtà-lòrt tháng bpee
every year	ทุกปี	thúk bpee
annual (adj)	รายปี	raai bpee
annually (adv)	ทุกปี	thúk bpee
4 times a year	ปีละสี่ครั้ง	bpee lá sèe khráng
date (e.g. today's ~)	วันที่	wan thêe
date (e.g. ~ of birth)	วันเดือนปี	wan deuan bpee
calendar	ปฏิทิน	bpà-dtì-thin
half a year	ครึ่งปี	khrêung bpee
six months	หกเดือน	hòk deuan
season (summer, etc.)	ฤดูกาล	réu-doo gaan
century	ศตวรรษ	sà-dtà-wát

23. Time. Miscellaneous

time	เวลา	way-laa
moment	ครูหนึ่ง	khrôo nèung

instant (n)	ครู่เดียว	khrôo dieow
instant (adj)	เพียงครู่เดียว	phiang khrôo dieow
lapse (of time)	ช่วงเวลา	chûang way-laa
life	ชีวิต	chee-wít
eternity	ตลอดกาล	dtà-lòrt gaan

epoch	สมัย	sà-măi
era	ยุค	yúk
cycle	วัฏจักร	wát-dtà-jàk
period	ช่วง	chûang
term (short-~)	ระยะเวลา	rá-yá way-laa

the future	อนาคต	a-naa-khót
future (as adj)	อนาคต	a-naa-khót
next time	ครั้งหน้า	khráng nâa
the past	อดีต	a-dèet
past (recent)	ที่ผ่านมา	thêe phàan maa
last time	ครั้งที่แล้ว	khráng thêe láew

later (adv)	ภายหลัง	phaai lăng
after (prep.)	หลังจาก	lăng jàak
nowadays (adv)	เวลานี้	way-laa née
now (at this moment)	ตอนนี้	dtorn-née
immediately (adv)	ทันที	than thee
soon (adv)	อีกไม่นาน	èek mâi naan
in advance (beforehand)	ล่วงหน้า	lûang nâa

a long time ago	นานมาแล้ว	naan maa láew
recently (adv)	เมื่อเร็ว ๆ นี้	mêua reo reo née
destiny	ชะตากรรม	chá-dtaa gam
recollections	ความทรงจำ	khwaam song jam
archives	จดหมายเหตุ	jòt măai hàyt
during ...	ระหว่าง...	rá-wàang...
long, a long time (adv)	นาน	naan
not long (adv)	ไม่นาน	mâi naan
early (in the morning)	ล่วงหน้า	lûang nâa
late (not early)	ช้า	cháa

forever (for good)	ตลอดกาล	dtà-lòrt gaan
to start (begin)	เริ่ม	rêrm
to postpone (vt)	เลื่อน	lêuan

at the same time	ในเวลาเดียวกัน	nai way-laa dieow gan
permanently (adv)	อย่างถาวร	yàang thăa-won
constant (noise, pain)	ต่อเนื่อง	dtòr nêuang
temporary (adj)	ชั่วคราว	chûa khraao
sometimes (adv)	บางครั้ง	baang khráng
rarely (adv)	ไม่บ่อย	mâi bòi
often (adv)	บ่อย	bòi

24. Lines and shapes

| square | สี่เหลี่ยมจัตุรัส | sèe lìam jàt-dtù-ràt |
| square (as adj) | สี่เหลี่ยมจัตุรัส | sèe lìam jàt-dtù-ràt |

circle	วงกลม	wong glom
round (adj)	กลม	glom
triangle	รูปสามเหลี่ยม	rôop sǎam lìam
triangular (adj)	สามเหลี่ยม	sǎam lìam

oval	รูปกลมรี	rôop glom ree
oval (as adj)	กลมรี	glom ree
rectangle	สี่เหลี่ยมมุมฉาก	sèe lìam mum chàak
rectangular (adj)	สี่เหลี่ยมมุมฉาก	sèe lìam mum chàak

pyramid	พีระมิด	phee-rá-mít
rhombus	รูปสี่เหลี่ยม ขนมเปียกปูน	rôop sèe lìam khà-nǒm bpìak bpoon
trapezium	รูปสี่เหลี่ยมคางหมู	rôop sèe lìam khaang mǒo
cube	ลูกบาศก์	lôok bàat
prism	ปริซึม	bprì seum

circumference	เส้นรอบวง	sên rôrp wong
sphere	ทรงกลม	song glom
ball (solid sphere)	ลูกกลม	lôok glom
diameter	เส้นผ่านศูนย์กลาง	sên phàan sǒon-glaang
radius	เส้นรัศมี	sên rát-sà-mĕe
perimeter (circle's ~)	เส้นรอบวง	sên rôrp wong
centre	กลาง	glaang

horizontal (adj)	แนวนอน	naew norn
vertical (adj)	แนวตั้ง	naew dtâng
parallel (n)	เส้นขนาน	sên khà-nǎan
parallel (as adj)	ขนาน	khà-nǎan

line	เส้น	sên
stroke	เส้น	sên
straight line	เส้นตรง	sên dtrorng
curve (curved line)	เส้นโค้ง	sên khóhng
thin (line, etc.)	บาง	baang
contour (outline)	เส้นขอบ	sâyn khòrp

intersection	เส้นตัด	sên dtàt
right angle	มุมฉาก	mum chàak
segment	เซกเมนต์	sâyk-mayn
sector (circular ~)	เซกเตอร์	sâyk-dtêr
side (of a triangle)	ข้าง	khâang
angle	มุม	mum

25. Units of measurement

weight	น้ำหนัก	nám nàk
length	ความยาว	khwaam yaao
width	ความกว้าง	khwaam gwâang
height	ความสูง	khwaam sǒong
depth	ความลึก	khwaam léuk
volume	ปริมาณ	bpà-rí-maan
area	บริเวณ	bor-rí-wayn
gram	กรัม	gram

milligram	มิลลิกรัม	min-lí gram
kilogram	กิโลกรัม	gì-loh gram
ton	ตัน	dtan
pound	ปอนด์	bporn
ounce	ออนซ์	orn

metre	เมตร	máyt
millimetre	มิลลิเมตร	min-lí mâyt
centimetre	เซ็นติเมตร	sen dtì mâyt
kilometre	กิโลเมตร	gì-loh máyt
mile	ไมล์	mai

inch	นิ้ว	níw
foot	ฟุต	fút
yard	หลา	lǎa

| square metre | ตารางเมตร | dtaa-raang máyt |
| hectare | เฮกตาร์ | hêek dtaa |

litre	ลิตร	lít
degree	องศา	ong-sǎa
volt	โวลต์	wohn
ampere	แอมแปร์	aem-bpae
horsepower	แรงม้า	raeng máa

quantity	จำนวน	jam-nuan
a little bit of ...	นิดนอย	nít nói
half	ครึ่ง	khrêung
dozen	โหล	lŏh
piece (item)	สวน	sùan

| size | ขนาด | khà-nàat |
| scale (map ~) | มาตราสวน | mâat-dtraa sùan |

minimal (adj)	นอยที่สุด	nói thêe sùt
the smallest (adj)	เล็กที่สุด	lék thêe sùt
medium (adj)	กลาง	glaang
maximal (adj)	สูงสุด	sǒong sùt
the largest (adj)	ใหญ่ที่สุด	yài têe sùt

26. Containers

canning jar (glass ~)	ขวดโหล	khùat lŏh
tin, can	กระปอง	grà-bpŏrng
bucket	ถัง	thǎng
barrel	ถัง	thǎng

wash basin (e.g., plastic ~)	กะทะ	gà-thá
tank (100L water ~)	ถังเก็บน้ำ	thǎng gèp nám
hip flask	กระติกน้ำ	grà-dtìk nám
jerrycan	ภาชนะ	phaa-chá-ná
tank (e.g., tank car)	ถังบรรจุ	thǎng ban-jù
mug	แกว	gâew
cup (of coffee, etc.)	ถวย	thûay

saucer	จานรอง	jaan rorng
glass (tumbler)	แก้ว	gâew
wine glass	แก้วไวน์	gâew wai
stock pot (soup pot)	หม้อ	môr

bottle (~ of wine)	ขวด	khùat
neck (of the bottle, etc.)	ปาก	bpàak

carafe (decanter)	คนโท	khon-thoh
pitcher	เหยือก	yèuak
vessel (container)	ภาชนะ	phaa-chá-ná
pot (crock, stoneware ~)	หม้อ	môr
vase	แจกัน	jae-gan

flacon, bottle (perfume ~)	กระติก	grà-dtìk
vial, small bottle	ขวดเล็ก	khùat lék
tube (of toothpaste)	หลอด	lòrt

sack (bag)	ถุง	thŭng
bag (paper ~, plastic ~)	ถุง	thŭng
packet (of cigarettes, etc.)	ซอง	sorng

box (e.g. shoebox)	กล่อง	glòrng
crate	ลัง	lang
basket	ตะกร้า	dtà-grâa

27. Materials

material	วัสดุ	wát-sà-dù
wood (n)	ไม้	máai
wood-, wooden (adj)	ไม้	máai

glass (n)	แก้ว	gâew
glass (as adj)	แกว	gâew

stone (n)	หิน	hĭn
stone (as adj)	หิน	hĭn

plastic (n)	พลาสติก	pláat-dtìk
plastic (as adj)	พลาสติก	pláat-dtìk

rubber (n)	ยาง	yaang
rubber (as adj)	ยาง	yaang

cloth, fabric (n)	ผ้า	phâa
fabric (as adj)	ผา	phâa

paper (n)	กระดาษ	grà-dàat
paper (as adj)	กระดาษ	grà-dàat

cardboard (n)	กระดาษแข็ง	grà-dàat khăeng
cardboard (as adj)	กระดาษแข็ง	grà-dàat khăeng
polyethylene	โพลีเอทิลีน	phoh-lee-ay-thí-leen
cellophane	เซลโลเฟน	sayn loh-fayn

| linoleum | เสื่อน้ำมัน | sèua náam man |
| plywood | ไม้อัด | máai àt |

porcelain (n)	เครื่องเคลือบดินเผา	khrêuang khlêuap din phǎo
porcelain (as adj)	เครื่องเคลือบดินเผา	khrêuang khlêuap din phǎo
clay (n)	ดินเหนียว	din nǐeow
clay (as adj)	ดินเหนียว	din nǐeow
ceramic (n)	เซรามิก	say-raa mík
ceramic (as adj)	เซรามิก	say-raa mík

28. Metals

metal (n)	โลหะ	loh-hà
metal (as adj)	โลหะ	loh-hà
alloy (n)	โลหะสัมฤทธิ์	loh-hà sǎm-rít

gold (n)	ทอง	thorng
gold, golden (adj)	ทอง	thorng
silver (n)	เงิน	ngern
silver (as adj)	เงิน	ngern

iron (n)	เหล็ก	lèk
iron-, made of iron (adj)	เหล็ก	lèk
steel (n)	เหล็กกล้า	lèk glâa
steel (as adj)	เหล็กกลา	lèk glâa
copper (n)	ทองแดง	thorng daeng
copper (as adj)	ทองแดง	thorng daeng

aluminium (n)	อะลูมิเนียม	a-loo-mí-niam
aluminium (as adj)	อะลูมิเนียม	a-loo-mí-niam
bronze (n)	ทองบรอนซ์	thorng-bron
bronze (as adj)	ทองบรอนซ์	thorng-bron

brass	ทองเหลือง	thorng lěuang
nickel	นิกเกิล	ník-gêrn
platinum	ทองคำขาว	thorng kham khǎao
mercury	ปรอท	bpa -ròrt
tin	ดีบุก	dee-bùk
lead	ตะกั่ว	dtà-gùa
zinc	สังกะสี	sǎng-gà-sěe

HUMAN BEING

Human being. The body

29. Humans. Basic concepts

human being	มนุษย์	má-nút
man (adult male)	ผู้ชาย	phôo chaai
woman	ผู้หญิง	phôo yǐng
child	เด็ก, ลูก	dèk, lôok
girl	เด็กผู้หญิง	dèk phôo yǐng
boy	เด็กผู้ชาย	dèk phôo chaai
teenager	วัยรุ่น	wai rûn
old man	ชายชรา	chaai chá-raa
old woman	หญิงชรา	yǐng chá-raa

30. Human anatomy

organism (body)	ร่างกาย	râang gaai
heart	หัวใจ	hǔa jai
blood	เลือด	lêuat
artery	เส้นเลือดแดง	sâyn lêuat daeng
vein	เสนเลือดดำ	sâyn lêuat dam
brain	สมอง	sà-mǒrng
nerve	เส้นประสาท	sên bprà-sàat
nerves	เสนประสาท	sên bprà-sàat
vertebra	กระดูกสันหลัง	grà-dòok sǎn-lǎng
spine (backbone)	สันหลัง	sǎn lǎng
stomach (organ)	กระเพาะอาหาร	grà phór aa-hǎan
intestines, bowels	ลำไส้	lam sâi
intestine (e.g. large ~)	ลำไส้	lam sâi
liver	ตับ	dtàp
kidney	ไต	dtai
bone	กระดูก	grà-dòok
skeleton	โครงกระดูก	khrohng grà-dòok
rib	ซี่โครง	sêe khrohng
skull	กะโหลก	gà-lòhk
muscle	กล้ามเนื้อ	glâam néua
biceps	กล้ามเนื้อไบเซ็ปส์	glâam néua bai-sép
triceps	กล้ามเนื้อไทรเซปส์	gglâam néua thrai-sâyp
tendon	เส้นเอ็น	sâyn en
joint	ข้อต่อ	khôr dtòr

lungs	ปอด	bpòrt
genitals	อวัยวะเพศ	a-wai-wá phâyt
skin	ผิวหนัง	phǐw nǎng

31. Head

head	หัว	hǔa
face	หน้า	nâa
nose	จมูก	jà-mòok
mouth	ปาก	bpàak
eye	ตา	dtaa
eyes	ตา	dtaa
pupil	รูม่านตา	roo mâan dtaa
eyebrow	คิ้ว	khíw
eyelash	ขนตา	khǒn dtaa
eyelid	เปลือกตา	bplèuak dtaa
tongue	ลิ้น	lín
tooth	ฟัน	fan
lips	ริมฝีปาก	rim fěe bpàak
cheekbones	โหนกแก้ม	nòhk gâem
gum	เหงือก	ngèuak
palate	เพดานปาก	phay-daan bpàak
nostrils	รูจมูก	roo jà-mòok
chin	คาง	khaang
jaw	ขากรรไกร	khǎa gan-grai
cheek	แก้ม	gâem
forehead	หน้าผาก	nâa phàak
temple	ขมับ	khà-màp
ear	หู	hǒo
back of the head	หลังศีรษะ	lǎng sěe-sà
neck	คอ	khor
throat	ลำคอ	lam khor
hair	ผม	phǒm
hairstyle	ทรงผม	song phǒm
haircut	ทรงผม	song phǒm
wig	ผมปลอม	phǒm bplorm
moustache	หนวด	nùat
beard	เครา	krao
to have (a beard, etc.)	ไว้ลอง	lorng wái
plait	ผมเปีย	phǒm bpia
sideboards	จอน	jorn
red-haired (adj)	ผมแดง	phǒm daeng
grey (hair)	ผมหงอก	phǒm ngòrk
bald (adj)	หัวล้าน	hǔa láan
bald patch	หัวล้าน	hǔa láan
ponytail	ผมทรงหางม้า	phǒm song hǎang máa
fringe	ผมม้า	phǒm máa

32. Human body

hand	มือ	meu
arm	แขน	khǎen
finger	นิ้ว	níw
toe	นิ้วเท้า	níw tháo
thumb	นิ้วโป้ง	níw bpôhng
little finger	นิ้วก้อย	níw gôi
nail	เล็บ	lép
fist	กำปั้น	gam bpân
palm	ฝ่ามือ	fàa meu
wrist	ข้อมือ	khôr meu
forearm	แขนช่วงล่าง	khǎen chûang lâang
elbow	ข้อศอก	khôr sòrk
shoulder	ไหล่	lài
leg	ขา	khǎa
foot	เท้า	tháo
knee	หัวเข่า	hǔa khào
calf	น่อง	nôrng
hip	สะโพก	sà-phôhk
heel	ส้นเท้า	sôn tháo
body	ร่างกาย	râang gaai
stomach	ท้อง	thórng
chest	อก	òk
breast	หน้าอก	nâa òk
flank	ข้าง	khâang
back	หลัง	lǎng
lower back	หลังส่วนล่าง	lǎng sùan lâang
waist	เอว	eo
navel (belly button)	สะดือ	sà-deu
buttocks	ก้น	gôn
bottom	ก้น	gôn
beauty spot	ไฝเสน่ห์	fǎi sà-này
birthmark (café au lait spot)	ปาน	bpaan
tattoo	รอยสัก	roi sàk
scar	แผลเป็น	phlǎe bpen

Clothing & Accessories

33. Outerwear. Coats

clothes	เสื้อผ้า	sêua phâa
outerwear	เสื้อนอก	sêua nôk
winter clothing	เสื้อกันหนาว	sêua gan năao
coat (overcoat)	เสื้อโค้ท	sêua khóht
fur coat	เสื้อโค้ทขนสัตว์	sêua khóht khŏn sàt
fur jacket	แจคเก็ตขนสัตว์	jáek-gèt khŏn sàt
down coat	แจ็คเก็ตกันหนาว	jàek-gèt gan năao
jacket (e.g. leather ~)	แจ๊คเก็ต	jáek-gèt
raincoat (trenchcoat, etc.)	เสื้อกันฝน	sêua gan fŏn
waterproof (adj)	ซึ่งกันน้ำได้	sêung gan náam dâai

34. Men's & women's clothing

shirt (button shirt)	เสื้อ	sêua
trousers	กางเกง	gaang-gayng
jeans	กางเกงยีนส์	gaang-gayng yeen
suit jacket	แจ็คเก็ตสูท	jàek-gèt sòot
suit	ชุดสูท	chút sòot
dress (frock)	ชุดเดรส	chút draet
skirt	กระโปรง	grà bprohng
blouse	เสื้อ	sêua
knitted jacket (cardigan, etc.)	แจ๊คเก็ตถัก	jáek-gèt thàk
jacket (of a woman's suit)	แจคเก็ต	jáek-gèt
T-shirt	เสื้อยืด	sêua yêut
shorts (short trousers)	กางเกงขาสั้น	gaang-gayng khăa sân
tracksuit	ชุดวอร์ม	chút wom
bathrobe	เสื้อคลุมอาบน้ำ	sêua khlum àap náam
pyjamas	ชุดนอน	chút norn
jumper (sweater)	เสื้อไหมพรม	sêua măi phrom
pullover	เสื้อกันหนาวแบบสวม	sêua gan năao bàep sŭam
waistcoat	เสื้อกั๊ก	sêua gák
tailcoat	เสื้อเทลโค้ต	sêua thayn-khóht
dinner suit	ชุดทักซิโด	chút thák sí dôh
uniform	เครื่องแบบ	khrêuang bàep
workwear	ชุดทำงาน	chút tam ngaan
boiler suit	ชุดเอี๊ยม	chút íam
coat (e.g. doctor's smock)	เสื้อคลุม	sêua khlum

35. Clothing. Underwear

underwear	ชุดชั้นใน	chút chán nai
pants	กางเกงในชาย	gaang-gayng nai chaai
panties	กางเกงในสตรี	gaang-gayng nai sàt-dtree
vest (singlet)	เสื้อชั้นใน	sêua chán nai
socks	ถุงเท้า	thŭng tháo
nightdress	ชุดนอนสตรี	chút norn sàt-dtree
bra	ยกทรง	yók song
knee highs (knee-high socks)	ถุงเท้ายาว	thŭng tháo yaao
tights	ถุงน่องเต็มตัว	thŭng nôrng dtem dtua
stockings (hold ups)	ถุงน่อง	thŭng nôrng
swimsuit, bikini	ชุดวายน้ำ	chút wâai náam

36. Headwear

hat	หมวก	mùak
trilby hat	หมวก	mùak
baseball cap	หมวกเบสบอล	mùak bàyt-bon
flatcap	หมวกติงลี่	mùak dting lêe
beret	หมวกเบเร่ต์	mùak bay-rây
hood	ฮูด	hóot
panama hat	หมวกปานามา	mùak bpaa-naa-maa
knit cap (knitted hat)	หมวกไหมพรม	mùak măi phrom
headscarf	ผ้าโพกศีรษะ	phâa phôhk sěe-sà
women's hat	หมวกสตรี	mùak sàt-dtree
hard hat	หมวกนิรภัย	mùak ní-rá-phai
forage cap	หมวกหนีบ	mùak nèep
helmet	หมวกกันน็อค	mùak ní-rá-phai
bowler	หมวกกลมทรงสูง	mùak glom song sŏong
top hat	หมวกทรงสูง	mùak song sŏong

37. Footwear

footwear	รองเท้า	rorng tháo
shoes (men's shoes)	รองเท้า	rorng tháo
shoes (women's shoes)	รองเท้า	rorng tháo
boots (e.g., cowboy ~)	รองเท้าบูท	rorng tháo bòot
carpet slippers	รองเท้าแตะในบ้าน	rorng tháo dtàe nai bâan
trainers	รองเท้ากีฬา	rorng tháo gee-laa
trainers	รองเท้าผ้าใบ	rorng tháo phâa bai
sandals	รองเท้าแตะ	rorng tháo dtàe
cobbler (shoe repairer)	คนซ่อมรองเท้า	khon sôrm rorng tháo
heel	สันรองเท้า	sôn rorng tháo

pair (of shoes)	คู่	khôo
lace (shoelace)	เชือกรองเท้า	chêuak rorng tháo
to lace up (vt)	ผูกเชือกรองเท้า	phòok chêuak rorng tháo
shoehorn	ที่ช้อนรองเท้า	thêe chón rorng tháo
shoe polish	ยาขัดรองเท้า	yaa khàt rorng tháo

38. Textile. Fabrics

cotton (n)	ฝ้าย	fâai
cotton (as adj)	ฝ้าย	fâai
flax (n)	แฟลกซ์	fláek
flax (as adj)	แฟลกซ์	fláek

silk (n)	ไหม	măi
silk (as adj)	ไหม	măi
wool (n)	ขนสัตว์	khŏn sàt
wool (as adj)	ขนสัตว์	khŏn sàt

velvet	กำมะหยี่	gam-má-yèe
suede	หนังกลับ	năng glàp
corduroy	ผ้าลูกฟูก	phâa lôok fôok

nylon (n)	ไนลอน	nai-lorn
nylon (as adj)	ไนลอน	nai-lorn
polyester (n)	โพลีเอสเตอร์	poh-lee-àyt-dtêr
polyester (as adj)	โพลีเอสเตอร์	poh-lee-àyt-dtêr

leather (n)	หนัง	năng
leather (as adj)	หนัง	năng
fur (n)	ขนสัตว์	khŏn sàt
fur (e.g. ~ coat)	ขนสัตว์	khŏn sàt

39. Personal accessories

gloves	ถุงมือ	thŭng meu
mittens	ถุงมือ	thŭng meu
scarf (muffler)	ผ้าพันคอ	phâa phan khor

glasses	แว่นตา	wâen dtaa
frame (eyeglass ~)	กรอบแว่น	gròrp wâen
umbrella	ร่ม	rôm
walking stick	ไม้เท้า	máai tháo
hairbrush	แปรงหวีผม	bpraeng wĕe phŏm
fan	พัด	phát

tie (necktie)	เนคไท	nâyk-thai
bow tie	โบว์หูกระต่าย	boh hŏo grà-dtàai
braces	สายเอี่ยม	săai íam
handkerchief	ผ้าเช็ดหน้า	phâa chét-nâa

| comb | หวี | wĕe |
| hair slide | ที่หนีบผม | têe nèep phŏm |

hairpin	กิ๊บ	gíp
buckle	หัวเข็มขัด	hǔa khěm khàt
belt	เข็มขัด	khěm khàt
shoulder strap	สายกระเป๋า	sǎai grà-bpǎo
bag (handbag)	กระเป๋า	grà-bpǎo
handbag	กระเป๋าถือ	grà-bpǎo thěu
rucksack	กระเป๋าสะพายหลัง	grà-bpǎo sà-phaai lǎng

40. Clothing. Miscellaneous

fashion	แฟชั่น	fae-chân
in vogue (adj)	คานิยม	khâa ní-yom
fashion designer	นักออกแบบแฟชั่น	nák òrk bàep fae-chân
collar	คอปกเสื้อ	khor bpòk sêua
pocket	กระเป๋า	grà-bpǎo
pocket (as adj)	กระเป๋า	grà-bpǎo
sleeve	แขนเสื้อ	khǎen sêua
hanging loop	ที่แขวนเสื้อ	thêe khwǎen sêua
flies (on trousers)	ซิปกางเกง	síp gaang-gayng
zip (fastener)	ซิป	síp
fastener	ซิป	síp
button	กระดุม	grà dum
buttonhole	รูกระดุม	roo grà dum
to come off (ab. button)	หลุดออก	lùt òrk
to sew (vi, vt)	เย็บ	yép
to embroider (vi, vt)	ปัก	bpàk
embroidery	ลายปัก	laai bpàk
sewing needle	เข็มเย็บผ้า	khěm yép phâa
thread	เสนตาย	sây-dâai
seam	รอยเย็บ	roi yép
to get dirty (vi)	สกปรก	sòk-gà-bpròk
stain (mark, spot)	รอยเปื้อน	roi bpêuan
to crease, to crumple	พับเป็นรอยยน	pháp bpen roi yôn
to tear, to rip (vt)	ฉีก	chèek
clothes moth	แมลงกินผ้า	má-laeng gin phâa

41. Personal care. Cosmetics

toothpaste	ยาสีฟัน	yaa sěe fan
toothbrush	แปรงสีฟัน	bpraeng sěe fan
to clean one's teeth	แปรงฟัน	bpraeng fan
razor	มีดโกน	mêet gohn
shaving cream	ครีมโกนหนวด	khreem gohn nùat
to shave (vi)	โกน	gohn
soap	สบู่	sà-bòo

shampoo	แชมพู	chaem-phoo
scissors	กรรไกร	gan-grai
nail file	ตะไบเล็บ	dtà-bai lép
nail clippers	กรรไกรตัดเล็บ	gan-grai dtàt lép
tweezers	แหนบ	nàep

cosmetics	เครื่องสำอาง	khrêuang săm-aang
face mask	มาสกหน้า	mâak nâa
manicure	การแตงเล็บ	gaan dtàeng lép
to have a manicure	แตงเล็บ	dtàeng lép
pedicure	การแตงเล็บเท้า	gaan dtàeng lép táo

make-up bag	กระเป๋าเครื่องสำอาง	grà-bpăo khrêuang săm-aang
face powder	แปงฝุ่น	bpâeng-fùn
powder compact	ตลับแปง	dtà-làp bpâeng
blusher	แปงทาแกม	bpâeng thaa gâem

perfume (bottled)	น้ำหอม	nám hŏrm
toilet water (lotion)	น้ำหอมออนๆ	náam hŏrm òn òn
lotion	โลชั่น	loh-chân
cologne	โคโลญจ์	khoh-lohn

eyeshadow	อายแชโดว์	aai-chae-doh
eyeliner	อายไลเนอร์	aai lai-ner
mascara	มาสคารา	mâat-khaa-râa

lipstick	ลิปสติก	líp-sà-dtìk
nail polish	น้ำยาทาเล็บ	nám yaa-thaa lép
hair spray	สเปรยฉีดผม	sà-bpray chèet phŏm
deodorant	ยาดับกลิ่น	yaa dàp glìn

cream	ครีม	khreem
face cream	ครีมทาหน้า	khreem thaa nâa
hand cream	ครีมทามือ	khreem thaa meu
anti-wrinkle cream	ครีมลดริ้วรอย	khreem lót ríw roi
day cream	ครีมกลางวัน	khreem klaang wan
night cream	ครีมกลางคืน	khreem klaang kheun
day (as adj)	กลางวัน	glaang wan
night (as adj)	กลางคืน	glaang kheun

tampon	ผ้าอนามัยแบบสอด	phâa a-naa-mai bàep sòrt
toilet paper (toilet roll)	กระดาษชำระ	grà-dàat cham-rá
hair dryer	เครื่องเป่าผม	khrêuang bpào phŏm

42. Jewellery

jewellery, jewels	เครื่องเพชรพลอย	khrêuang phét phloi
precious (e.g. ~ stone)	เพชรพลอย	phét phloi
hallmark stamp	ตราฮอลมาร์ค	dtraa hon-mâak

ring	แหวน	wăen
wedding ring	แหวนแตงงาน	wăen dtàeng ngaan
bracelet	กำไลขอมือ	gam-lai khôr meu
earrings	ตุมหู	dtûm hŏo

necklace (~ of pearls)	สร้อยคอ	sôi khor
crown	มงกุฎ	mong-gùt
bead necklace	สร้อยคอลูกปัด	sôi khor lôok bpàt

diamond	เพชร	phét
emerald	มรกต	mor-rá-gòt
ruby	พลอยสีทับทิม	phloi sěe tháp-thim
sapphire	ไพลิน	phai-lin
pearl	ไข่มุก	khài múk
amber	อำพัน	am phan

43. Watches. Clocks

watch (wristwatch)	นาฬิกา	naa-lí-gaa
dial	หน้าปัด	nâa bpàt
hand (clock, watch)	เข็ม	khěm
metal bracelet	สายนาฬิกาข้อมือ	sǎai naa-lí-gaa khôr meu
watch strap	สายรัดข้อมือ	sǎai rát khôr meu

battery	แบตเตอรี่	bàet-dter-rêe
to be flat (battery)	หมด	mòt
to change a battery	เปลี่ยนแบตเตอรี่	bplìan bàet-dter-rêe
to run fast	เดินเร็วเกินไป	dern reo gern bpai
to run slow	เดินช้า	dern cháa

wall clock	นาฬิกาแขวนผนัง	naa-lí-gaa khwǎen phà-nǎng
hourglass	นาฬิกาทราย	naa-lí-gaa saai
sundial	นาฬิกาแดด	naa-lí-gaa dàet
alarm clock	นาฬิกาปลุก	naa-lí-gaa bplùk
watchmaker	ช่างซ่อมนาฬิกา	châang sôrm naa-lí-gaa
to repair (vt)	ซ่อม	sôrm

Food. Nutricion

44. Food

meat	เนื้อ	néua
chicken	ไก่	gài
poussin	เนื้อลูกไก่	néua lôok gài
duck	เป็ด	bpèt
goose	หาน	hàan
game	สัตว์ที่ล่า	sàt thêe lâa
turkey	ไกงวง	gài nguang

pork	เนื้อหมู	néua mǒo
veal	เนื้อลูกวัว	néua lôok wua
lamb	เนื้อแกะ	néua gàe
beef	เนื้อวัว	néua wua
rabbit	เนื้อกระต่าย	néua grà-dtàai

sausage (bologna, etc.)	ไส้กรอก	sâi gròrk
vienna sausage (frankfurter)	ไสกรอกเวียนนา	sâi gròrk wian-naa
bacon	หมูเบคอน	mǒo bay-khorn
ham	แฮม	haem
gammon	แฮมแกมมอน	haem gaem-morn

pâté	ปาเต	bpaa dtay
liver	ตับ	dtàp
mince (minced meat)	เนื้อสับ	néua sàp
tongue	ลิ้น	lín

egg	ไข่	khài
eggs	ไข่	khài
egg white	ไข่ขาว	khài khǎao
egg yolk	ไขแดง	khài daeng

fish	ปลา	bplaa
seafood	อาหารทะเล	aa hǎan thá-lay
crustaceans	สัตว์พวกกุ้งกั้งปู	sàt phûak gûng gâng bpoo
caviar	ไขปลา	khài-bplaa

crab	ปู	bpoo
prawn	กุ้ง	gûng
oyster	หอยนางรม	hǒi naang rom
spiny lobster	กุ้งมังกร	gûng mang-gon
octopus	ปลาหมึก	bplaa mèuk
squid	ปลาหมึกกล้วย	bplaa mèuk-glûay

sturgeon	ปลาสเตอร์เจียน	bpláa sà-dtêr jian
salmon	ปลาแซลมอน	bplaa saen-morn
halibut	ปลาตาเดียว	bplaa dtaa-dieow
cod	ปลาค็อด	bplaa khót

mackerel	ปลาแม็คเคอเร็ล	bplaa máek-kay-a-rĕn
tuna	ปลาทูนา	bplaa thoo-nâa
eel	ปลาไหล	bplaa lăi

trout	ปลาเทราท์	bplaa thrau
sardine	ปลาซาร์ดีน	bplaa saa-deen
pike	ปลาไพค	bplaa phai
herring	ปลาเฮอริง	bplaa her-ring

bread	ขนมปัง	khà-nŏm bpang
cheese	เนยแข็ง	noie khăeng
sugar	น้ำตาล	nám dtaan
salt	เกลือ	gleua

rice	ข้าว	khâao
pasta (macaroni)	พาสต้า	phâat-dtâa
noodles	กวยเตี๋ยว	gŭay-dtĭeow

butter	เนย	noie
vegetable oil	น้ำมันพืช	nám man phêut
sunflower oil	น้ำมันดอกทานตะวัน	nám man dòrk thaan dtà-wan
margarine	เนยเทียม	noie thiam

olives	มะกอก	má-gòrk
olive oil	น้ำมันมะกอก	nám man má-gòrk

milk	นม	nom
condensed milk	นมข้น	nom khôn
yogurt	โยเกิร์ต	yoh-gèrt
soured cream	ชาวรครีม	saao khreem
cream (of milk)	ครีม	khreem

mayonnaise	มาย็องเนส	maa-yorng-nâyt
buttercream	สวนผสมของเนย	sùan phà-sŏm khŏrng
	และน้ำตาล	noie láe nám dtaan

groats (barley ~, etc.)	เมล็ดธัญพืช	má-lét than-yá-phêut
flour	แป้ง	bpâeng
tinned food	อาหารกระป๋อง	aa-hăan grà-bpŏrng

cornflakes	คอร์นเฟลค	khorn-flâyk
honey	น้ำผึ้ง	nám phêung
jam	แยม	yaem
chewing gum	หมากฝรั่ง	màak fà-ràng

45. Drinks

water	น้ำ	nám
drinking water	น้ำดื่ม	nám dèum
mineral water	น้ำแร่	nám râe

still (adj)	ไม่มีฟอง	mâi mee forng
carbonated (adj)	น้ำอัดลม	nám àt lom
sparkling (adj)	มีฟอง	mee forng

| ice | น้ำแข็ง | nám khăeng |
| with ice | ใส่น้ำแข็ง | sài nám khăeng |

non-alcoholic (adj)	ไม่มีแอลกอฮอล์	mâi mee aen-gor-hor
soft drink	เครื่องดื่มที่ไม่มี แอลกอฮอล	krêuang dèum têe mâi mee aen-gor-hor
refreshing drink	เครื่องดื่มให้ ความสดชื่น	khrêuang dèum hâi khwaam sòt chêun
lemonade	น้ำเลมอนเนด	nám lay-morn-nâyt

spirits	เหล้า	lăo
wine	ไวน์	wai
white wine	ไวน์ขาว	wai khăao
red wine	ไวน์แดง	wai daeng

liqueur	สุรา	sù-raa
champagne	แชมเปญ	chaem-bpayn
vermouth	เหล้าองุ่นขาวซึ่งมี กลิ่นหอม	lâo a-ngùn khăao sêung mee glìn hŏrm

whisky	เหล้าวิสกี้	lăo wít-sa -gêe
vodka	เหล้าวอดก้า	lăo wórt-gâa
gin	เหล้ายิน	lăo yin
cognac	เหล้าคอนยัก	lăo khorn yák
rum	เหลารัม	lăo ram

coffee	กาแฟ	gaa-fae
black coffee	กาแฟดำๆ	gaa-fae dam
white coffee	กาแฟใส่นม	gaa-fae sài nom
cappuccino	กาแฟคาปูชิโน	gaa-fae khaa bpoo chí noh
instant coffee	กาแฟสำเร็จรูป	gaa-fae săm-rèt rôop

milk	นม	nom
cocktail	ค็อกเทล	khók-tayn
milkshake	มิลค์เชค	min-châyk

juice	น้ำผลไม้	nám phŏn-lá-máai
tomato juice	น้ำมะเขือเทศ	nám má-khĕua thâyt
orange juice	น้ำส้ม	nám sôm
freshly squeezed juice	น้ำผลไม้คั้นสด	nám phŏn-lá-máai khán sòt

beer	เบียร์	bia
lager	เบียร์ไลท์	bia lai
bitter	เบียร์ดาร์ค	bia dàak

tea	ชา	chaa
black tea	ชาดำ	chaa dam
green tea	ชาเขียว	chaa khĭeow

46. Vegetables

vegetables	ผัก	phàk
greens	ผักใบเขียว	phàk bai khĭeow
tomato	มะเขือเทศ	má-khĕua thâyt

cucumber	แตงกวา	dtaeng-gwaa
carrot	แครอท	khae-rót
potato	มันฝรั่ง	man fà-ràng
onion	หัวหอม	hǔa hǒrm
garlic	กระเทียม	grà-thiam
cabbage	กะหล่ำปลี	gà-làm bplee
cauliflower	ดอกกะหล่ำ	dòrk gà-làm
Brussels sprouts	กะหล่ำดาว	gà-làm-daao
broccoli	บร็อคโคลี่	bròrk-khoh-lêe
beetroot	บีทรูท	bee-trôot
aubergine	มะเขือยาว	má-khěua-yaao
courgette	แตงซูคินี	dtaeng soo-khí-nee
pumpkin	ฟักทอง	fák-thorng
turnip	หัวผักกาด	hǔa-phàk-gàat
parsley	ผักชีฝรั่ง	phàk chee fà-ràng
dill	ผักชีลาว	phàk-chee-laao
lettuce	ผักกาดหอม	phàk gàat hǒrm
celery	คื่นช่าย	khêun-châai
asparagus	หน่อไม้ฝรั่ง	nòr máai fà-ràng
spinach	ผักขม	phàk khǒm
pea	ถั่วลันเตา	thùa-lan-dtao
beans	ถั่ว	thùa
maize	ข้าวโพด	khâao-phôht
kidney bean	ถั่วรูปไต	thùa rôop dtai
sweet paper	พริกหยวก	phrík-yùak
radish	หัวไชเท้า	hǔa chai tháo
artichoke	อาร์ติโชค	aa dtì chôhk

47. Fruits. Nuts

fruit	ผลไม้	phǒn-lá-máai
apple	แอปเปิ้ล	àep-bpêrn
pear	แพร	phae
lemon	มะนาว	má-naao
orange	ส้ม	sôm
strawberry (garden ~)	สตรอว์เบอร์รี่	sà-dtror-ber-rêe
tangerine	ส้มแมนดาริน	sôm maen daa rin
plum	พลัม	phlam
peach	ลูกทอ	lôok thór
apricot	แอปริคอท	ae-bprì-khôrt
raspberry	ราสเบอร์รี่	râat-ber-rêe
pineapple	สับปะรด	sàp-bpà-rót
banana	กล้วย	glûay
watermelon	แตงโม	dtaeng moh
grape	องุ่น	a-ngùn
sour cherry	เชอรี่	cher-rêe
sweet cherry	เชอรี่ป่า	cher-rêe bpàa

melon	เมลอน	may-lorn
grapefruit	สมโอ	sôm oh
avocado	อะโวคาโด	a-who-khaa-doh
papaya	มะละกอ	má-lá-gor
mango	มะม่วง	má-mûang
pomegranate	ทับทิม	tháp-thim

redcurrant	เรดเคอร์แรนท์	râyt-khêr-raen
blackcurrant	แบล็คเคอร์แรนท์	blàek khêr-raen
gooseberry	กูสเบอร์รี่	gòot-ber-rêe
bilberry	บิลเบอร์รี่	bil-ber-rêe
blackberry	แบล็คเบอร์รี่	blàek ber-rêe

raisin	ลูกเกด	lôok gàyt
fig	มะเดื่อฝรั่ง	má dèua fà-ràng
date	ลูกอินทผลัม	lôok in-thá-plǎm

peanut	ถั่วลิสง	thùa-lí-sǒng
almond	อัลมอนด์	an-morn
walnut	วอลนัต	wor-lá-nát
hazelnut	เฮเซลนัท	hay sayn nát
coconut	มะพร้าว	má-phráao
pistachios	ถั่วพิสตาชิโอ	thùa phít dtaa chí oh

48. Bread. Sweets

bakers' confectionery (pastry)	ขนม	khà-nǒm
bread	ขนมปัง	khà-nǒm bpang
biscuits	คุกกี้	khúk-gêe

chocolate (n)	ช็อกโกแลต	chók-goh-láet
chocolate (as adj)	ช็อกโกแลต	chók-goh-láet
candy (wrapped)	ลูกกวาด	lôok gwàat
cake (e.g. cupcake)	ขนมเค้ก	khà-nǒm kháyk
cake (e.g. birthday ~)	ขนมเค้ก	khà-nǒm kháyk

pie (e.g. apple ~)	ขนมพาย	khà-nǒm phaai
filling (for cake, pie)	ไส้ในขนม	sâi nai khà-nǒm

jam (whole fruit jam)	แยม	yaem
marmalade	แยมผิวส้ม	yaem phǐw sôm
wafers	วาฟเฟิล	waaf-fern
ice-cream	ไอศกรีม	ai-sà-greem
pudding (Christmas ~)	พุดดิ้ง	phút-dîng

49. Cooked dishes

course, dish	มื้ออาหาร	méu aa-hǎan
cuisine	อาหาร	aa-hǎan
recipe	ตำราอาหาร	dtam-raa aa-hǎan
portion	สวน	sùan
salad	สลัด	sà-làt

soup	ซุป	súp
clear soup (broth)	ซุปน้ำใส	súp nám-sǎi
sandwich (bread)	แซนด์วิช	saen-wít
fried eggs	ไข่ทอด	khài thôrt

hamburger (beefburger)	แฮมเบอร์เกอร์	haem-ber-gêr
beefsteak	สเต็กเนื้อ	sà-dtèk néua

side dish	เครื่องเคียง	khrêuang khiang
spaghetti	สปาเก็ตตี้	sà-bpaa-gèt-dtêe
mash	มันฝรั่งบด	man fà-ràng bòt
pizza	พิซซ่า	phít-sâa
porridge (oatmeal, etc.)	ข้าวต้ม	khâao-dtôm
omelette	ไข่เจียว	khài jieow

boiled (e.g. ~ beef)	ต้ม	dtôm
smoked (adj)	รมควัน	rom khwan
fried (adj)	ทอด	thôrt
dried (adj)	ตากแห้ง	dtàak hâeng
frozen (adj)	แช่แข็ง	châe khǎeng
pickled (adj)	ดอง	dorng

sweet (sugary)	หวาน	wǎan
salty (adj)	เค็ม	khem
cold (adj)	เย็น	yen
hot (adj)	ร้อน	rórn
bitter (adj)	ขม	khǒm
tasty (adj)	อร่อย	à-ròi

to cook in boiling water	ต้ม	dtôm
to cook (dinner)	ทำอาหาร	tham aa-hǎan
to fry (vt)	ทอด	thôrt
to heat up (food)	อุ่น	ùn

to salt (vt)	ใส่เกลือ	sài gleua
to pepper (vt)	ใส่พริกไทย	sài phrík thai
to grate (vt)	ขูด	khòot
peel (n)	เปลือก	bplèuak
to peel (vt)	ปอกเปลือก	bpòrk bplêuak

50. Spices

salt	เกลือ	gleua
salty (adj)	เค็ม	khem
to salt (vt)	ใส่เกลือ	sài gleua

black pepper	พริกไทย	phrík thai
red pepper (milled ~)	พริกแดง	phrík daeng
mustard	มัสตาร์ด	mát-dtàat
horseradish	ฮอสแรดิช	hórt rae dìt

condiment	เครื่องปรุงรส	khrêuang bprung rót
spice	เครื่องเทศ	khrêuang thâyt
sauce	ซอส	sós

vinegar	น้ำส้มสายชู	nám sôm săai choo
anise	เทียนสัตตบุษย์	thian-sàt-dtà-bùt
basil	ใบโหระพา	bai hŏh rá phaa
cloves	กานพลู	gaan-phloo
ginger	ขิง	khĭng
coriander	ผักชีลา	pàk-chee-laa
cinnamon	อบเชย	òp-choie

sesame	งา	ngaa
bay leaf	ใบกระวาน	bai grà-waan
paprika	พริกป่น	phrík bpòn
caraway	เทียนตากบ	thian dtaa gòp
saffron	หญ้าฝรั่น	yâa fà-ràn

51. Meals

food	อาหาร	aa-hăan
to eat (vi, vt)	กิน	gin

breakfast	อาหารเช้า	aa-hăan cháo
to have breakfast	ทานอาหารเช้า	thaan aa-hăan cháo
lunch	ขาวเที่ยง	khâao thîang
to have lunch	ทานอาหารเที่ยง	thaan aa-hăan thîang
dinner	อาหารเย็น	aa-hăan yen
to have dinner	ทานอาหารเย็น	thaan aa-hăan yen

appetite	ความอยากอาหาร	kwaam yàak aa hăan
Enjoy your meal!	กินใหอรอย!	gin hâi a-ròi

to open (~ a bottle)	เปิด	bpèrt
to spill (liquid)	ทำหก	tham hòk
to spill out (vi)	ทำหกออกมา	tham hòk òrk maa
to boil (vi)	ตูม	dtôm
to boil (vt)	ตูม	dtôm
boiled (~ water)	ตม	dtôm
to chill, cool down (vt)	แชเย็น	châe yen
to chill (vi)	แชเย็น	châe yen

taste, flavour	รสชาติ	rót châat
aftertaste	รส	rót

to slim down (lose weight)	ลดน้ำหนัก	lót nám nàk
diet	อาหารพิเศษ	aa-hăan phí-sàyt
vitamin	วิตามิน	wí-dtaa-min
calorie	แคลอรี่	khae-lor-rêe
vegetarian (n)	คนกินเจ	khon gin jay
vegetarian (adj)	มังสวิรัติ	mang-sà-wí-rát

fats (nutrient)	ไขมัน	khăi man
proteins	โปรตีน	bproh-dteen
carbohydrates	คาร์โบไฮเดรต	kaa-boh-hai-dràyt
slice (of lemon, ham)	แผน	phàen
piece (of cake, pie)	ชิ้น	chín
crumb (of bread, cake, etc.)	เศษ	sàyt

52. Table setting

spoon	ช้อน	chórn
knife	มีด	mêet
fork	สอม	sôrm

cup (e.g., coffee ~)	แก้ว	gâew
plate (dinner ~)	จาน	jaan
saucer	จานรอง	jaan rorng
serviette	ผ้าเช็ดปาก	phâa chét bpàak
toothpick	ไม้จิ้มฟัน	máai jîm fan

53. Restaurant

restaurant	ร้านอาหาร	ráan aa-hǎan
coffee bar	ร้านกาแฟ	ráan gaa-fae
pub, bar	ร้านเหล้า	ráan lâo
tearoom	รานน้ำชา	ráan nám chaa

waiter	คนเสิร์ฟชาย	khon sèrf chaai
waitress	คนเสิร์ฟหญิง	khon sèrf yǐng
barman	บาร์เทนเดอร์	baa-thayn-dêr

menu	เมนู	may-noo
wine list	รายการไวน์	raai gaan wai
to book a table	จองโต๊ะ	jorng dtó

course, dish	มื้ออาหาร	méu aa-hǎan
to order (meal)	สั่ง	sàng
to make an order	สั่งอาหาร	sàng aa-hǎan

aperitif	เครื่องดื่มเหล้ากอนอาหาร	khrêuang dèum lâo gòrn aa-hǎan
starter	ของกินเล่น	khǒrng gin lâyn
dessert, pudding	ของหวาน	khǒrng wǎan

bill	คิดเงิน	khít ngern
to pay the bill	จวยคาอาหาร	jàai khâa aa hǎan
to give change	ให้เงินทอน	hâi ngern thorn
tip	เงินทิป	ngern thíp

Family, relatives and friends

54. Personal information. Forms

name (first name)	ชื่อ	chêu
surname (last name)	นามสกุล	naam sà-gun
date of birth	วันเกิด	wan gèrt
place of birth	สถานที่เกิด	sà-thăan thêe gèrt
nationality	สัญชาติ	săn-châat
place of residence	ที่อยู่อาศัย	thêe yòo aa-săi
country	ประเทศ	bprà-thâyt
profession (occupation)	อาชีพ	aa-chêep
gender, sex	เพศ	phâyt
height	ความสูง	khwaam sŏong
weight	น้ำหนัก	nám nàk

55. Family members. Relatives

mother	มารดา	maan-daa
father	บิดา	bì-daa
son	ลูกชาย	lôok chaai
daughter	ลูกสาว	lôok săao
younger daughter	ลูกสาวคนเล็ก	lôok săao khon lék
younger son	ลูกชายคนเล็ก	lôok chaai khon lék
eldest daughter	ลูกสาวคนโต	lôok săao khon dtoh
eldest son	ลูกชายคนโต	lôok chaai khon dtoh
elder brother	พี่ชาย	phêe chaai
younger brother	น้องชาย	nórng chaai
elder sister	พี่สาว	phêe săao
younger sister	น้องสาว	nórng săao
cousin (masc.)	ลูกพี่ลูกน้อง	lôok phêe lôok nórng
cousin (fem.)	ลูกพี่ลูกน้อง	lôok phêe lôok nórng
mummy	แม่	mâe
dad, daddy	พ่อ	phôr
parents	พ่อแม่	phôr mâe
child	เด็ก, ลูก	dèk, lôok
children	เด็กๆ	dèk dèk
grandmother	ย่า, ยาย	yâa, yaai
grandfather	ปู่, ตา	bpòo, dtaa
grandson	หลานชาย	lăan chaai
granddaughter	หลานสาว	lăan săao

grandchildren	หลานๆ	lăan
uncle	ลุง	lung
aunt	ป้า	bpâa
nephew	หลานชาย	lăan chaai
niece	หลานสาว	lăan săao

mother-in-law (wife's mother)	แม่ยาย	mâe yaai
father-in-law (husband's father)	พ่อสามี	phôr săa-mee
son-in-law (daughter's husband)	ลูกเขย	lôok khŏie
stepmother	แม่เลี้ยง	mâe líang
stepfather	พ่อเลี้ยง	phôr líang

infant	ทารก	thaa-rók
baby (infant)	เด็กเล็ก	dèk lék
little boy, kid	เด็ก	dèk

wife	ภรรยา	phan-rá-yaa
husband	สามี	săa-mee
spouse (husband)	สามี	săa-mee
spouse (wife)	ภรรยา	phan-rá-yaa

married (masc.)	แต่งงานแล้ว	dtàeng ngaan láew
married (fem.)	แตงงานแลว	dtàeng ngaan láew
single (unmarried)	เป็นโสด	bpen sòht
bachelor	ชายโสด	chaai sòht
divorced (masc.)	หย่าแล้ว	yàa láew
widow	แม่หม้าย	mâe mâai
widower	พ่อหม้าย	phôr mâai

relative	ญาติ	yâat
close relative	ญาติใกล้ชิด	yâat glâi chít
distant relative	ญาติห่างๆ	yâat hàang hàang
relatives	ญาติๆ	yâat

orphan (boy)	เด็กชายกำพร้า	dèk chaai gam phráa
orphan (girl)	เด็กหญิงกำพรา	dèk yĭng gam phráa
guardian (of a minor)	ผู้ปกครอง	phôo bpòk khrorng
to adopt (a boy)	บุญธรรม	bun tham
to adopt (a girl)	บุญธรรม	bun tham

56. Friends. Colleagues

friend (masc.)	เพื่อน	phêuan
friend (fem.)	เพื่อน	phêuan
friendship	มิตรภาพ	mít-dtrà-phâap
to be friends	เป็นเพื่อน	bpen phêuan

pal (masc.)	เพื่อนสนิท	phêuan sà-nìt
pal (fem.)	เพื่อนสนิท	phêuan sà-nìt
partner	หุ้นส่วน	hûn sùan
chief (boss)	หัวหน้า	hŭa-nâa

superior (n)	ผู้บังคับบัญชา	phôo bang-kháp ban-chaa
owner, proprietor	เจ้าของ	jâo khǒrng
subordinate (n)	ลูกน้อง	lôok nórng
colleague	เพื่อนร่วมงาน	phêuan rûam ngaan
acquaintance (person)	ผู้คุ้นเคย	phôo khún khoie
fellow traveller	เพื่อนร่วมทาง	pêuan rûam thaang
classmate	เพื่อนรุ่น	phêuan rûn
neighbour (masc.)	เพื่อนบ้านผู้ชาย	phêuan bâan pôo chaai
neighbour (fem.)	เพื่อนบ้านผู้หญิง	phêuan bâan phôo yǐng
neighbours	เพื่อนบ้าน	phêuan bâan

57. Man. Woman

woman	ผู้หญิง	phôo yǐng
girl (young woman)	หญิงสาว	yǐng sǎao
bride	เจ้าสาว	jâo sǎao
beautiful (adj)	สวย	sǔay
tall (adj)	สูง	sǒong
slender (adj)	ผอม	phǒrm
short (adj)	เตี้ย	dtîa
blonde (n)	ผมสีทอง	phǒm sěe thorng
brunette (n)	ผมสีคล้ำ	phǒm sěe khlám
ladies' (adj)	สตรี	sàt-dtree
virgin (girl)	บริสุทธิ์	bor-rí-sùt
pregnant (adj)	ตั้งครรภ์	dtâng khan
man (adult male)	ผู้ชาย	phôo chaai
blonde haired man	ผมสีทอง	phǒm sěe thorng
dark haired man	ผมสีคล้ำ	phǒm sěe khlám
tall (adj)	สูง	sǒong
short (adj)	เตี้ย	dtîa
rude (rough)	หยาบคาย	yàap kaai
stocky (adj)	แข็งแรง	khǎeng raeng
robust (adj)	กำยำ	gam-yam
strong (adj)	แข็งแรง	khǎeng raeng
strength	ความแข็งแรง	khwaam khǎeng raeng
plump, fat (adj)	ท้วม	thúam
swarthy (dark-skinned)	ผิวดำ	phǐw dam
slender (well-built)	ผอม	phǒrm
elegant (adj)	สง่า	sà-ngàa

58. Age

age	อายุ	aa-yú
youth (young age)	วัยเยาว์	wai yao

young (adj)	หนุ่ม	nùm
younger (adj)	อายุน้อยกว่า	aa-yú nói gwàa
older (adj)	อายุสูงกว่า	aa-yú sŏong gwàa
young man	ชายหนุ่ม	chaai nùm
teenager	วัยรุ่น	wai rûn
guy, fellow	คนหนุ่ม	khon nùm
old man	ชายชรา	chaai chá-raa
old woman	หญิงชรา	yǐng chá-raa
adult (adj)	ผู้ใหญ่	phôo yài
middle-aged (adj)	วัยกลาง	wai glaang
elderly (adj)	วัยชรา	wai chá-raa
old (adj)	แก่	gàe
retirement	การเกษียณอายุ	gaan gà-sǐan aa-yú
to retire (from job)	เกษียณ	gà-sǐan
retiree, pensioner	ผู้เกษียณอายุ	phôo gà-sǐan aa-yú

59. Children

child	เด็ก, ลูก	dèk, lôok
children	เด็กๆ	dèk dèk
twins	แฝด	fàet
cradle	เปล	bplay
rattle	ของเล่นกุ๊งกิ๊ง	khŏrng lên gúng-gîng
nappy	ผ้าอ้อม	phâa ôrm
dummy, comforter	จุกนม	jùk-nom
pram	รถเข็นเด็ก	rót khěn dèk
nursery	โรงเรียนอนุบาล	rohng rian a-nú-baan
babysitter	คนเฝ้าเด็ก	khon fâo dèk
childhood	วัยเด็ก	wai dèk
doll	ตุ๊กตา	dtúk-dtaa
toy	ของเล่น	khŏrng lên
construction set (toy)	ชุดของเล่นก่อสร้าง	chút khŏrng lên gòr sâang
well-bred (adj)	มีกิริยา มารยาทดี	mee gì-rí-yaa maa-rá-yâat dee
ill-bred (adj)	ไม่มีมารยาท	mâi mee maa-rá-yâat
spoilt (adj)	เสียคน	sǐa khon
to be naughty	ซน	son
mischievous (adj)	ซน	son
mischievousness	ความเกเร	kwaam gay-ray
mischievous child	เด็กเกเร	dèk gay-ray
obedient (adj)	ที่เชื่อฟัง	thêe chêua fang
disobedient (adj)	ที่ไม่เชื่อฟัง	thêe mâi chêua fang
docile (adj)	ที่เชื่อฟังผู้ใหญ่	thée chêua fang phôo yài
clever (intelligent)	ฉลาด	chà-làat
child prodigy	เด็กมีพรสวรรค์	dèk mee phon sà-wǎn

60. Married couples. Family life

to kiss (vt)	จูบ	jòop
to kiss (vi)	จูบ	jòop
family (n)	ครอบครัว	khrôrp khrua
family (as adj)	ครอบครัว	khrôrp khrua
couple	ตัวเมีย	phǔa mia
marriage (state)	การแตงงาน	gaan dtàeng ngaan
hearth (home)	บาน	bâan
dynasty	วงศตระกูล	wong dtrà-goon

date	การออกเดท	gaan òrk dàyt
kiss	การจูบ	gaan jòop

love (for sb)	ความรัก	khwaam rák
to love (sb)	รัก	rák
beloved	ที่รัก	thêe rák

tenderness	ความละเมียดละไม	khwaam lá-mîat lá-mai
tender (affectionate)	ละเมียดละไม	lá-mîat lá-mai
faithfulness	ความซื่อ	khwaam sêu
faithful (adj)	ซื่อ	sêu
care (attention)	การดูแล	gaan doo lae
caring (~ father)	ชอบดูแล	chôrp doo lae

newlyweds	คู่แต่งงานใหม่	khôo dtàeng ngaan mài
honeymoon	ฮันนีมูน	han-nee-moon
to get married (ab. woman)	แตงงาน	dtàeng ngaan
to get married (ab. man)	แตงงาน	dtàeng ngaan
wedding	การสมรส	gaan sǒm rót
golden wedding	การสมรส ครบรอบ 50 ปี	gaan sǒm rót khróp rôrp hâa-sìp bpee
anniversary	วันครบรอบ	wan khróp rôrp

lover (masc.)	คู่รัก	khôo rák
mistress (lover)	เมียนอย	mia nói

adultery	การดูบชู้	gaan khóp chóo
to cheat on ... (commit adultery)	คบชู้	khóp chóo
jealous (adj)	หึงหวง	hěung hǔang
to be jealous	หึง	hěung
divorce	การหย่าร้าง	gaan yàa ráang
to divorce (vi)	หย่า	yàa

to quarrel (vi)	ทะเลาะ	thá-lór
to be reconciled (after an argument)	ประนีประนอม	bprà-nee-bprà-nom
together (adv)	ด้วยกัน	dûay gan
sex	เพศสัมพันธ์	phâyt sǎm-phan

happiness	ความสุข	khwaam sùk
happy (adj)	มีความสุข	mee khwaam sùk
misfortune (accident)	เหตุราย	hàyt ráai
unhappy (adj)	ไม่มีความสุข	mâi mee khwaam sùk

Character. Feelings. Emotions

61. Feelings. Emotions

feeling (emotion)	ความรู้สึก	khwaam róo sèuk
feelings	ความรู้สึก	khwaam róo sèuk
to feel (vt)	รู้สึก	róo sèuk
hunger	ความหิว	khwaam hǐw
to be hungry	หิว	hǐw
thirst	ความกระหาย	khwaam grà-hǎai
to be thirsty	กระหาย	grà-hǎai
sleepiness	ความง่วง	khwaam ngûang
to feel sleepy	ง่วง	ngûang
tiredness	ความเหนื่อย	khwaam nèuay
tired (adj)	เหนื่อย	nèuay
to get tired	เหนื่อย	nèuay
mood (humour)	อารมณ์	aa-rom
boredom	ความเบื่อ	khwaam bèua
to be bored	เบื่อ	bèua
seclusion	ความเหงา	khwaam ngǎo
to seclude oneself	ปลีกวิเวก	bplèek wí-wâyk
to worry (make anxious)	ทำให้...เป็นห่วง	tham hâi...bpen hùang
to be worried	กังวล	gang-won
worrying (n)	ความเป็นห่วง	khwaam bpen hùang
anxiety	ความวิตกกังวล	khwaam wí-dtòk gang-won
preoccupied (adj)	เป็นห่วงใหญ่	bpen hùang yài
to be nervous	กระวนกระวาย	grà won grà waai
to panic (vi)	ตื่นตระหนก	dtèun dtrà-nòk
hope	ความหวัง	khwaam wǎng
to hope (vi, vt)	หวัง	wǎng
certainty	ความแน่ใจ	khwaam nâe jai
certain, sure (adj)	แน่ใจ	nâe jai
uncertainty	ความไม่มั่นใจ	khwaam mâi mân jai
uncertain (adj)	ไม่มั่นใจ	mâi mân jai
drunk (adj)	เมา	mao
sober (adj)	ไม่เมา	mâi mao
weak (adj)	อ่อนแอ	òrn ae
happy (adj)	มีความสุข	mee khwaam sùk
to scare (vt)	ทำให้...กลัว	tham hâi...glua
fury (madness)	ความโกรธเคือง	khwaam gròht kheuang
rage (fury)	ความเดือดดาล	khwaam dèuat daan
depression	ความหดหู่	khwaam hòt-hòo
discomfort (unease)	อึดอัด	èut àt

comfort	สบาย	sà-baai
to regret (be sorry)	เสียดาย	sǐa daai
regret	ความเสียดาย	khwaam sǐa daai
bad luck	โชคราย	chôhk ráai
sadness	ความเศรา	khwaam sâo

shame (remorse)	ความละอายใจ	khwaam lá-aai jai
gladness	ความปิติ	khwaam bpì-dtì
enthusiasm, zeal	ความกระตือรือร้น	khwaam grà-dteu-reu-rón
enthusiast	คนที่กระตือรือรน	khon thêe grà-dteu-reu-rón
to show enthusiasm	แสดงความ กระตือรือรน	sà-daeng khwaam grà-dteu-reu-rón

62. Character. Personality

character	นิสัย	ní-sǎi
character flaw	ขอเสีย	khôr sǐa
mind	สติ	sà-dtì
reason	สติ	sà-dtì

conscience	มโนธรรม	má-noh tham
habit (custom)	นิสัย	ní-sǎi
ability (talent)	ความสามารถ	khwaam sǎa-mâat
can (e.g. ~ swim)	สามารถ	sǎa-mâat

patient (adj)	อดทน	òt thon
impatient (adj)	ใจรอนใจเร็ว	jai rórn jai reo
curious (inquisitive)	อยากรู้อยากเห็น	yàak róo yàak hěn
curiosity	ความอยากรู้อยากเห็น	khwaam yàak róo yàak hěn

modesty	ความถอมตน	khwaam thòrm dton
modest (adj)	ถอมตน	thòrm dton
immodest (adj)	หยาบโลน	yàap lohn

laziness	ความขี้เกียจ	khwaam khêe gìat
lazy (adj)	ขี้เกียจ	khêe gìat
lazy person (masc.)	คนขี้เกียจ	khon khêe gìat

cunning (n)	ความเจ้าเล่ห์	khwaam jâo lây
cunning (as adj)	เจาเลห	jâo lây
distrust	ความหวาดระแวง	khwaam wàat rá-waeng
distrustful (adj)	เคลือบแคลง	khlêuap-khlaeng

generosity	ความเอื้อเฟื้อ	khwaam êua féua
generous (adj)	มีน้ำใจ	mee nám jai
talented (adj)	มีพรสวรรค์	mee phon sà-wǎn
talent	พรสวรรค	phon sà-wǎn

courageous (adj)	กล้าหาญ	glâa hǎan
courage	ความกล้าหาญ	khwaam glâa hǎan
honest (adj)	ชื่อสัตย์	sêu sàt
honesty	ความชื่อสัตย์	khwaam sêu sàt
careful (cautious)	ระมัดระวัง	rá mát rá-wang
brave (courageous)	กลา	glâa

serious (adj)	เอาจริงเอาจัง	ao jing ao jang
strict (severe, stern)	เขมงวด	khêm ngûat
decisive (adj)	เด็ดเดี่ยว	dèt dìeow
indecisive (adj)	ไม่เด็ดขาด	mâi dèt khàat
shy, timid (adj)	อาย	aai
shyness, timidity	ความขวยอาย	khwaam khǔay aai
confidence (trust)	ความไว้ใจ	khwaam wái jai
to believe (trust)	ไว้เนื้อเชื่อใจ	wái néua chêua jai
trusting (credulous)	เชื่อใจ	chêua jai
sincerely (adv)	อย่างจริงใจ	yàang jing jai
sincere (adj)	จริงใจ	jing jai
sincerity	ความจริงใจ	khwaam jing jai
open (person)	เปิดเผย	bpèrt phǒie
calm (adj)	ใจเย็น	jai yen
frank (sincere)	จริงใจ	jing jai
naïve (adj)	หลงเชื่อ	lǒng chêua
absent-minded (adj)	ใจลอย	jai loi
funny (odd)	ตลก	dtà-lòk
greed, stinginess	ความโลภ	khwaam lôhp
greedy, stingy (adj)	โลภ	lôhp
stingy (adj)	ขี้เหนียว	khêe nǐeow
evil (adj)	เลว	leo
stubborn (adj)	ดื้อ	dêu
unpleasant (adj)	ไม่น่าพึงพอใจ	mâi nâa pheung phor jai
selfish person (masc.)	คนที่เห็นแก่ตัว	khon thêe hěn gàe dtua
selfish (adj)	เห็นแก่ตัว	hěn gàe dtua
coward	คนขี้ขลาด	khon khêe khlàat
cowardly (adj)	ขี้ขลาด	khêe khlàat

63. Sleep. Dreams

to sleep (vi)	นอน	norn
sleep, sleeping	ความนอน	khwaam norn
dream	ความฝัน	khwaam fǎn
to dream (in sleep)	ฝัน	fǎn
sleepy (adj)	ง่วง	ngûang
bed	เตียง	dtiang
mattress	ฟูกนอน	fôok norn
blanket (eiderdown)	ผ้าห่ม	phâa hòm
pillow	หมอน	mǒrn
sheet	ผ้าปูที่นอน	phâa bpoo thêe norn
insomnia	อาการนอนไม่หลับ	aa-gaan norn mâi làp
sleepless (adj)	นอนไม่หลับ	norn mâi làp
sleeping pill	ยานอนหลับ	yaa-norn-làp
to take a sleeping pill	กินยานอนหลับ	gin yaa-norn-làp
to feel sleepy	ง่วง	ngûang

to yawn (vi)	หาว	hăao
to go to bed	ไปนอน	bpai norn
to make up the bed	ปูที่นอน	bpoo thêe norn
to fall asleep	หลับ	làp
nightmare	ฝันร้าย	făn ráai
snore, snoring	การกรน	gaan-kron
to snore (vi)	กรน	gron
alarm clock	นาฬิกาปลุก	naa-lí-gaa bplùk
to wake (vt)	ปลุก	bplùk
to wake up	ตื่น	dtèun
to get up (vi)	ลุกขึ้น	lúk khêun
to have a wash	ล้างหน้าล้างตา	láang nâa láang dtaa

64. Humour. Laughter. Gladness

humour (wit, fun)	อารมณ์ขัน	aa-rom khăn
sense of humour	อารมณ์	aa-rom
to enjoy oneself	เริงรื่น	rerng rêun
cheerful (merry)	เริงรื่น	rerng rêun
merriment (gaiety)	ความรื่นเริง	khwaam rêun-rerng
smile	รอยยิ้ม	roi yím
to smile (vi)	ยิ้ม	yím
to start laughing	เริ่มหัวเราะ	rêrm hŭa rór
to laugh (vi)	หัวเราะ	hŭa rór
laugh, laughter	การหัวเราะ	gaan hŭa rór
anecdote	เรื่องขำขัน	rêuang khăm khăn
funny (anecdote, etc.)	ตลก	dtà-lòk
funny (odd)	ขบขัน	khòp khăn
to joke (vi)	ล้อเล่น	lór lên
joke (verbal)	ตลก	dtà-lòk
joy (emotion)	ความสุขสันต์	khwaam sùk-săn
to rejoice (vi)	โมทนา	moh-thá-naa
joyful (adj)	ยินดี	yin dee

65. Discussion, conversation. Part 1

communication	การสื่อสาร	gaan sèu săan
to communicate	สื่อสาร	sèu săan
conversation	การสนทนา	gaan sŏn-thá-naa
dialogue	บทสนทนา	bòt sŏn-thá-naa
discussion (discourse)	การหารือ	gaan hăa-reu
dispute (debate)	การโต้แย้ง	gaan dtôh yáeng
to dispute, to debate	โต้แย้ง	dtôh yáeng
interlocutor	คู่สนทนา	khôo sŏn-tá-naa
topic (theme)	หัวข้อ	hŭa khôr

point of view	แง่คิด	ngâe khít
opinion (point of view)	ความคิดเห็น	khwaam khít hěn
speech (talk)	สุนทรพจน์	sǔn tha ra phót

discussion (of a report, etc.)	การหารือ	gaan hǎa-reu
to discuss (vt)	หารือ	hǎa-reu
talk (conversation)	การสนทนา	gaan sǒn-thá-naa
to talk (to chat)	คุยกัน	khui gan
meeting (encounter)	การพบกัน	gaan phóp gan
to meet (vi, vt)	พบ	phóp

proverb	สุภาษิต	sù-phaa-sìt
saying	คำกล่าว	kham glàao
riddle (poser)	ปริศนา	bprìt-sà-nǎa
to pose a riddle	ถามปริศนา	thǎam bprìt-sà-nǎa
password	รหัสผ่าน	rá-hàt phàan
secret	ความลับ	khwaam láp

oath (vow)	คำสาบาน	kham sǎa-baan
to swear (an oath)	สาบาน	sǎa baan
promise	คำสัญญา	kham sǎn-yaa
to promise (vt)	สัญญา	sǎn-yaa

advice (counsel)	คำแนะนำ	kham náe nam
to advise (vt)	แนะนำ	náe nam
to follow one's advice	ทำตามคำแนะนำ	tham dtaam kham náe nam
to listen to ... (obey)	เชื่อฟัง	chêua fang

news	ข่าว	khàao
sensation (news)	ข่าวดัง	khàao dang
information (report)	ข้อมูล	khôr moon
conclusion (decision)	ข้อสรุป	khôr sà-rùp
voice	เสียง	sǐang
compliment	คำชมเชย	kham chom choie
kind (nice)	ใจดี	jai dee

word	คำ	kham
phrase	วลี	wá-lee
answer	คำตอบ	kham dtòrp

truth	ความจริง	khwaam jing
lie	การโกหก	gaan goh-hòk

thought	ความคิด	khwaam khít
idea (inspiration)	ความคิด	khwaam khít
fantasy	จินตนาการ	jin-dtà-naa gaan

66. Discussion, conversation. Part 2

respected (adj)	ที่นับถือ	thêe náp thěu
to respect (vt)	นับถือ	náp thěu
respect	ความนับถือ	khwaam náp thěu
Dear ... (letter)	ทาน	thâan
to introduce (sb to sb)	แนะนำ	náe nam

to make acquaintance	รู้จัก	róo jàk
intention	ความตั้งใจ	khwaam dtâng jai
to intend (have in mind)	ตั้งใจ	dtâng jai
wish	การขอพร	gaan khŏr phon
to wish (~ good luck)	ขอ	khŏr

surprise (astonishment)	ความประหลาดใจ	khwaam bprà-làat jai
to surprise (amaze)	ทำให้...ประหลาดใจ	tham hâi...bprà-làat jai
to be surprised	ประหลาดใจ	bprà-làat jai

to give (vt)	ให้	hâi
to take (get hold of)	รับ	ráp
to give back	ให้คืน	hâi kheun
to return (give back)	เอาคืน	ao kheun

to apologize (vi)	ขอโทษ	khŏr thôht
apology	คำขอโทษ	kham khŏr thôht
to forgive (vt)	ให้อภัย	hâi a-phai

to talk (speak)	คุยกัน	khui gan
to listen (vi)	ฟัง	fang
to hear out	ฟังจนจบ	fang jon jòp
to understand (vt)	เข้าใจ	khâo jai

to show (to display)	แสดง	sà-daeng
to look at ...	ดู	doo
to call (yell for sb)	เรียก	rîak
to distract (disturb)	รบกวน	róp guan
to disturb (vt)	รุบกวน	róp guan
to pass (to hand sth)	ส่ง	sòng

demand (request)	ข้อร้องขอ	khŏr rórng khŏr
to request (ask)	ร้องขอ	rórng khŏr
demand (firm request)	ขอเรียกร้อง	khŏr rîak rórng
to demand (request firmly)	เรียกร้อง	rîak rórng

to tease (call names)	แซว	saew
to mock (make fun of)	ล้อเลียน	lór lian
mockery, derision	ขอลอเลียน	khŏr lór lian
nickname	ชื่อเล่น	chêu lên

insinuation	การพูดเป็นนัย	gaan phôot bpen nai
to insinuate (imply)	พูดเป็นนัย	phôot bpen nai
to mean (vt)	หมายความว่า	măai khwaam wâa

description	คำพรรณนา	kham phan-ná-naa
to describe (vt)	พรรณนา	phan-ná-naa
praise (compliments)	คำชม	kham chom
to praise (vt)	ชม	chom

disappointment	ความผิดหวัง	khwaam phìt wăng
to disappoint (vt)	ทำให้...ผิดหวัง	tham hâi...phìt wăng
to be disappointed	ผิดหวัง	phìt wăng

| supposition | ข้อสมมุติ | khŏr sŏm mút |
| to suppose (assume) | สมมุติ | sŏm mút |

| warning (caution) | คำเตือน | kham dteuan |
| to warn (vt) | เตือน | dteuan |

67. Discussion, conversation. Part 3

| to talk into (convince) | เกลี้ยกล่อม | glîak-glôrm |
| to calm down (vt) | ทำให้...สงบ | tham hâi...sà-ngòp |

silence (~ is golden)	ความเงียบ	khwaam ngîap
to be silent (not speaking)	เงียบ	ngîap
to whisper (vi, vt)	กระซิบ	grà síp
whisper	เสียงกระซิบ	sĭang grà síp

frankly, sincerely (adv)	พูดตรงๆ	phôot dtrorng dtrorng
in my opinion ...	ในสายตาของ	nai sǎai dtaa-kǒrng
	ผม/ฉัน...	phǒm/chǎn...

detail (of the story)	รายละเอียด	raai lá-ìat
detailed (adj)	โดยละเอียด	doi lá-ìat
in detail (adv)	อย่างละเอียด	yàang lá-ìat

| hint, clue | คำบอกใบ้ | kham bòrk bâi |
| to give a hint | บอกใบ้ | bòrk bâi |

look (glance)	การมอง	gaan morng
to have a look	มอง	morng
fixed (look)	จ้อง	jôrng
to blink (vi)	กระพริบตา	grà phríp dtaa
to wink (vi)	ขยิบตา	khà-yìp dtaa
to nod (in assent)	พยักหน้า	phá-yák nâa

sigh	การถอนหายใจ	gaan thǒrn hǎai jai
to sigh (vi)	ถอนหายใจ	thǒrn hǎai-jai
to shudder (vi)	สั่น	sàn
gesture	อิริยาบถ	i-rí-yaa-bòt
to touch (one's arm, etc.)	สัมผัส	sǎm-phàt
to seize (e.g., ~ by the arm)	จับ	jàp
to tap (on the shoulder)	แตะ	dtàe

Look out!	ระวัง!	rá-wang
Really?	จริงหรือ?	jing rěu
Are you sure?	คุณแน่ใจหรือ?	khun nâe jai rěu
Good luck!	ขอให้โชคดี!	khǒr hâi chôhk dee
I see!	ฉันเข้าใจ!	chǎn khâo jai
What a pity!	น่าเสียดาย!	nâa sǐa-daai

68. Agreement. Refusal

consent	การยินยอม	gaan yin yorm
to consent (vi)	ยินยอม	yin yorm
approval	คำอนุมัติ	kham a-nú-mát
to approve (vt)	อนุมัติ	a-nú-mát

| refusal | คำปฏิเสธ | kham bpà-dtì-sàyt |
| to refuse (vi, vt) | ปฏิเสธ | bpà-dtì-sàyt |

Great!	เยี่ยม!	yîam
All right!	ดีเลย!	dee loie
Okay! (I agree)	โอเค!	oh-khay

forbidden (adj)	ไม่ได้รับอนุญาต	mâi dâai ráp a-nú-yâat
it's forbidden	ห้าม	hâam
it's impossible	มันเป็นไปไม่ได้	man bpen bpai mâi dâai
incorrect (adj)	ไม่ถูกต้อง	mâi thòok dtôrng

to reject (~ a demand)	ปฏิเสธ	bpà-dtì-sàyt
to support (cause, idea)	สนับสนุน	sà-nàp-sà-nǔn
to accept (~ an apology)	ยอมรับ	yorm ráp

to confirm (vt)	ยืนยัน	yeun yan
confirmation	คำยืนยัน	kham yeun yan
permission	คำอนุญาต	kham a-nú-yâat
to permit (vt)	อนุญาต	a-nú-yâat
decision	การตัดสินใจ	gaan dtàt sǐn jai
to say nothing (hold one's tongue)	ไม่พูดอะไร	mâi phôot a-rai

condition (term)	เงื่อนไข	ngêuan khǎi
excuse (pretext)	ข้ออ้าง	khôr âang
praise (compliments)	คำชม	kham chom
to praise (vt)	ชม	chom

69. Success. Good luck. Failure

success	ความสำเร็จ	khwaam sǎm-rèt
successfully (adv)	ให้เป็นผลสำเร็จ	hâi bpen phǒn sǎm-rèt
successful (adj)	ที่สำเร็จ	thêe sǎm-rèt

luck (good luck)	โชค	chôhk
Good luck!	ขอให้โชคดี!	khǒr hâi chôhk dee
lucky (e.g. ~ day)	มีโชค	mee chôhk
lucky (fortunate)	มีโชคดี	mee chôhk dee

failure	ความล้มเหลว	khwaam lóm lěo
misfortune	โชคร้าย	chôhk ráai
bad luck	โชคร้าย	chôhk ráai
unsuccessful (adj)	ไม่ประสบความสำเร็จ	mâi bprà-sòp khwaam sǎm-rèt
catastrophe	ความล้มเหลว	khwaam lóm lěo

pride	ความภาคภูมิใจ	khwaam phâak phoom jai
proud (adj)	ภูมิใจ	phoom jai
to be proud	ภูมิใจ	phoom jai

winner	ผู้ชนะ	phôo chá-ná
to win (vi)	ชนะ	chá-ná
to lose (not win)	แพ้	pháe

try	ความพยายาม	khwaam phá-yaa-yaam
to try (vi)	พยายาม	phá-yaa-yaam
chance (opportunity)	โอกาส	oh-gàat

70. Quarrels. Negative emotions

shout (scream)	เสียงตะโกน	sĭang dtà-gohn
to shout (vi)	ตะโกน	dtà-gohn
to start to cry out	เริ่มตะโกน	rêrm dtà-gohn

quarrel	การทะเลาะ	gaan thá-lór
to quarrel (vi)	ทะเลาะ	thá-lór
fight (squabble)	ความทะเลาะ	khwaam thá-lór
to make a scene	ตีโพยตีพาย	dtee phoi dtee phaai
conflict	ความขัดแย้ง	khwaam khàt yáeng
misunderstanding	การเขาใจผิด	gaan khâo jai phìt

insult	คำดูถูก	kham doo thòok
to insult (vt)	ดูถูก	doo thòok
insulted (adj)	โดนดูถูก	dohn doo thòok
resentment	ความเคียดแค้น	khwaam khîat-kháen
to offend (vt)	ลวงเกิน	lûang gern
to take offence	ถือสา	thĕu săa

indignation	ความโกรธแค้น	khwaam gròht kháen
to be indignant	ขุ่นเคือง	khùn kheuang
complaint	คำร้อง	kham rórng
to complain (vi, vt)	บ่น	bòn

apology	คำขอโทษ	kham khŏr thôht
to apologize (vi)	ขอโทษ	khŏr thôht
to beg pardon	ขออภัย	khŏr a-phai

criticism	คำวิจารณ์	kham wí-jaan
to criticize (vt)	วิจารณ์	wí-jaan
accusation (charge)	การกลาวหา	gaan glàao hăa
to accuse (vt)	กลาวหา	glàao hăa

revenge	การแก้แค้น	gaan gâe kháen
to avenge (get revenge)	แก้แค้น	gâe kháen
to pay back	แก้แค้น	gâe kháen

disdain	ความดูหมิ่น	khwaam doo mìn
to despise (vt)	ดูหมิ่น	doo mìn
hatred, hate	ความเกลียดชัง	khwaam glìat chang
to hate (vt)	เกลียด	glìat

nervous (adj)	กระวนกระวาย	grà won grà waai
to be nervous	กระวนกระวาย	grà won grà waai
angry (mad)	โกรธ	gròht
to make angry	ทำให้...โกรธ	tham hâi...gròht

humiliation	ความเสียดเย้ย	khwaam sìat yóie
to humiliate (vt)	ฉีกหนา	chèek nâa

to humiliate oneself	ฉีกหน้าตนเอง	chèek nâa dton ayng
shock	ความตกตะลึง	khwaam dtòk dtà-leung
to shock (vt)	ทำให้...ตกตะลึง	tham hâi...dtòk dtà-leung

trouble (e.g. serious ~)	ปัญหา	bpan-hǎa
unpleasant (adj)	ไม่น่าพึงพอใจ	mâi nâa pheung phor jai

fear (dread)	ความกลัว	khwaam glua
terrible (storm, heat)	เเย	yâe
scary (e.g. ~ story)	น่ากลัว	nâa glua
horror	ความกลัว	khwaam glua
awful (crime, news)	เเยมาก	yâe mâak

to begin to tremble	เริ่มตัวสั่น	rêrm dtua sàn
to cry (weep)	ร้องไห้	rórng hâi
to start crying	เริ่มร้องไห้	rêrm rórng hâi
tear	น้ำตา	nám dtaa

fault	ความผิด	khwaam phìt
guilt (feeling)	ผิด	phìt
dishonor (disgrace)	เสียเกียรติ	sǐa gìat
protest	การประท้วง	gaan bprà-thúang
stress	ความวาวุ่นใจ	khwaam wáa-wûn-jai

to disturb (vt)	รบกวน	róp guan
to be furious	โกรธจัด	gròht jàt
angry (adj)	โกรธ	gròht
to end (~ a relationship)	ยุติ	yút-dtì
to swear (at sb)	ดุด่า	dù dàa

to scare (become afraid)	ตกใจ	dtòk jai
to hit (strike with hand)	ตี	dtee
to fight (street fight, etc.)	สู้	sôo

to settle (a conflict)	ยุติ	yút-dtì
discontented (adj)	ไม่พอใจ	mâi phor jai
furious (adj)	โกรธจัด	gròht jàt

It's not good!	มันไม่ค่อยดี	man mâi khôi dee
It's bad!	มันไม่ดีเลย	man mâi dee loie

Medicine

illness	โรค	rôhk
to be ill	ป่วย	bpùay
health	สุขภาพ	sùk-khà-phâap

runny nose (coryza)	น้ำมูกไหล	nám môok lǎi
tonsillitis	ตอมทอนซิลอักเสบ	dtòm thorn-sin àk-sàyp
cold (illness)	หวัด	wàt
to catch a cold	เป็นหวัด	bpen wàt

bronchitis	โรคหลอดลมอักเสบ	rôhk lòrt lom àk-sàyp
pneumonia	โรคปอดบวม	rôhk bpòrt-buam
flu, influenza	ไขหวัดใหญ่	khâi wàt yài

shortsighted (adj)	สายตาสั้น	sǎai dtaa sân
longsighted (adj)	สายตายาว	sǎai dtaa yaao
strabismus (crossed eyes)	ตาเหล ,	dtaa lày
squint-eyed (adj)	เป็นตาเหล่	bpen dtaa kǎy rěu lày
cataract	ตอกระจก	dtôr grà-jòk
glaucoma	ตอหิน	dtôr hǐn

stroke	โรคหลอดเลือดสมอง	rôhk lòrt lêuat sà-mǒrng
heart attack	อาการหัวใจวาย	aa-gaan hǔa jai waai
myocardial infarction	กลามเนื้อหัวใจตาย เหตุขาดเลือด	glâam néua hǔa jai dtaai hàyt khàat lêuat
paralysis	อัมพาต	am-má-phâat
to paralyse (vt)	ทำให้เป็นอัมพาต	tham hâi bpen am-má-phâat

allergy	ภูมิแพ้	phoom pháe
asthma	โรคหืด	rôhk hèut
diabetes	โรคเบาหวาน	rôhk bao wǎan

toothache	อาการปวดฟัน	aa-gaan bpùat fan
caries	ฟันผุ	fan phù

diarrhoea	อาการทูองเสีย	aa-gaan thórng sǐa
constipation	อาการทองผูก	aa-gaan thórng phòok
stomach upset	อาการปวดทอง	aa-gaan bpùat thórng
food poisoning	ภาวะอาหารเป็นพิษ	phaa-wá aa hǎan bpen pít
to get food poisoning	กินอาหารเป็นพิษ	gin aa hǎan bpen phít

arthritis	โรคข้ออักเสบ	rôhk khôr àk-sàyp
rickets	โรคกระดูกออน	rôhk grà-dòok òrn
rheumatism	โรครูมาติ๊ก	rôhk roo-maa-dtík
atherosclerosis	ภาวะหลอดเลือดแข็ง	phaa-wá lòrt lêuat khǎeng
gastritis	โรคกระเพาะอาหาร	rôhk grà-phór aa-hǎan
appendicitis	ไสติ่งอักเสบ	sâi dtìng àk-sàyp

| cholecystitis | โรคถุงน้ำดีอักเสบ | rôhk thŭng nám dee àk-sàyp |
| ulcer | แผลเปื่อย | phlăe bpèuay |

measles	โรคหัด	rôhk hàt
rubella (German measles)	โรคหัดเยอรมัน	rôhk hàt yer-rá-man
jaundice	โรคดีซาน	rôhk dee sâan
hepatitis	โรคตับอักเสบ	rôhk dtàp àk-sàyp

schizophrenia	โรคจิตเภท	rôhk jìt-dtà-phâyt
rabies (hydrophobia)	โรคพิษสุนัขบ้า	rôhk phít sù-nák bâa
neurosis	โรคประสาท	rôhk bprà-sàat
concussion	สมองกระทบ กระเทือน	sà-mŏrng grà-thóp grà-theuan

cancer	มะเร็ง	má-reng
sclerosis	กวรแข็งตัวของ เนื้อเยื่อรางกาย	gaan kăeng dtua kŏng néua yêua râang gaai
multiple sclerosis	โรคปลอกประสาท เสื่อมแข็ง	rôhk bplòk bprà-sàat sèuam kăeng

alcoholism	โรคพิษสุราเรื้อรัง	rôhk phít sù-raa réua rang
alcoholic (n)	คนขี้เหลา	khon khêe lâo
syphilis	โรคซิฟิลิส	rôhk sí-fí-lít
AIDS	โรคเอดส	rôhk àyt

tumour	เนื้องอก	néua ngôk
malignant (adj)	ราย	ráai
benign (adj)	ไมราย	mâi ráai

fever	ไข้	khâi
malaria	ไข้มาลาเรีย	kâi maa-laa-ria
gangrene	เนื้อตายเนา	néua dtaai nâo
seasickness	ภาวะเมวๅคลื่น	phaa-wá mao khlêun
epilepsy	โรคลมบาหมู	rôhk lom bâa-mŏo

epidemic	โรคระบาด	rôhk rá-bàat
typhus	โรครากสาดใหญ่	rôhk râak-sàat yài
tuberculosis	วัณโรค	wan-ná-rôhk
cholera	อหิวาตกโรค	a-hì-wâat-gà-rôhk
plague (bubonic ~)	กาฬโรค	gaan-lá-rôhk

72. Symptoms. Treatments. Part 1

symptom	อาการ	aa-gaan
temperature	อุณหภูมิ	un-hà-phoom
high temperature (fever)	อุณหภูมิสูง	un-hà-phoom sŏong
pulse (heartbeat)	ชีพจร	chêep-phá-jon

dizziness (vertigo)	อาการเวียนหัว	aa-gaan wian hŭa
hot (adj)	รอน	rórn
shivering	หนาวสั่น	năao sàn
pale (e.g. ~ face)	หนาเชียว	nâa sieow
cough	การไอ	gaan ai
to cough (vi)	ไอ	ai

to sneeze (vi)	จาม	jaam
faint	การเป็นลม	gaan bpen lom
to faint (vi)	เป็นลม	bpen lom

bruise (hématome)	ฟกช้ำ	fók chám
bump (lump)	บวม	buam
to bang (bump)	ชน	chon
contusion (bruise)	รอยฟกช้ำ	roi fók chám
to get a bruise	ได้รอยช้ำ	dâai roi chám

to limp (vi)	กะโผลกกะเผลก	gà-phlòhk-gà-phlàyk
dislocation	ขอหลุด	khôr lùt
to dislocate (vt)	ทำขอหลุด	tham khôr lùt
fracture	กระดูกหัก	grà-dòok hàk
to have a fracture	หักกระดูก	hàk grà-dòok

cut (e.g. paper ~)	รอยบาด	roi bàat
to cut oneself	ทำบาด	tham bàat
bleeding	การเลือดไหล	gaan lêuat lǎi

| burn (injury) | แผลไฟไหม้ | phlǎe fai mâi |
| to get burned | ได้รับแผลไฟไหม้ | dâai ráp phlǎe fai mâi |

to prick (vt)	ตำ	dtam
to prick oneself	ตำตัวเอง	dtam dtua ayng
to injure (vt)	ทำให้บาดเจ็บ	tham hâi bàat jèp
injury	การบาดเจ็บ	gaan bàat jèp
wound	แผล	phlǎe
trauma	แผลบาดเจ็บ	phlǎe bàat jèp

to be delirious	คลุ้มคลั่ง	khlúm khlâng
to stutter (vi)	พูดตะกุกตะกัก	phôot dtà-gùk-dtà-gàk
sunstroke	โรคลมแดด	rôhk lom dàet

73. Symptoms. Treatments. Part 2

| pain, ache | ความเจ็บปวด | khwaam jèp bpùat |
| splinter (in foot, etc.) | เสี้ยน | sîan |

sweat (perspiration)	เหงื่อ	ngèua
to sweat (perspire)	เหงื่อออก	ngèua òrk
vomiting	การอาเจียน	gaan aa-jian
convulsions	การชัก	gaan chák

pregnant (adj)	ตั้งครรภ์	dtâng khan
to be born	เกิด	gèrt
delivery, labour	การคลอด	gaan khlôrt
to deliver (~ a baby)	คลอดบุตร	khlôrt bùt
abortion	การแท้งบุตร	gaan tháeng bùt

breathing, respiration	การหายใจ	gaan hǎai-jai
in-breath (inhalation)	การหายใจเข้า	gaan hǎai-jai khâo
out-breath (exhalation)	การหายใจออก	gaan hǎai-jai òrk
to exhale (breathe out)	หายใจออก	hǎai-jai òrk

to inhale (vi)	หายใจเข้า	hǎai-jai khâo
disabled person	คนพิการ	khon phí-gaan
cripple	พิการ	phí-gaan
drug addict	ผู้ติดยาเสพติด	phôo dtìt yaa-sàyp-dtìt

deaf (adj)	หูหนวก	hǒo nùak
mute (adj)	เป็นใบ้	bpen bâi
deaf mute (adj)	หูหนวกเป็นใบ้	hǒo nùak bpen bâi

mad, insane (adj)	บ้า	bâa
madman (demented person)	คนบ้า	khon bâa
madwoman	คนบ้า	khon bâa
to go insane	เสียสติ	sǐa sà-dtì

gene	ยีน	yeun
immunity	ภูมิคุ้มกัน	phoom khúm gan
hereditary (adj)	เป็นกรรมพันธุ์	bpen gam-má-phan
congenital (adj)	แต่กำเนิด	dtàe gam-nèrt

virus	เชื้อไวรัส	chéua wai-rát
microbe	จุลินทรีย์	jù-lin-see
bacterium	แบคทีเรีย	bàek-tee-ria
infection	การติดเชื้อ	gaan dtìt chéua

74. Symptoms. Treatments. Part 3

hospital	โรงพยาบาล	rohng phá-yaa-baan
patient	ผู้ป่วย	phôo bpùay

diagnosis	การวินิจฉัยโรค	gaan wí-nít-chǎi rôhk
cure	การรักษา	gaan rák-sǎa
medical treatment	การรักษาทางการแพทย์	gaan rák-sǎa thaang gaan phâet
to get treatment	รับการรักษา	ráp gaan rák-sǎa
to treat (~ a patient)	รักษา	rák-sǎa
to nurse (look after)	รักษา	rák-sǎa
care (nursing ~)	การดูแลรักษา	gaan doo lae rák-sǎa

operation, surgery	การผ่าตัด	gaan phàa dtàt
to bandage (head, limb)	พันแผล	phan phlǎe
bandaging	การพันแผล	gaan phan phlǎe

vaccination	การฉีดวัคซีน	gaan chèet wák-seen
to vaccinate (vt)	ฉีดวัคซีน	chèet wák-seen
injection	การฉีดยา	gaan chèet yaa
to give an injection	ฉีดยา	chèet yaa

attack	มีอาการเฉียบพลัน	mee aa-gaan chìap phlan
amputation	การตัดอวัยวะออก	gaan dtàt a-wai-wá òrk
to amputate (vt)	ตัด	dtàt
coma	อาการโคม่า	aa-gaan khoh-mâa
to be in a coma	อยู่ในอาการโคม่า	yòo nai aa-gaan khoh-mâa
intensive care	หน่วยอภิบาล	nùay à-phí-baan

to recover (~ from flu)	ฟื้นตัว	féun dtua
condition (patient's ~)	อาการ	aa-gaan
consciousness	สติสัมปชัญญะ	sà-dtì săm-bpà-chan-yá
memory (faculty)	ความทรงจำ	khwaam song jam

to pull out (tooth)	ถอน	thŏrn
filling	การอุด	gaan ùt
to fill (a tooth)	อุด	ùt

hypnosis	การสะกดจิต	gaan sà-gòt jìt
to hypnotize (vt)	สะกดจิต	sà-gòt jìt

75. Doctors

doctor	แพทย์	phâet
nurse	พยาบาล	phá-yaa-baan
personal doctor	แพทย์ส่วนตัว	phâet sùan dtua

dentist	ทันตแพทย์	than-dtà phâet
optician	จักษุแพทย์	jàk-sù phâet
general practitioner	อายุรแพทย์	aa-yú-rá-phâet
surgeon	ศัลยแพทย์	săn-yá-phâet

psychiatrist	จิตแพทย์	jìt-dtà-phâet
paediatrician	กุมารแพทย์	gù-maan phâet
psychologist	นักจิตวิทยา	nák jìt wít-thá-yaa
gynaecologist	นรีแพทย์	ná-ree phâet
cardiologist	หทัยแพทย์	hà-thai phâet

76. Medicine. Drugs. Accessories

medicine, drug	ยา	yaa
remedy	ยา	yaa
to prescribe (vt)	จ่ายยา	jàai yaa
prescription	ใบสั่งยา	bai sàng yaa

tablet, pill	ยาเม็ด	yaa mét
ointment	ยาทา	yaa thaa
ampoule	หลอดยา	lòrt yaa
mixture, solution	ยาส่วนผสม	yaa sùan phà-sŏm
syrup	น้ำเชื่อม	nám chêuam
capsule	ยาเม็ด	yaa mét
powder	ยาผง	yaa phŏng

gauze bandage	ผ้าพันแผล	phâa phan phlăe
cotton wool	สำลี	săm-lee
iodine	ไอโอดีน	ai oh-deen

plaster	พลาสเตอร์	phláat-dtêr
eyedropper	ที่หยอดตา	thêe yòrt dtaa
thermometer	ปรอท	bpa -ròrt
syringe	เข็มฉีดยา	khĕm chèet-yaa

| wheelchair | รถเข็นคนพิการ | rót khĕn khon phí-gaan |
| crutches | ไม้ค้ำยัน | máai khám yan |

painkiller	ยาแก้ปวด	yaa gâe bpùat
laxative	ยาระบาย	yaa rá-baai
spirits (ethanol)	เอธานอล	ay-thaa-norn
medicinal herbs	สมุนไพร ทางการแพทย์	sà-mŭn phrai thaang gaan phâet
herbal (~ tea)	สมุนไพร	sà-mŭn phrai

77. Smoking. Tobacco products

tobacco	ยาสูบ	yaa sòop
cigarette	บุหรี่	bù rèe
cigar	ซิการ์	sí-gâa
pipe	ไปป์	bpai
packet (of cigarettes)	ซอง	sorng

matches	ไม้ขีด	máai khèet
matchbox	กลองไม้ขีด	glòrng máai khèet
lighter	ไฟแช็ก	fai cháek
ashtray	ที่เขี่ยบุหรี่	thêe khìa bù rèe
cigarette case	กลองใส่บุหรี่	glòrng sài bù rèe

| cigarette holder | ที่ต่อบุหรี่ | thêe dtòr bù rèe |
| filter (cigarette tip) | ตัวกรองบุหรี่ | dtua grorng bù rèe |

to smoke (vi, vt)	สูบ	sòop
to light a cigarette	จุดบุหรี่	jùt bù rèe
smoking	การสูบบุหรี่	gaan sòop bù rèe
smoker	ผู้สูบบุหรี่	pôo sòop bù rèe

cigarette end	ก้นบุหรี่	gôn bù rèe
smoke, fumes	ควันบุหรี่	khwan bù rèe
ash	ขี้บุหรี่	khêe bù rèe

HUMAN HABITAT

City

city, town	เมือง	meuang
capital city	เมืองหลวง	meuang lŭang
village	หมู่บ้าน	mòo bâan
city map	แผนที่เมือง	phăen thêe meuang
city centre	ใจกลางเมือง	jai glaang-meuang
suburb	ชานเมือง	chaan meuang
suburban (adj)	ชานเมือง	chaan meuang
outskirts	รอบนอกเมือง	rôrp nôrk meuang
environs (suburbs)	เขตรอบเมือง	khàyt rôrp-meuang
city block	บล็อกผังเมือง	blòrk phăng meuang
residential block (area)	บล็อกที่อยูอาศัย	blòrk thêe yòo aa-săi
traffic	การจราจร	gaan jà-raa-jon
traffic lights	ไฟจราจร	fai jà-raa-jon
public transport	ขนส่งมวลชน	khŏn sòng muan chon
crossroads	สี่แยก	sèe yâek
zebra crossing	ทางม้าลาย	thaang máa laai
pedestrian subway	อุโมงค์คนเดิน	u-mohng kon dern
to cross (~ the street)	ข้าม	khâam
pedestrian	คนเดินเท้า	khon dern tháo
pavement	ทางเท้า	thaang tháo
bridge	สะพาน	sà-phaan
embankment (river walk)	ทางเลียบแม่น้ำ	thaang lîap mâe náam
fountain	น้ำพุ	nám phú
allée (garden walkway)	ทางเลียบสวน	thaang lîap sŭan
park	สวน	sŭan
boulevard	ถนนกว้าง	thà-nŏn gwâang
square	จัตุรัส	jàt-dtù-ràt
avenue (wide street)	ถนนใหญ่	thà-nŏn yài
street	ถนน	thà-nŏn
side street	ซอย	soi
dead end	ทางตัน	thaang dtan
house	บ้าน	bâan
building	อาคาร	aa-khaan
skyscraper	ตึกระฟ้า	dtèuk rá-fáa
facade	ด้านหน้าอาคาร	dâan-nâa aa-khaan
roof	หลังคา	lăng khaa

window	หน้าต่าง	nâa dtàang
arch	ซุมประตู	súm bprà-dtoo
column	เสา	săo
corner	มุม	mum

shop window	หน้าต่างร้านค้า	nâa dtàang ráan kháa
signboard (store sign, etc.)	ป้ายราน	bpâai ráan
poster (e.g., playbill)	โปสเตอร์	bpòht-dtêr
advertising poster	ป้ายโฆษณา	bpâai khôht-sà-naa
hoarding	กระดานปิดประกาศโฆษณา	grà-daan bpìt bprà-gàat khôht-sà-naa

rubbish	ขยะ	khà-yà
rubbish bin	ถังขยะ	thăng khà-yà
to litter (vi)	ทิ้งขยะ	thíng khà-yà
rubbish dump	ที่ทิ้งขยะ	thêe thíng khà-yà

telephone box	ตู้โทรศัพท์	dtôo thoh-rá-sàp
lamppost	เสาโคม	săo khohm
bench (park ~)	ม้านั่ง	máa nâng

police officer	เจ้าหน้าที่ตำรวจ	jâo nâa-thêe dtam-rùat
police	ตำรวจ	dtam-rùat
beggar	ขอทาน	khŏr thaan
homeless (n)	คนไร้บ้าน	khon rái bâan

79. Urban institutions

shop	ร้านค้า	ráan kháa
chemist, pharmacy	ร้านขายยา	ráan khăai yaa
optician (spectacles shop)	รานตัดแว่น	ráan dtàt wâen
shopping centre	ศูนย์กวรค้า	sŏon gaan kháa
supermarket	ซูเปอร์มาร์เก็ต	soo-bper-maa-gèt

bakery	ร้านขนมปัง	ráan khà-nŏm bpang
baker	คนอบขนมปัง	khon òp khà-nŏm bpang
cake shop	ร้านขนม	ráan khà-nŏm
grocery shop	ร้านขายของชำ	ráan khăai khŏrng cham
butcher shop	รานขายเนื้อ	ráan khăai néua

greengrocer	ร้านขายผัก	ráan khăai phàk
market	ตลาด	dtà-làat

coffee bar	ร้านกาแฟ	ráan gaa-fae
restaurant	รานอาหาร	ráan aa-hăan
pub, bar	บาร์	baa
pizzeria	รานพิซซ่า	ráan phís-sâa

hairdresser	ร้านทำผม	ráan tham phŏm
post office	โรงไปรษณีย์	rohng bprai-sà-nee
dry cleaners	ร้านซักแหง	ráan sák hâeng
photo studio	ห้องถายภาพ	hôrng thàai phâap
shoe shop	ร้านขายรองเท้า	ráan khăai rorng táo
bookshop	รานขายหนังสือ	ráan khăai năng-sĕu

sports shop	ร้านขายอุปกรณ์กีฬา	ráan khǎai u-bpà-gon gee-laa
clothes repair shop	ร้านซ่อมเสื้อผ้า	ráan sôrm sêua phâa
formal wear hire	ร้านเช่าเสื้อออกงาน	ráan châo sêua òrk ngaan
video rental shop	ร้านเช่าวิดีโอ	ráan châo wí-dee-oh
circus	โรงละครสัตว์	rohng lá-khon sàt
zoo	สวนสัตว์	sǔan sàt
cinema	โรงภาพยนตร์	rohng phâap-phá-yon
museum	พิพิธภัณฑ์	phí-phítha phan
library	หองสมุด	hôrng sà-mùt
theatre	โรงละคร	rohng lá-khon
opera (opera house)	โรงอุปรากร	rohng ù-bpà-raa-gon
nightclub	ไนท์คลับ	nai-khláp
casino	คาสิโน	khaa-sì-noh
mosque	สุเหร่า	sù-ráo
synagogue	โบสถ์ยิว	bòht yiw
cathedral	อาสนวิหาร	aa sǒn wí-hǎan
temple	วิหาร	wí-hǎan
church	โบสถ์	bòht
college	วิทยาลัย	wít-thá-yaa-lai
university	มหาวิทยาลัย	má-hǎa wít-thá-yaa-lai
school	โรงเรียน	rohng rian
prefecture	ศาลากลางจังหวัด	sǎa-laa glaang jang-wàt
town hall	ศาลาเทศบาล	sǎa-laa thâyt-sà-baan
hotel	โรงแรม	rohng raem
bank	ธนาคาร	thá-naa-khaan
embassy	สถานทูต	sà-thǎan thôot
travel agency	บริษัททัวร์	bor-rí-sàt thua
information office	สำนักงาน	sǎm-nák ngaan
	ศูนย์ข้อมูล	sǒon khôr moon
currency exchange	ร้านแลกเงิน	ráan lâek ngern
underground, tube	รถไฟใต้ดิน	rót fai dtâi din
hospital	โรงพยาบาล	rohng phá-yaa-baan
petrol station	ปั๊มน้ำมัน	bpám náam man
car park	ลานจอดรถ	laan jòrt rót

80. Signs

signboard (store sign, etc.)	ป้ายร้าน	bpâai ráan
notice (door sign, etc.)	ป้ายเตือน	bpâai dteuan
poster	โปสเตอร์	bpòht-dtêr
direction sign	ป้ายบอกทาง	bpâai bòrk thaang
arrow (sign)	ลูกศร	lôok sǒn
caution	คำเตือน	kham dteuan
warning sign	ป้ายเตือน	bpâai dteuan
to warn (vt)	เตือน	dteuan

rest day (weekly ~)	วันหยุด	wan yùt
timetable (schedule)	ตารางเวลา	dtaa-raang way-laa
opening hours	เวลาทำการ	way-laa tham gaan

WELCOME!	ยินดีต้อนรับ!	yin dee dtôrn ráp
ENTRANCE	ทางเขา	thaang khâo
WAY OUT	ทางออก	thaang òrk

PUSH	ผลัก	phlàk
PULL	ดึง	deung
OPEN	เปิด	bpèrt
CLOSED	ปิด	bpìt

| WOMEN | หญิง | yǐng |
| MEN | ชาย | chaai |

DISCOUNTS	ลดราคา	lót raa-khaa
SALE	ขายของลดราคา	khǎai khǒrng lót raa-khaa
NEW!	ใหม่!	mài
FREE	ฟรี	free

ATTENTION!	โปรดทราบ!	bpròht sâap
NO VACANCIES	ไม่มีห้องว่าง	mâi mee hôrng wâang
RESERVED	จองแล้ว	jorng láew

| ADMINISTRATION | สำนักงาน | sǎm-nák ngaan |
| STAFF ONLY | เฉพาะพนักงาน | chà-phór phá-nák ngaan |

BEWARE OF THE DOG!	ระวังสุนัข!	rá-wang sù-nák
NO SMOKING	ห้ามสูบบุหรี่	hâam sòop bù rèe
DO NOT TOUCH!	ห้ามแตะ!	hâam dtàe

DANGEROUS	อันตราย	an-dtà-raai
DANGER	อันตราย	an-dtà-raai
HIGH VOLTAGE	ไฟฟ้าแรงสูง	fai fáa raeng sǒong
NO SWIMMING!	ห้ามว่ายน้ำ!	hâam wâai náam
OUT OF ORDER	เสีย	sǐa

FLAMMABLE	อันตรายติดไฟ	an-dtà-raai dtìt fai
FORBIDDEN	ห้าม	hâam
NO TRESPASSING!	ห้ามผ่าน!	hâam phàan
WET PAINT	สีพื้นเปียก	sěe phéun bpìak

81. Urban transport

bus, coach	รถเมล์	rót may
tram	รถราง	rót raang
trolleybus	รถโดยสารประจำทางไฟฟ้า	rót doi sǎan bprà-jam thaang fai fáa

| route (bus ~) | เส้นทาง | sên thaang |
| number (e.g. bus ~) | หมายเลข | mǎai lâyk |

| to go by ... | ไปด้วย | bpai dûay |
| to get on (~ the bus) | ขึ้น | khêun |

to get off …	ลง	long
stop (e.g. bus ~)	ป้าย	bpâai
next stop	ป้ายถัดไป	bpâai thàt bpai
terminus	ป้ายสุดท้าย	bpâai sùt tháai
timetable	ตารางเวลา	dtaa-raang way-laa
to wait (vt)	รอ	ror

| ticket | ตั๋ว | dtŭa |
| fare | ค่าตั๋ว | khâa dtŭa |

cashier (ticket seller)	คนขายตั๋ว	khon khăai dtŭa
ticket inspection	การตรวจตั๋ว	gaan dtrùat dtŭa
ticket inspector	พนักงานตรวจตั๋ว	phá-nák ngaan dtrùat dtŭa

to be late (for …)	ไปสาย	bpai săai
to miss (~ the train, etc.)	พลาด	phlâat
to be in a hurry	รีบเร่ง	rêep râyng

taxi, cab	แท็กซี่	tháek-sêe
taxi driver	คนขับแท็กซี่	khon khàp tháek-sêe
by taxi	โดยแท็กซี่	doi tháek-sêe
taxi rank	ป้ายจอดแท็กซี่	bpâai jòrt tháek sêe
to call a taxi	เรียกแท็กซี่	rîak tháek sêe
to take a taxi	ขึ้นรถแท็กซี่	khêun rót tháek-sêe

traffic	การจราจร	gaan jà-raa-jon
traffic jam	การจราจรติดขัด	gaan jà-raa-jon dtìt khàt
rush hour	ชั่วโมงเร่งด่วน	chûa mohng râyng dùan
to park (vi)	จอด	jòrt
to park (vt)	จอด	jòrt
car park	ลานจอดรถ	laan jòrt rót

underground, tube	รถไฟใต้ดิน	rót fai dtâi din
station	สถานี	sà-thăa-nee
to take the tube	ขึ้นรถไฟใต้ดิน	khêun rót fai dtâi din
train	รถไฟ	rót fai
train station	สถานีรถไฟ	sà-thăa-nee rót fai

82. Sightseeing

monument	อนุสาวรีย์	a-nú-săa-wá-ree
fortress	ป้อม	bpôrm
palace	วัง	wang
castle	ปราสาท	bpraa-sàat
tower	หอ	hŏr
mausoleum	สุสาน	sù-săan

architecture	สถาปัตยกรรม	sà-thăa-bpàt-dtà-yá-gam
medieval (adj)	ยุคกลาง	yúk glaang
ancient (adj)	โบราณ	boh-raan
national (adj)	แห่งชาติ	hàeng châat
famous (monument, etc.)	ที่มีชื่อเสียง	thêe mee chêu-sĭang
tourist	นักท่องเที่ยว	nák thôrng thîeow
guide (person)	มัคคุเทศก์	mák-khú-thâyt

excursion, sightseeing tour	ทัศนศึกษา	thát-sà-ná-sèuk-săa
to show (vt)	แสดง	sà-daeng
to tell (vt)	เลา	lâo

to find (vt)	หาพบ	hăa phóp
to get lost (lose one's way)	หลงทาง	lŏng thaang
map (e.g. underground ~)	แผนที่	phăen thêe
map (e.g. city ~)	แผนที่	phăen thêe

souvenir, gift	ของที่ระลึก	khŏrng thêe rá-léuk
gift shop	รานขาย ของที่ระลึก	ráan khăai khŏrng thêe rá-léuk
to take pictures	ถูยภาพ	thàai phâap
to have one's picture taken	ได้รับการ ถายภาพให	dâai ráp gaan thàai phâap hâi

83. Shopping

to buy (purchase)	ซื้อ	séu
shopping	ของซื้อ	khŏrng séu
to go shopping	ไปซื้อของ	bpai séu khŏrng
shopping	การชอปปิง	gaan chóp bping

| to be open (ab. shop) | เปิด | bpèrt |
| to be closed | ปิด | bpìt |

footwear, shoes	รองเท้า	rorng tháo
clothes, clothing	เสื้อผา	sêua phâa
cosmetics	เครื่องสำอาง	khrêuang săm-aang
food products	อาหาร	aa-hăan
gift, present	ของขวัญ	khŏrng khwăn

| shop assistant (masc.) | พนักงานขาย | phá-nák ngaan khăai |
| shop assistant (fem.) | พนักงานขาย | phá-nák ngaan khăai |

cash desk	ที่จ่ายเงิน	thêe jàai ngern
mirror	กระจก	grà-jòk
counter (shop ~)	เดานเตอร์	khao-dtêr
fitting room	หองลองเสื้อผา	hôrng lorng sêua phâa

to try on	ลอง	lorng
to fit (ab. dress, etc.)	เหมาะ	mò
to fancy (vt)	ชอบ	chôrp

price	ราคา	raa-khaa
price tag	ป้ายราคา	bpâai raa-khaa
to cost (vt)	ราคา	raa-khaa
How much?	ราคาเท่าไหร่?	raa-khaa thâo rài
discount	ลดราคา	lót raa-khaa

inexpensive (adj)	ไม่แพง	mâi phaeng
cheap (adj)	ถูก	thòok
expensive (adj)	แพง	phaeng
It's expensive	มันราคาแพง	man raa-khaa phaeng

hire (n)	การเช่า	gaan châo
to hire (~ a dinner jacket)	เช่า	châo
credit (trade credit)	สินเชื่อ	sĭn chêua
on credit (adv)	ซื้อเงินเชื่อ	séu ngern chêua

84. Money

money	เงิน	ngern
currency exchange	การแลกเปลี่ยนสกุลเงิน	gaan lâek bplìan sà-gun ngern
exchange rate	อัตราแลกเปลี่ยนสกุลเงิน	àt-dtraa lâek bplìan sà-gun ngern
cashpoint	เอทีเอ็ม	ay-thee-em
coin	เหรียญ	rĭan

| dollar | ดอลลาร์ | dorn-lâa |
| euro | ยูโร | yoo-roh |

lira	ลีราอิตาลี	lee-raa ì-dtaa-lee
Deutschmark	มาร์ค	mâak
franc	ฟรังค์	frang
pound sterling	ปอนด์สเตอร์ลิง	bporn sà-dtêr-ling
yen	เยน	yayn

debt	หนี้	nêe
debtor	ลูกหนี้	lôok nêe
to lend (money)	ให้ยืม	hâi yeum
to borrow (vi, vt)	ขอยืม	khŏr yeum

bank	ธนาคาร	thá-naa-khaan
account	บัญชี	ban-chee
to deposit (vt)	ฝาก	fàak
to deposit into the account	ฝากเงินเข้าบัญชี	fàak ngern khâo ban-chee
to withdraw (vt)	ถอน	thŏrn

credit card	บัตรเครดิต	bàt khray-dìt
cash	เงินสด	ngern sòt
cheque	เช็ค	chék
to write a cheque	เขียนเช็ค	khĭan chék
chequebook	สมุดเช็ค	sà-mùt chék

wallet	กระเป๋าเงิน	grà-bpăo ngern
purse	กระเป๋าสตางค์	grà-bpăo sà-dtaang
safe	ตู้เซฟ	dtôo sâyf

heir	ทายาท	thaa-yâat
inheritance	มรดก	mor-rá-dòrk
fortune (wealth)	เงินจำนวนมาก	ngern jam-nuan mâak

lease	สัญญาเช่า	săn-yaa châo
rent (money)	ค่าเช่า	kâa châo
to rent (sth from sb)	เช่า	châo
price	ราคา	raa-khaa
cost	ราคา	raa-khaa

sum	จำนวนเงินรวม	jam-nuan ngern ruam
to spend (vt)	จ่าย	jàai
expenses	ค่าจ่าย	khâa jàai
to economize (vi, vt)	ประหยัด	bprà-yàt
economical	ประหยัด	bprà-yàt
to pay (vi, vt)	จ่าย	jàai
payment	การจ่ายเงิน	gaan jàai ngern
change (give the ~)	เงินทอน	ngern thorn
tax	ภาษี	phaa-sěe
fine	ค่าปรับ	khâa bpràp
to fine (vt)	ปรับ	bpràp

85. Post. Postal service

post office	โรงไปรษณีย์	rohng bprai-sà-nee
post (letters, etc.)	จดหมาย	jòt măai
postman	บุรุษไปรษณีย์	bù-rùt bprai-sà-nee
opening hours	เวลาทำการ	way-laa tham gaan
letter	จดหมาย	jòt măai
registered letter	จดหมายลงทะเบียน	jòt măai long thá-bian
postcard	ไปรษณียบัตร	bprai-sà-nee-yá-bàt
telegram	โทรเลข	thoh-rá-lâyk
parcel	พัสดุ	phát-sà-dù
money transfer	การโอนเงิน	gaan ohn ngern
to receive (vt)	รับ	ráp
to send (vt)	ฝาก	fàak
sending	การฝาก	gaan fàak
address	ที่อยู่	thêe yòo
postcode	รหัสไปรษณีย์	rá-hàt bprai-sà-nee
sender	ผู้ฝาก	phôo fàak
receiver	ผู้รับ	phôo ráp
name (first name)	ชื่อ	chêu
surname (last name)	นามสกุล	naam sà-gun
postage rate	อัตราค่าส่งไปรษณีย์	àt-dtraa khâa sòng bprai-sà-nee
standard (adj)	มาตรฐาน	mâat-dtrà-thăan
economical (adj)	ประหยัด	bprà-yàt
weight	น้ำหนัก	nám nàk
to weigh (~ letters)	มีน้ำหนัก	mee nám nàk
envelope	ซอง	sorng
postage stamp	แสตมป์ไปรษณีย์	sà-dtaem bprai-sà-nee
to stamp an envelope	แสตมป์ตราประทับบนซอง	sà-dtaem dtraa bprà-tháp bon song

Dwelling. House. Home

86. House. Dwelling

house	บ้าน	bâan
at home (adv)	ที่บาน	thêe bâan
yard	สนาม	sà-năam
fence (iron ~)	รั้ว	rúa
brick (n)	อิฐ	ìt
brick (as adj)	อิฐ	ìt
stone (n)	หิน	hĭn
stone (as adj)	หิน	hĭn
concrete (n)	คอนกรีต	khorn-grèet
concrete (as adj)	คอนกรีต	khorn-grèet
new (new-built)	ใหม่	mài
old (adj)	เก่า	gào
decrepit (house)	เสื่อมสภาพ	sèuam sà-phâap
modern (adj)	ทันสมัย	than sà-măi
multistorey (adj)	ที่มีหลายชั้น	thêe mee lăai chán
tall (~ building)	สูง	sŏong
floor, storey	ชั้น	chán
single-storey (adj)	ชั้นเดียว	chán dieow
ground floor	ชั้นลาง	chán lâang
top floor	ชั้นบนสุด	chán bon sùt
roof	หลังคา	lăng khaa
chimney	ปลองควัน	bplòrng khwan
roof tiles	กระเบื้องหลังคา	grà-bêuang lăng khaa
tiled (adj)	กระเบื้อง	grà-bêuang
loft (attic)	หองใตหลังคา	hôrng dtâi lăng-khaa
window	หน้าตาง	nâa dtàang
glass	แกว	gâew
window ledge	ชั้นติดผนัง	chán dtìt phà-năng
	ใตหนาตาง	dtâi nâa dtàang
shutters	ชัตเตอร์	chát-dtêr
wall	ฝาผนัง	făa phà-năng
balcony	ระเบียง	rá-biang
downpipe	รางน้ำ	raang náam
upstairs (to be ~)	ชั้นบน	chán bon
to go upstairs	ขึ้นไปขางบน	khêun bpai khâang bon
to come down (the stairs)	ลง	long
to move (to new premises)	ยายไป	yáai bpai

87. House. Entrance. Lift

entrance	ทางเข้า	thaang khâo
stairs (stairway)	บันได	ban-dai
steps	ขั้นบันได	khân ban-dai
banisters	ราวบันได	raao ban-dai
lobby (hotel ~)	ห้องโถง	hôrng thŏhng

postbox	ตู้จดหมาย	dtôo jòt măai
waste bin	ถุงขยะ	thăng khà-yà
refuse chute	ช่องทิ้งขยะ	chôhng thíng khà-yà

lift	ลิฟต์	líf
goods lift	ลิฟต์ขนของ	líf khŏn khŏrng
lift cage	กรงลิฟต์	grorng líf
to take the lift	ขึ้นลิฟต์	khêun líf

flat	อพาร์ตเมนต์	a-phâat-mayn
residents (~ of a building)	ผู้อาศัย	phôo aa-săi
neighbour (masc.)	เพื่อนบ้าน	phêuan bâan
neighbour (fem.)	เพื่อนบ้าน	phêuan bâan
neighbours	เพื่อนบ้าน	phêuan bâan

88. House. Electricity

electricity	ไฟฟ้า	fai fáa
light bulb	หลอดไฟฟ้า	lòrt fai fáa
switch	ปุ่มปิดเปิดไฟ	bpùm bpìt bpèrt fai
fuse (plug fuse)	ฟิวส์	fiw

cable, wire (electric ~)	สายไฟฟ้า	săai fai fáa
wiring	การเดินสายไฟ	gaan dern săai fai
electricity meter	มิเตอร์วัดไฟฟ้า	mí-dtêr wát fai fáa
readings	คามิเตอร์	khâa mí-dtêr

89. House. Doors. Locks

door	ประตู	bprà-dtoo
gate (vehicle ~)	ประตูรั้ว	bprà-dtoo rúa
handle, doorknob	ลูกบิดประตู	lôok bìt bprà-dtoo
to unlock (unbolt)	ไข	khăi
to open (vt)	เปิด	bpèrt
to close (vt)	ปิด	bpìt

key	ลูกกุญแจ	lôok gun-jae
bunch (of keys)	พวง	phuang
to creak (door, etc.)	ออดแอด	órt-áet
creak	เสียงออดแอด	sĭang órt-áet
hinge (door ~)	บานพับ	baan pháp
doormat	ที่เช็ดเท้า	thêe chét tháo
door lock	แม่กุญแจ	mâe gun-jae

keyhole	รูกุญแจ	roo gun-jae
crossbar (sliding bar)	ไม้ที่วางขวาง	máai thêe waang khwǎang
door latch	กลอนประตู	glorn bprà-dtoo
padlock	ดอกกุญแจ	dòrk gun-jae

to ring (~ the door bell)	กดออด	gòt òrt
ringing (sound)	เสียงดัง	sǐang dang
doorbell	กระดิ่งประตู	grà-dìng bprà-dtoo
doorbell button	ปุ่มออดหน้าประตู	bpùm òrt nâa bprà-dtoo
knock (at the door)	เสียงเคาะ	sǐang khór
to knock (vi)	เคาะ	khór

code	รหัส	rá-hàt
combination lock	กุญแจรหัส	gun-jae rá-hàt
intercom	อินเตอร์คอม	in-dtêr-khom
number (on the door)	เลข	lâyk
doorplate	ป้ายหน้าประตู	bpâai nâa bprà-dtoo
peephole	ช่องตาแมว	chôrng dtaa maew

90. Country house

village	หมู่บ้าน	mòo bâan
vegetable garden	สวนผัก	sǔan phàk
fence	รั้ว	rúa
picket fence	รั้วปักดิน	rúa bpàk din
wicket gate	ประตูรั้วเล็กๆ	bprà-dtoo rúa lék lék

granary	ยุ้งฉาง	yúng chǎang
cellar	ห้องใต้ดิน	hôrng dtâi din
shed (garden ~)	โรงนา	rohng naa
water well	บ่อน้ำ	bòr náam

stove (wood-fired ~)	เตา	dtao
to stoke the stove	จุดไฟ	jùt fai
firewood	ฟืน	feun
log (firewood)	ทอน	thôrn

veranda	เฉลียงหน้าบ้าน	chà-lǐang nâa bâan
deck (terrace)	ระเบียง	rá-biang
stoop (front steps)	บันไดทางเข้าบ้าน	ban-dai thaang khâo bâan
swing (hanging seat)	ชิงช้า	ching cháa

91. Villa. Mansion

country house	บ้านสไตล์คันทรี่	bâan sà-dtai khan trêe
country-villa	คฤหาสน์	khá-réu-hàat
wing (~ of a building)	สวน	sùan

garden	สวน	sǔan
park	สวน	sǔan
conservatory (greenhouse)	เรือนกระจกเขตร้อน	reuan grà-jòk khàyt rórn
to look after (garden, etc.)	ดูแล	doo lae

swimming pool	สระว่ายน้ำ	sà wâai náam
gym (home gym)	โรงยิม	rohng-yim
tennis court	สนามเทนนิส	sà-nǎam then-nít
home theater (room)	หองฉายหนัง	hôrng chǎai nǎng
garage	โรงรถ	rohng rót

| private property | ทรัพย์สินส่วนบุคคล | sáp sǐn sùan bùk-khon |
| private land | ที่ดินส่วนบุคคล | thêe din sùan bùk-khon |

| warning (caution) | คำเตือน | kham dteuan |
| warning sign | ป้ายเตือน | bpâai dteuan |

security	ผู้รักษา	phôo rák-sǎa
	ความปลอดภัย	khwaam bplòrt phai
security guard	ยาม	yaam
burglar alarm	สัญญาณกันขโมย	sǎn-yaan gan khà-moi

92. Castle. Palace

castle	ปราสาท	bpraa-sàat
palace	วัง	wang
fortress	ป้อม	bpôrm

wall (round castle)	กำแพง	gam-phaeng
tower	หอ	hǒr
keep, donjon	หอกลาง	hǒr klaang

portcullis	ประตูชักรอก	bprà-dtoo chák rôrk
subterranean passage	ทางใต้ดิน	taang dtâi din
moat	คูเมือง	khoo meuang
chain	โซ่	sôh
arrow loop	ช่องยิงธนู	chôrng ying thá-noo

magnificent (adj)	ภัทร	phát
majestic (adj)	โอ่โถง	òh thǒhng
impregnable (adj)	ที่ไม่สามารถ	thêe mâi sǎa-mâat
	เจาะเขาไปถึง	jòr khâo bpai thěung
medieval (adj)	ยุคกลาง	yúk glaang

93. Flat

flat	อพาร์ตเมนต์	a-phâat-mayn
room	หอง	hôrng
bedroom	หองนอน	hôrng norn
dining room	หองรับประทาน	hôrng ráp bprà-thaan
	อาหาร	aa-hǎan
living room	หองนั่งเล่น	hôrng nâng lên
study (home office)	หองทำงาน	hôrng tham ngaan

entry room	หองเข้า	hôrng khâo
bathroom	หองน้ำ	hôrng náam
water closet	หองสวม	hôrng sûam

ceiling	เพดาน	phay-daan
floor	พื้น	phéun
corner	มุม	mum

94. Flat. Cleaning

to clean (vi, vt)	ทำความสะอาด	tham khwaam sà-àat
to put away (to stow)	เก็บ	gèp
dust	ฝุ่น	fùn
dusty (adj)	มีฝุ่นเยอะ	mee fùn yúh
to dust (vt)	ปัดกวาด	bpàt gwàat
vacuum cleaner	เครื่องดูดฝุ่น	khrêuang dòot fùn
to vacuum (vt)	ดูดฝุ่น	dòot fùn
to sweep (vi, vt)	กวาด	gwàat
sweepings	ฝุ่นกวาด	fùn gwàat
order	ความสะอาด	khwaam sà-àat
disorder, mess	ความไม่เป็นระเบียบ	khwaam mâi bpen rá-bìap
mop	ไม้ถูพื้น	mái thǒo phéun
duster	ผ้าเช็ดพื้น	phâa chét phéun
short broom	ไม้กวาดสั้น	máai gwàat sân
dustpan	ที่ตักผง	têe dtàk phǒng

95. Furniture. Interior

furniture	เครื่องเรือน	khrêuang reuan
table	โต๊ะ	dtó
chair	เก้าอี้	gâo-êe
bed	เตียง	dtiang
sofa, settee	โซฟา	soh-faa
armchair	เก้าอี้เท้าแขน	gâo-êe tháo khǎen
bookcase	ตู้หนังสือ	dtôo nǎng-sěu
shelf	ชั้นวาง	chán waang
wardrobe	ตู้เสื้อผ้า	dtôo sêua phâa
coat rack (wall-mounted ~)	ที่แขวนเสื้อ	thêe khwǎen sêua
coat stand	ไม้แขวนเสื้อ	mái khwǎen sêua
chest of drawers	ตู้ลิ้นชัก	dtôo lín chák
coffee table	โต๊ะกาแฟ	dtó gaa-fae
mirror	กระจก	grà-jòk
carpet	พรม	phrom
small carpet	พรมเช็ดเท้า	phrom chét tháo
fireplace	เตาผิง	dtao phǐng
candle	เทียน	thian
candlestick	เชิงเทียน	cherng thian
drapes	ผ้าแขวน	phâa khwǎen

| wallpaper | วอลเปเปอร์ | worn-bpay-bper |
| blinds (jalousie) | บานเกล็ดหน้าต่าง | baan glèt nâa dtàang |

table lamp	โคมไฟตั้งโต๊ะ	khohm fai dtâng dtó
wall lamp (sconce)	ไฟติดผนัง	fai dtìt phà-năng
standard lamp	โคมไฟตั้งพื้น	khohm fai dtâng phéun
chandelier	โคมระย้า	khohm rá-yáa

leg (of a chair, table)	ขา	khăa
armrest	ที่พักแขน	thêe phák khăen
back (backrest)	พนักพิง	phá-nák phing
drawer	ลิ้นชัก	lín chák

96. Bedding

bedclothes	ชุดผ้าปูที่นอน	chút phâa bpoo thêe norn
pillow	หมอน	mŏrn
pillowslip	ปลอกหมอน	bplòk mŏrn
duvet	ผ้าผวย	phâa phŭay
sheet	ผ้าปู	phâa bpoo
bedspread	ผ้าคลุมเตียง	phâa khlum dtiang

97. Kitchen

kitchen	ห้องครัว	hôrng khrua
gas	แก๊ส	gáet
gas cooker	เตาแก๊ส	dtao gàet
electric cooker	เตาไฟฟ้า	dtao fai-fáa
oven	เตาอบ	dtao òp
microwave oven	เตาอบไมโครเวฟ	dtao òp mai-khroh-we p

refrigerator	ตู้เย็น	dtôo yen
freezer	ตู้แช่แข็ง	dtôo châe khăeng
dishwasher	เครื่องล้างจาน	khrêuang láang jaan

mincer	เครื่องบดเนื้อ	khrêuang bòt néua
juicer	เครื่องคั้น น้ำผลไม้	khrêuang khán náam phŏn-lá-mái
toaster	เครื่องปิ้ง ขนมปัง	khrêuang bpîng khà-nŏm bpang
mixer	เครื่องปั่น	khrêuang bpàn

coffee machine	เครื่องชงกาแฟ	khrêuang chong gaa-fae
coffee pot	หม้อกาแฟ	môr gaa-fae
coffee grinder	เครื่องบดกาแฟ	khrêuang bòt gaa-fae

kettle	กาน้ำ	gaa náam
teapot	กาน้ำชา	gaa náam chaa
lid	ฝา	făa
tea strainer	ที่กรองชา	thêe grorng chaa
spoon	ช้อน	chórn
teaspoon	ช้อนชา	chórn chaa

soup spoon	ช้อนซุป	chórn súp
fork	ส้อม	sôrm
knife	มีด	mêet

tableware (dishes)	ถ้วยชาม	thûay chaam
plate (dinner ~)	จาน	jaan
saucer	จานรอง	jaan rorng

shot glass	แก้วช็อต	gâew chórt
glass (tumbler)	แก้ว	gâew
cup	ถ้วย	thûay

sugar bowl	โถน้ำตาล	thǒh náam dtaan
salt cellar	กระปุกเกลือ	grà-bpùk gleua
pepper pot	กระปุกพริกไท	grà-bpùk phrík thai
butter dish	ที่ใส่เนย	thêe sài noie

stock pot (soup pot)	หม้อต้ม	môr dtôm
frying pan (skillet)	กระทะ	grà-thá
ladle	กระบวย	grà-buay
colander	กระชอน	grà chorn
tray (serving ~)	ถาด	thàat

bottle	ขวด	khùat
jar (glass)	ขวดโหล	khùat lǒh
tin (can)	กระป๋อง	grà-bpǒrng

bottle opener	ที่เปิดขวด	thêe bpèrt khùat
tin opener	ที่เปิดกระป๋อง	thêe bpèrt grà-bpǒrng
corkscrew	ที่เปิดจุก	thêe bpèrt jùk
filter	ที่กรอง	thêe grorng
to filter (vt)	กรอง	grorng

| waste (food ~, etc.) | ขยะ | khà-yà |
| waste bin (kitchen ~) | ถังขยะ | thǎng khà-yà |

98. Bathroom

bathroom	ห้องน้ำ	hôrng náam
water	น้ำ	nám
tap	ก็อกน้ำ	gòk náam
hot water	น้ำร้อน	nám rórn
cold water	น้ำเย็น	nám yen

toothpaste	ยาสีฟัน	yaa sěe fan
to clean one's teeth	แปรงฟัน	bpraeng fan
toothbrush	แปรงสีฟัน	bpraeng sěe fan

to shave (vi)	โกน	gohn
shaving foam	โฟมโกนหนวด	fohm gohn nùat
razor	มีดโกน	mêet gohn

| to wash (one's hands, etc.) | ล้าง | láang |
| to have a bath | อาบ | àap |

shower	ฝักบัว	fàk bua
to have a shower	อาบน้ำฝักบัว	àap náam fàk bua
bath	อ่างอาบน้ำ	àang àap náam
toilet (toilet bowl)	โถชักโครก	thŏh chák khrôhk
sink (washbasin)	อ่างล้างหน้า	àang láang-nâa
soap	สบู่	sà-bòo
soap dish	ที่ใส่สบู่	thêe sài sà-bòo
sponge	ฟองน้ำ	forng náam
shampoo	แชมพู	chaem-phoo
towel	ผ้าเช็ดตัว	phâa chét dtua
bathrobe	เสื้อคลุมอาบน้ำ	sêua khlum àap náam
laundry (laundering)	การซักผ้า	gaan sák phâa
washing machine	เครื่องซักผ้า	khrêuang sák phâa
to do the laundry	ซักผ้า	sák phâa
washing powder	ผงซักฟอก	phŏng sák-fôrk

99. Household appliances

TV, telly	ทีวี	thee-wee
tape recorder	เครื่องบันทึกเทป	khrêuang ban-théuk thâyp
video	เครื่องบันทึกวิดีโอ	khrêuang ban-théuk wí-dee-oh
radio	วิทยุ	wít-thá-yú
player (CD, MP3, etc.)	เครื่องเล่น	khrêuang lên
video projector	โปรเจ็คเตอร์	bproh-jèk-dtêr
home cinema	เครื่องฉายภาพยนตร์ที่บ้าน	khhrêuang chǎai phâap-phá-yon thêe bâan
DVD player	เครื่องเล่น DVD	khrêuang lên dee-wee-dee
amplifier	เครื่องขยายเสียง	khrêuang khà-yǎai sǐang
video game console	เครื่องเกมคอนโซล	khrêuang gaym khorn sohn
video camera	กล้องถ่ายวิดีโอ	glôrng thàai wí-dee-oh
camera (photo)	กล้องถ่ายรูป	glôrng thàai rôop
digital camera	กล้องดิจิตอล	glôrng dì-jì-dton
vacuum cleaner	เครื่องดูดฝุ่น	khrêuang dòot fùn
iron (e.g. steam ~)	เตารีด	dtao rêet
ironing board	กระดานรองรีด	grà-daan rorng rêet
telephone	โทรศัพท์	thoh-rá-sàp
mobile phone	มือถือ	meu thěu
typewriter	เครื่องพิมพ์ดีด	khrêuang phim dèet
sewing machine	จักรเย็บผ้า	jàk yép phâa
microphone	ไมโครโฟน	mai-khroh-fohn
headphones	หูฟัง	hǒo fang
remote control (TV)	รีโมตทีวี	ree môht thee wee
CD, compact disc	CD	see-dee
cassette, tape	เทป	thâyp
vinyl record	จานเสียง	jaan sǐang

100. Repairs. Renovation

renovations	การซ่อมแซม	gaan sôrm saem
to renovate (vt)	ซ่อมแซม	sôrm saem
to repair, to fix (vt)	ซ่อมแซม	sôrm saem
to put in order	สะสาง	sà-sǎang
to redo (do again)	ทำใหม่	tham mài
paint	สี	sěe
to paint (~ a wall)	ทาสี	thaa sěe
house painter	ช่างทาสีบ้าน	châang thaa sěe bâan
paintbrush	แปรงทาสี	bpraeng thaa sěe
whitewash	สารฟอกขาว	sǎan fôrk khǎao
to whitewash (vt)	ฟอกขาว	fôrk khǎao
wallpaper	วอลเปเปอร์	worn-bpay-bper
to wallpaper (vt)	ติดวอลเปเปอร์	dtìt wor lá-bpay-bper
varnish	น้ำมันชักเงา	náam man chák ngao
to varnish (vt)	เคลือบ	khlêuap

101. Plumbing

water	น้ำ	nám
hot water	น้ำร้อน	nám rórn
cold water	น้ำเย็น	nám yen
tap	ก๊อกน้ำ	gòk náam
drop (of water)	หยด	yòt
to drip (vi)	ตก	dtòk
to leak (ab. pipe)	รั่ว	rûa
leak (pipe ~)	การรั่ว	gaan rûa
puddle	หลมน้ำ	lòm nám
pipe	ท่อ	thôr
valve (e.g., ball ~)	วาล์ว	waao
to be clogged up	อุดตัน	ùt dtan
tools	เครื่องมือ	khrêuang meu
adjustable spanner	ประแจคอม้า	bprà-jae kor máa
to unscrew (lid, filter, etc.)	คลายเกลียวออก	khlaai glieow òrk
to screw (tighten)	ขันให้แน่น	khǎn hâi nâen
to unclog (vt)	แก้การอุดตัน	gâe gaan ùt dtan
plumber	ช่างประปา	châang bprà-bpaa
basement	ชั้นใต้ดิน	chán dtâi din
sewerage (system)	ระบบท่อน้ำทิ้ง	rá-bòp thôr náam thíng

102. Fire. Conflagration

fire (accident)	ไฟไหม้	fai mâi
flame	เปลวไฟ	bpleo fai

spark	ประกายไฟ	bprà-gaai fai
smoke (from fire)	ควัน	khwan
torch (flaming stick)	คบเพลิง	khóp phlerng
campfire	กองไฟ	gorng fai
petrol	น้ำมันเชื้อเพลิง	nám man chéua phlerng
paraffin	น้ำมันก๊าด	nám man gáat
flammable (adj)	ติดไฟได้	dtìt fai dâai
explosive (adj)	ที่ระเบิดได้	thêe rá-bèrt dâai
NO SMOKING	ห้ามสูบบุหรี่	hâam sòop bù rèe
safety	ความปลอดภัย	khwaam bplòrt phai
danger	อันตราย	an-dtà-raai
dangerous (adj)	อันตราย	an-dtà-raai
to catch fire	ติดไฟ	dtìt fai
explosion	การระเบิด	gaan rá-bèrt
to set fire	เผา	phǎo
arsonist	ผู้ลอบวางเพลิง	phôo lôp waang phlerng
arson	การลอบวางเพลิง	gaan lôp waang phlerng
to blaze (vi)	ไฟลุกโชน	fai lúk-chohn
to burn (be on fire)	ไหม้	mâi
to burn down	เผาให้ราบ	phǎo hâi râap
to call the fire brigade	เรียกนักดับเพลิง	rîak nák dàp phlerng
firefighter, fireman	นักดับเพลิง	nák dàp phlerng
fire engine	รถดับเพลิง	rót dàp phlerng
fire brigade	สถานีดับเพลิง	sà-thǎa-nee dàp phlerng
fire engine ladder	บันไดรถดับเพลิง	ban-dai rót dàp phlerng
fire hose	ท่อดับเพลิง	thôr dàp phlerng
fire extinguisher	ที่ดับเพลิง	thêe dàp phlerng
helmet	หมวกนิรภัย	mùak ní-rá-phai
siren	สัญญาณเตือนภัย	sǎn-yaan dteuan phai
to cry (for help)	ร้อง,	rórng
to call for help	ขอช่วย	khǒr chûay
rescuer	นักกู้ภัย	nák gôo phai
to rescue (vt)	ช่วยชีวิต	chûay chee-wít
to arrive (vi)	มา	maa
to extinguish (vt)	ดับเพลิง	dàp phlerng
water	น้ำ	nám
sand	ทราย	saai
ruins (destruction)	ซาก	sâak
to collapse (building, etc.)	ถล่ม	thà-lòm
to fall down (vi)	ถล่มทลาย	thà-lòm thá-laai
to cave in (ceiling, floor)	ถลม	thà-lòm
piece of debris	ส่วนสะเก็ด	sùan sà-gèt
ash	ขี้เถา	khêe thâo
to suffocate (die)	ขาดอากาศตาย	khàat aa-gàat dtaai
to be killed (perish)	เสียชีวิต	sǐa chee-wít

HUMAN ACTIVITIES

Job. Business. Part 1

103. Office. Working in the office

office (company ~)	สำนักงาน	sǎm-nák ngaan
office (director's ~)	ห้องทำงาน	hôrng tham ngaan
reception desk	แผนกต้อนรับ	phà-nàek dtôrn ráp
secretary	เลขา	lay-khǎa
secretary (fem.)	เลขา	lay-khǎa
director	ผู้อำนวยการ	phôo am-nuay gaan
manager	ผู้จัดการ	phôo jàt gaan
accountant	คนทำบัญชี	khon tham ban-chee
employee	พนักงาน	phá-nák ngaan
furniture	เครื่องเรือน	khrêuang reuan
desk	โต๊ะ	dtó
desk chair	เก้าอี้สำนักงาน	gâo-êe sǎm-nák ngaan
drawer unit	ตู้มีลิ้นชัก	dtôo mee lín chák
coat stand	ไม้แขวนเสื้อ	mái khwǎen sêua
computer	คอมพิวเตอร์	khorm-phiw-dtêr
printer	เครื่องพิมพ์	khrêuang phim
fax machine	เครื่องโทรสาร	khrêuang thoh-rá-sǎan
photocopier	เครื่องอัดสำเนา	khrêuang àt sǎm-nao
paper	กระดาษ	grà-dàat
office supplies	เครื่องใช้สำนักงาน	khrêuang chái sǎm-nák ngaan
mouse mat	แผ่นรองเมาส์	phàen rorng mao
sheet of paper	ใบ	bai
binder	แฟ้ม	fáem
catalogue	บัญชีรายชื่อ	ban-chee raai chêu
phone directory	สมุดโทรศัพท์	sà-mùt thoh-rá-sàp
documentation	เอกสาร	àyk sǎan
brochure (e.g. 12 pages ~)	โบรชัวร์	broh-chua
leaflet (promotional ~)	ใบปลิว	bai bpliw
sample	ตัวอย่าง	dtua yàang
training meeting	การประชุมฝึกอบรม	gaan bprà-chum fèuk òp-rom
meeting (of managers)	การประชุม	gaan bprà-chum
lunch time	การพักเที่ยง	gaan phák thîang
to make a copy	ทำสำเนา	tham sǎm-nao
to make multiple copies	ทำสำเนาหลายฉบับ	tham sǎm-nao lǎai chà-bàp
to receive a fax	รับโทรสาร	ráp thoh-rá-sǎan

to send a fax	ส่งโทรสาร	sòng thoh-rá-săan
to call (by phone)	โทรศัพท์	thoh-rá-sàp
to answer (vt)	รับสาย	ráp săai
to put through	โอนสาย	ohn săai

to arrange, to set up	นัด	nát
to demonstrate (vt)	สาธิต	săa-thít
to be absent	ขาด	khàat
absence	การขาด	gaan khàat

104. Business processes. Part 1

| business | ธุรกิจ | thú-rá gìt |
| occupation | อาชีพ | aa-chêep |

firm	บริษัท	bor-rí-sàt
company	บริษัท	bor-rí-sàt
corporation	บริษัท	bor-rí-sàt
enterprise	บริษัท	bor-rí-sàt
agency	สำนักงาน	săm-nák ngaan

agreement (contract)	ข้อตกลง	khôr dtòk long
contract	สัญญา	săn-yaa
deal	ข้อตกลง	khôr dtòk long
order (to place an ~)	การสั่ง	gaan sàng
terms (of the contract)	เงื่อนไข	ngêuan khăi

wholesale (adv)	ขายส่ง	khăai sòng
wholesale (adj)	ขายส่ง	khăai sòng
wholesale (n)	การขายส่ง	gaan khăai sòng
retail (adj)	ขายปลีก	khăai bplèek
retail (n)	การขายปลีก	gaan khăai bplèek

competitor	คู่แข่ง	khôo khàeng
competition	การแข่งขัน	gaan khàeng khăn
to compete (vi)	แข่งขัน	khàeng khăn

| partner (associate) | พันธมิตร | phan-thá-mít |
| partnership | หางหุนสวน | hâang hûn sùan |

crisis	วิกฤติ	wí-grìt
bankruptcy	การล้มละลาย	gaan lóm lá-laai
to go bankrupt	ล้มละลาย	lóm lá-laai
difficulty	ความยากลำบาก	khwaam yâak lam-bàak
problem	ปัญหา	bpan-hăa
catastrophe	ความหายนะ	khwaam hăa-yá-ná

economy	เศรษฐกิจ	sàyt-thà-gìt
economic (~ growth)	ทางเศรษฐกิจ	thaang sàyt-thà-gìt
economic recession	เศรษฐกิจถดถอย	sàyt-thà-gìt thòt thŏi

goal (aim)	เป้าหมาย	bpâo măai
task	งาน	ngaan
to trade (vi)	แลกเปลี่ยน	lâek bplìan

network (distribution ~)	เครือข่าย	khreua khàai
inventory (stock)	คลังสินค้า	khlang sĭn kháa
range (assortment)	ประเภทสินค้า ตางๆ	bprà-phâyt sĭn kháa dtàang dtàang

leader (leading company)	ผู้นำ	phôo nam
large (~ company)	ขนาดใหญ่	khà-nàat yài
monopoly	การผูกขาด	gaan phòok khàat

theory	ทฤษฎี	thrít-sà-dee
practice	การดำเนินการ	gaan dam-nern gaan
experience (in my ~)	ประสบการณ์	bprà-sòp gaan
trend (tendency)	แนวโน้ม	naew nóhm
development	การพัฒนา	gaan phát-thá-naa

105. Business processes. Part 2

| profit (foregone ~) | กำไร | gam-rai |
| profitable (~ deal) | กำไร | gam-rai |

delegation (group)	คณะผู้แทน	khá-ná phôo thaen
salary	เงินเดือน	ngern deuan
to correct (an error)	แก้ไข	gâe khăi
business trip	การเดินทางไป ทำธุรกิจ	gaan dern taang bpai tham thú-rá gìt
commission	คณะ	khá-ná

to control (vt)	ควบคุม	khûap khum
conference	งานประชุม	ngaan bprà-chum
licence	ใบอนุญาต	bai a-nú-yâat
reliable (~ partner)	พึ่งพาได้	phêung phaa dâai

initiative (undertaking)	การริเริ่ม	gaan rí-rêrm
norm (standard)	มาตรฐาน	mâat-dtrà-thăan
circumstance	ภาวะ	phaa-wá
duty (of an employee)	หน้าที่	nâa thêe

organization (company)	องค์การ	ong gaan
organization (process)	การจัด	gaan jàt
organized (adj)	ที่ถูกจัด	thêe thòok jàt
cancellation	การยกเลิก	gaan yók lêrk
to cancel (call off)	ยกเลิก	yók lêrk
report (official ~)	รายงาน	raai ngaan

patent	สิทธิบัตร	sìt-thí bàt
to patent (obtain patent)	จดสิทธิบัตร	jòt sìt-thí bàt
to plan (vt)	วางแผน	waang phăen

bonus (money)	โบนัส	boh-nát
professional (adj)	ทางวิชาชีพ	thaang wí-chaa chêep
procedure	กระบวนการ	grà-buan gaan

| to examine (contract, etc.) | ปรึกษาหารือ | bprèuk-săa hăa-reu |
| calculation | การนับ | gaan náp |

reputation	ความมีหน้ามีตา	khwaam mee nâa mee dtaa
risk	ความเสี่ยง	khwaam sìang
to manage, to run	บริหาร	bor-rí-hăan
information (report)	ขอมูล	khôr moon
property	ทรัพย์สิน	sáp sĭn
union	สหภาพ	sà-hà phâap
life insurance	การประกันชีวิต	gaan bprà-gan chee-wít
to insure (vt)	ประกันภัย	bprà-gan phai
insurance	การประกันภัย	gaan bprà-gan phai
auction (~ sale)	การขายเลหลัง	gaan khăai lay-lăng
to notify (inform)	แจง	jâeng
management (process)	การบริหาร	gaan bor-rí-hăan
service (~ industry)	บริการ	bor-rí-gaan
forum	การประชุมฟอรั่ม	gaan bprà-chum for-râm
to function (vi)	ดำเนินการ	dam-nern gaan
stage (phase)	ขั้น	khân
legal (~ services)	ทางกฎหมาย	thaang gòt măai
lawyer (legal advisor)	ทนายความ	thá-naai khwaam

106. Production. Works

plant	โรงงาน	rohng ngaan
factory	โรงงาน	rohng ngaan
workshop	ห้องทำงาน	hôrng tham ngaan
works, production site	ที่ผลิต	thêe phà-lìt
industry (manufacturing)	อุตสาหกรรม	út-saa há-gam
industrial (adj)	ทางอุตสาหกรรม	thaang ùt-săa-hà-gam
heavy industry	อุตสาหกรรมหนัก	ùt-săa-hà-gam nàk
light industry	อุตสาหกรรมเบา	ùt-săa-hà-gam bao
products	ผลิตภัณฑ์	phà-lìt-dtà-phan
to produce (vt)	ผลิต	phà-lìt
raw materials	วัตถุดิบ	wát-thù dìp
foreman (construction ~)	คนคุมงาน	khon khum ngaan
workers team (crew)	ทีมคนงาน	theem khon ngaan
worker	คนงาน	khon ngaan
working day	วันทำงาน	wan tham ngaan
pause (rest break)	หยุดพัก	yùt phák
meeting	การประชุม	gaan bprà-chum
to discuss (vt)	หารือ	hăa-reu
plan	แผน	phăen
to fulfil the plan	ทำตามแผน	tham dtaam phăen
rate of output	อัตราผลลัพธ์	àt-dtraa phŏn láp
quality	คุณภาพ	khun-ná-phâap
control (checking)	การควบคุม	gaan khûap khum
quality control	การควบคุมคุณภาพ	gaan khûap khum khun-ná-phâap

workplace safety	ความปลอดภัย ในที่ทำงาน	khwaam bplòrt phai nai thêe tham ngaan
discipline	วินัย	wí-nai
violation (of safety rules, etc.)	การละเมิด	gaan lá-mêrt
to violate (rules)	ละเมิด	lá-mêrt
strike	การประท้วงหยุดงาน	gaan bprà-thúang yùt ngaan
striker	ผู้ประท้วงหยุดงาน	phôo bprà-thúang yùt ngaan
to be on strike	ประท้วงหยุดงาน	bprà-thúang yùt ngaan
trade union	สหภาพแรงงาน	sà-hà-phâap raeng ngaan
to invent (machine, etc.)	ประดิษฐ์	bprà-dìt
invention	สิ่งประดิษฐ์	sìng bprà-dìt
research	การวิจัย	gaan wí-jai
to improve (make better)	ทำให้ดีขึ้น	tham hâi dee khêun
technology	เทคโนโลยี	thék-noh-loh-yee
technical drawing	ภาพรางทางเทคนิค	phâap-râang thaang thék-nìk
load, cargo	ของบรรทุก	khŏrng ban-thúk
loader (person)	คนงานยกของ	khon ngaan yók khŏrng
to load (vehicle, etc.)	บรรทุก	ban-thúk
loading (process)	การบรรทุก	gaan ban-thúk
to unload (vi, vt)	ขนออก	khŏn òrk
unloading	การขนออก	gaan khŏn òrk
transport	การขนส่ง	gaan khŏn sòng
transport company	บริษัทขนสง	bor-rí-sàt khŏn sòng
to transport (vt)	ขนสง	khŏn sòng
wagon	ตู้รถไฟรถ	dtôo rót fai
tank (e.g., oil ~)	ถัง	thăng
lorry	รถบรรทุก	rót ban-thúk
machine tool	เครื่องมือกล	khrêuang meu gon
mechanism	กลไก	gon-gai
industrial waste	ของเสียจากโรงงาน	khŏrng sĭa jàak rohng ngaan
packing (process)	การทำหีบหอ	gaan tham hèep hòr
to pack (vt)	แพ็คหีบหอ	pháek hèep hòr

107. Contract. Agreement

contract	สัญญา	săn-yaa
agreement	ขอตกลง	khôr dtòk long
addendum	ภาคผนวก	phâak phà-nùak
to sign a contract	ลงนามในสัญญา	long naam nai săn-yaa
signature	ลายมือชื่อ	laai meu chêu
to sign (vt)	ลงนาม	long naam
seal (stamp)	ตราประทับ	dtraa bprà-tháp
subject of the contract	หัวข้อของสัญญา	hŭa khôr khŏrng săn-yaa
clause	ขอ	khôr
parties (in contract)	ฝ่าย	fàai

legal address	ที่อยู่ตามกฎหมาย	thêe yòo dtaam gòt mǎai
to violate the contract	การละเมิดสัญญา	gaan lá-mêrt sǎn-yaa
commitment (obligation)	พันธสัญญา	phan-thá-sǎn-yaa
responsibility	ความรับผิดชอบ	khwaam ráp phìt chôp
force majeure	เหตุสุดวิสัย	hàyt sùt wí-sǎi
dispute	ความขัดแย้ง	khwaam khàt yáeng
penalties	บทลงโทษ	bòt long thôht

108. Import & Export

import	การนำเข้า	gaan nam khâo
importer	ผู้นำเข้า	phôo nam khâo
to import (vt)	นำเข้า	nam khâo
import (as adj.)	นำเข้า	nam khâo

export (exportation)	การส่งออก	gaan sòng òrk
exporter	ผู้ส่งออก	phôo sòng òrk
to export (vt)	ส่งออก	sòng òrk
export (as adj.)	ส่งออก	sòng òrk

| goods (merchandise) | สินค้า | sǐn kháa |
| consignment, lot | สินค้าที่ส่งไป | sǐn kháa thêe sòng bpai |

weight	น้ำหนัก	nám nàk
volume	ปริมาณ	bpà-rí-maan
cubic metre	ลูกบาศก์เมตร	lôok bàat máyt

manufacturer	ผู้ผลิต	phôo phà-lìt
transport company	บริษัทขนส่ง	bor-rí-sàt khǒn sòng
container	ตู้คอนเทนเนอร์	dtôo khorn thay ná-ner

border	ชายแดน	chaai daen
customs	ด่านศุลกากร	dàan sǔn-lá-gaa-gon
customs duty	ภาษีศุลกากร	phaa-sěe sǔn-lá-gaa-gon
customs officer	เจ้าหน้าที่ศุลกากร	jâo nâa-thêe sǔn-lá-gaa-gon
smuggling	การลักลอบ	gaan lák-lôrp
contraband (smuggled goods)	สินค้าที่ผิดกฎหมาย	sǐn kháa thêe phìt gòt mǎai

109. Finances

share, stock	หุ้น	hûn
bond (certificate)	ตราสารหนี้	dtraa sǎan nêe
promissory note	ตั๋วสัญญาใช้เงิน	dtǔa sǎn-yaa chái ngern

| stock exchange | ตลาดหลักทรัพย์ | dtà-làat làk sáp |
| stock price | ราคาหุ้น | raa-khaa hûn |

| to go down (become cheaper) | ถูกลง | thòok long |
| to go up (become more expensive) | แพงขึ้น | phaeng khêun |

share	ปันผล	bpan phǒn
controlling interest	ส่วนได้เสียที่ มีอำนาจควบคุม	sùan dâai sǐa têe mee am-nâat khûap khum

investment	การลงทุน	gaan long thun
to invest (vt)	ลงทุน	long thun
percent	เปอร์เซ็นต์	bper-sen
interest (on investment)	ดอกเบี้ย	dòrk bîa

profit	กำไร	gam-rai
profitable (adj)	ได้กำไร	dâai gam-rai
tax	ภาษี	phaa-sěe

currency (foreign ~)	สกุลเงิน	sà-gun ngern
national (adj)	แห่งชาติ	hàeng châat
exchange (currency ~)	การแลกเปลี่ยน	gaan lâek bplìan

accountant	นักบัญชี	nák ban-chee
accounting	การทำบัญชี	gaan tham ban-chee

bankruptcy	การล้มละลาย	gaan lóm lá-laai
collapse, ruin	การพังพินาศ	gaan phang phí-nâat
ruin	ความพินาศ	khwaam phí-nâat
to be ruined (financially)	ล้มละลาย	lóm lá-laai
inflation	เงินเฟ้อ	ngern fér
devaluation	การลดค่าเงิน	gaan lót khâa ngern

capital	เงินทุน	ngern thun
income	รายได้	raai dâai
turnover	การหมุนเวียน	gaan mǔn wian
resources	ทรัพยากร	sáp-pá-yaa-gon
monetary resources	แหล่งเงินทุน	làeng ngern thun

overheads	ค่าใช้จ่าย	khâa chái jàai
to reduce (expenses)	ลด	lót

110. Marketing

marketing	การตลาด	gaan dtà-làat
market	ตลาด	dtà-làat
market segment	ส่วนตลาด	sùan dtà-làat
product	ผลิตภัณฑ์	phà-lìt-dtà-phan
goods (merchandise)	สินค้า	sǐn kháa

brand	ยี่ห้อ	yêe hôr
trademark	เครื่องหมายการค้า	khrêuang mǎai gaan kháa
logotype	โลโก้	loh-gôh
logo	โลโก้	loh-gôh

demand	อุปสงค์	u-bpà-sǒng
supply	อุปทาน	u-bpà-thaan
need	ความต้องการ	khwaam dtôrng gaan
consumer	ผู้บริโภค	phôo bor-rí-phôhk
analysis	การวิเคราะห์	gaan wí-khrór

to analyse (vt)	วิเคราะห์	wí-khrór
positioning	การวางตำแหน่ง	gaan waang dtam-nàeng
	ผลิตภัณฑ์	phà-lìt-dtà-phan
to position (vt)	วางตำแหน่ง	waang dtam-nàeng
	ผลิตภัณฑ์	phà-lìt-dtà-phan

price	ราคา	raa-khaa
pricing policy	นโยบาย	ná-yoh-baai
	การตั้งราคา	gaan dtâng raa-khaa
price formation	การตั้งราคา	gaan dtâng raa-khaa

111. Advertising

advertising	การโฆษณา	gaan khôht-sà-naa
to advertise (vt)	โฆษณา	khôht-sà-naa
budget	งบประมาณ	ngóp bprà-maan

ad, advertisement	การโฆษณา	gaan khôht-sà-naa
TV advertising	การโฆษณา	gaan khôht-sà-naa thaang
	ทางทีวี	thee wee
radio advertising	การโฆษณา	gaan khôht-sà-naa thaang
	ทางวิทยุ	wít-thá-yú
outdoor advertising	การโฆษณา	gaan khôht-sà-naa
	แบบกลางแจ้ง	bàep glaang jâeng

mass medias	สื่อสารมวลชน	sèu săan muan chon
periodical (n)	หนังสือรายคาบ	năng-sĕu raai khâap
image (public appearance)	ภาพลักษณ์	phâap-lák

| slogan | คำขวัญ | kham khwăn |
| motto (maxim) | คติพจน์ | khá-dtì phót |

campaign	การรณรงค์	gaan ron-ná-rorng
advertising campaign	การรณรงค์	gaan ron-ná-rorng
	โฆษณา	khôht-sà-naa
target group	กลุ่มเป้าหมาย	glùm bpâo-măai

business card	นามบัตร	naam bàt
leaflet (promotional ~)	ใบปลิว	bai bpliw
brochure (e.g. 12 pages ~)	โบรชัวร์	broh-chua
pamphlet	แผ่นพับ	phàen pháp
newsletter	จดหมายข่าว	jòt măai khàao

signboard (store sign, etc.)	ป้ายร้าน	bpâai ráan
poster	โปสเตอร์	bpòht-dtêr
hoarding	กระดานปิดประกาศ	grà-daan bpìt bprà-gàat
	โฆษณา	khôht-sà-naa

112. Banking

| bank | ธนาคาร | thá-naa-khaan |
| branch (of a bank) | สาขา | săa-khăa |

consultant	พนักงาน	phá-nák ngaan
	ธนาคาร	thá-naa-khaan
manager (director)	ผู้จัดการ	phôo jàt gaan

bank account	บัญชีธนาคาร	ban-chee thá-naa-kaan
account number	หมายเลขบัญชี	măai lâyk ban-chee
current account	กระแสรายวัน	grà-săe raai wan
deposit account	บัญชีออมทรัพย์	ban-chee orm sáp

to open an account	เปิดบัญชี	bpèrt ban-chee
to close the account	ปิดบัญชี	bpìt ban-chee
to deposit into the account	ฝากเงินเข้าบัญชี	fàak ngern khâo ban-chee
to withdraw (vt)	ถอน	thŏrn

deposit	การฝาก	gaan fàak
to make a deposit	ฝาก	fàak
wire transfer	การโอนเงิน	gaan ohn ngern
to wire, to transfer	โอนเงิน	ohn ngern

sum	จำนวนเงินรวม	jam-nuan ngern ruam
How much?	เท่าไหร่?	thâo rài

signature	ลายมือชื่อ	laai meu chêu
to sign (vt)	ลงนาม	long naam

credit card	บัตรเครดิต	bàt khray-dìt
code (PIN code)	รหัส	rá-hàt
credit card number	หมายเลขบัตรเครดิต	măai lâyk bàt khray-dìt
cashpoint	เอทีเอ็ม	ay-thee-em

cheque	เช็ค	chék
to write a cheque	เขียนเช็ค	khĭan chék
chequebook	สมุดเช็ค	sà-mùt chék

loan (bank ~)	เงินกู้	ngern gôo
to apply for a loan	ขอสินเชื่อ	khŏr sĭn chêua
to get a loan	กู้เงิน	gôo ngern
to give a loan	ให้กู้เงิน	hâi gôo ngern
guarantee	การรับประกัน	gaan ráp bprà-gan

113. Telephone. Phone conversation

telephone	โทรศัพท์	thoh-rá-sàp
mobile phone	มือถือ	meu thĕu
answerphone	เครื่องพูดตอบ	khrêuang phôot dtòp

to call (by phone)	โทรศัพท์	thoh-rá-sàp
call, ring	การโทรศัพท์	gaan thoh-rá-sàp

to dial a number	หมุนหมายเลขโทรศัพท์	mŭn măai lâyk thoh-rá-sàp
Hello!	สวัสดี!	sà-wàt-dee
to ask (vt)	ถาม	thăam
to answer (vi, vt)	รับสาย	ráp săai
to hear (vt)	ได้ยิน	dâai yin

well (adv)	ดี	dee
not well (adv)	ไม่ดี	mâi dee
noises (interference)	เสียงรบกวน	sĭang róp guan
receiver	ตัวรับสัญญาณ	dtua ráp săn-yaan
to pick up (~ the phone)	รับสาย	ráp săai
to hang up (~ the phone)	วางสาย	waang săai
busy (engaged)	ไม่ว่าง	mâi wâang
to ring (ab. phone)	ดัง	dang
telephone book	สมุดโทรศัพท์	sà-mùt thoh-rá-sàp
local (adj)	ในประเทศ	nai bprà-thâyt
local call	โทรในประเทศ	thoh nai bprà-thâyt
trunk (e.g. ~ call)	ระยะไกล	rá-yá glai
trunk call	โทรระยะไกล	thoh-rá-yá glai
international (adj)	ต่างประเทศ	dtàang bprà-thâyt
international call	โทรต่างประเทศ	thoh dtàang bprà-thâyt

114. Mobile telephone

mobile phone	มือถือ	meu thĕu
display	หน้าจอ	nâa jor
button	ปุ่ม	bpùm
SIM card	ซิมการ์ด	sím gàat
battery	แบตเตอรี่	bàet-dter-rêe
to be flat (battery)	หมด	mòt
charger	ที่ชาร์จ	thêe châat
menu	เมนู	may-noo
settings	การตั้งค่า	gaan dtâng khâa
tune (melody)	เสียงเพลง	sĭang phlayng
to select (vt)	เลือก	lêuak
calculator	เครื่องคิดเลข	khrêuang khít lâyk
voice mail	ข้อความเสียง	khôr khwaam sĭang
alarm clock	นาฬิกาปลุก	naa-lí-gaa bplùk
contacts	รายชื่อผู้ติดต่อ	raai chêu phôo dtìt dtòr
SMS (text message)	SMS	es-e-mes
subscriber	ผู้สมัครรับบริการ	phôo sà-màk ráp bor-rí-gaan

115. Stationery

ballpoint pen	ปากกาลูกลื่น	bpàak gaa lôok lêun
fountain pen	ปากกาหมึกซึม	bpàak gaa mèuk seum
pencil	ดินสอ	din-sŏr
highlighter	ปากกาเน้น	bpàak gaa náyn
felt-tip pen	ปากกาเมจิค	bpàak gaa may jìk
notepad	สมุดจด	sà-mùt jòt

diary	สมุดบันทึกรายวัน	sà-mùt ban-théuk raai wan
ruler	ไม้บรรทัด	máai ban-thát
calculator	เครื่องคิดเลข	khrêuang khít lâyk
rubber	ยางลบ	yaang lóp
drawing pin	เป๊ก	bpáyk
paper clip	ลวดหนีบกระดาษ	lûat nèep grà-dàat

glue	กาว	gaao
stapler	ที่เย็บกระดาษ	thêe yép grà-dàat
hole punch	ที่เจาะรูกระดาษ	thêe jòr roo grà-dàat
pencil sharpener	ที่เหลาดินสอ	thêe lăo din-sŏr

116. Various kinds of documents

account (report)	รายการ	raai gaan
agreement	ขอตกลง	khôr dtòk long
application form	ใบสมัคร	bai sà-màk
authentic (adj)	แท้	tháe
badge (identity tag)	ป้ายชื่อ	bpâai chêu
business card	นามบัตร	naam bàt

certificate (~ of quality)	ใบรับรอง	bai ráp rorng
cheque (e.g. draw a ~)	เช็ค	chék
bill (in restaurant)	คิดเงิน	khít ngern
constitution	รัฐธรรมนูญ	rát-thà-tham-má-noon

contract (agreement)	สัญญา	săn-yaa
copy	สำเนา	săm-nao
copy (of a contract, etc.)	ฉบับ	chà-bàp

customs declaration	แบบฟอร์มการเสีย ภาษีศุลกากร	bàep form gaan sĭa phaa-sĕe sŭn-lá-gaa-gon
document	เอกสาร	àyk săan
driving licence	ใบอนุญาตขับขี่	bai a-nú-yâat khàp khèe
addendum	ภาคผนวก	phâak phà-nùak
form	แบบฟอร์ม	bàep form

ID card (e.g., warrant card)	บัตรประจำตัว	bàt bprà-jam dtua
inquiry (request)	คำร้องขอ	kham rórng khŏr
invitation card	บัตรเชิญ	bàt chern
invoice	ใบกำกับสินค้า	bai gam-gàp sĭn kháa

law	กฎหมาย	gòt măai
letter (mail)	จดหมาย	jòt măai
letterhead	แบบฟอร์ม	bàep form
list (of names, etc.)	รายชื่อ	raai chêu
manuscript	ต้นฉบับ	dtôn chà-bàp
newsletter	จดหมายข่าว	jòt măai khàao
note (short letter)	ข้อความสั้นๆ	khôr khwaam sân sân

pass (for worker, visitor)	บัตรผ่าน	bàt phàan
passport	หนังสือเดินทาง	năng-sĕu dern-thaang
permit	ใบอนุญาต	bai a-nú-yâat
curriculum vitae, CV	ประวัติย่อ	bprà-wàt yôr

debt note, IOU	รายการหนี้	raai gaan nêe
receipt (for purchase)	ใบเสร็จ	bai sèt
till receipt	ใบเสร็จ	bai sèt
report (mil.)	รายงาน	raai ngaan

to show (ID, etc.)	แสดง	sà-daeng
to sign (vt)	ลงนาม	long naam
signature	ลายมือชื่อ	laai meu chêu
seal (stamp)	ตราประทับ	dtraa bprà-tháp
text	ข้อความ	khôr khwaam
ticket (for entry)	ตั๋ว	dtŭa

to cross out	ขีดฆ่า	khèet khâa
to fill in (~ a form)	กรอก	gròrk

waybill (shipping invoice)	รายการสินค้าขนส่ง	raai gaan sĭn kháa khŏn sòng
will (testament)	พินัยกรรม	phí-nai-gam

117. Kinds of business

accounting services	บริการทำบัญชี	bor-rí-gaan tham ban-chee
advertising	การโฆษณา	gaan khôht-sà-naa
advertising agency	บริษัทโฆษณา	bor-rí-sàt khôht-sà-naa
air-conditioners	เครื่องปรับอากาศ	khrêuang bpràp-aa-gàat
airline	สายการบิน	săai gaan bin

alcoholic beverages	เครื่องดื่มแอลกอฮอล์	khrêuang dèum aen-gor-hor
antiques (antique dealers)	ของเก่า	khŏrng gào
art gallery (contemporary ~)	หอศิลป์	hŏr sĭn
audit services	บริการตรวจสอบบัญชี	bor-rí-gaan dtrùat sòrp ban-chee

banking industry	การธนาคาร	gaan thá-naa-khaan
beauty salon	ช่างเสริมสวย	châang sĕrm sŭay
bookshop	ร้านขายหนังสือ	ráan khăai năng-sĕu
brewery	โรงงานต้มเหล้า	rohng ngaan dtôm lâu
business centre	ศูนย์ธุรกิจ	sŏon thú-rá gìt
business school	โรงเรียนธุรกิจ	rohng rian thú-rá gìt

casino	คาสิโน	khaa-sì-noh
chemist, pharmacy	ร้านขายยา	ráan khăai yaa
cinema	โรงภาพยนตร์	rohng phâap-phá-yon
construction	การก่อสร้าง	gaan gòr sâang
consulting	การปรึกษา	gaan bprèuk-săa

dental clinic	คลินิกทันตกรรม	khlí-nìk than-ta-gam
design	การออกแบบ	gaan òrk bàep
dry cleaners	ร้านซักแห้ง	ráan sák hâeng

employment agency	สำนักงานจัดหางาน	săm-nák ngaan jàt hăa ngaan
financial services	บริการด้านการเงิน	bor-rí-gaan dâan gaan ngern
food products	ผลิตภัณฑ์อาหาร	phà-lìt-dtà-phan aa hăan
furniture (e.g. house ~)	เครื่องเรือน	khrêuang reuan

clothing, garment	เสื้อผ้า	sêua phâa
hotel	โรงแรม	rohng raem
ice-cream	ไอศกรีม	ai-sà-greem
industry (manufacturing)	อุตสาหกรรม	út-saa há-gam
insurance	การประกัน	gaan bprà-gan
Internet	อินเทอร์เน็ต	in-thêr-nét
investments (finance)	การลงทุน	gaan long thun
jeweller	ช่างทำเครื่อง เพชรพลอย	châang tham khrêuang phét phloi
jewellery	เครื่องเพชรพลอย	khrêuang phét phloi
laundry (shop)	โรงซักรีดผ้า	rohng sák rêet phâa
legal adviser	คนที่ปรึกษา ทางกฎหมาย	khon thêe bprèuk-săa thaang gòt măai
light industry	อุตสาหกรรมเบา	ùt-săa-hà-gam bao
magazine	นิตยสาร	nít-dtà-yá-săan
mail order selling	การขายสินค้า ทางไปรษณีย์	gaan khăai sĭn kháa thaang bprai-sà-nee
medicine	การแพทย์	gaan phâet
museum	พิพิธภัณฑ์	phí-phítha phan
news agency	สำนักข่าว	săm-nák khàao
newspaper	หนังสือพิมพ์	năng-sĕu phim
nightclub	ไนท์คลับ	nai-khláp
oil (petroleum)	น้ำมัน	nám man
courier services	บริการจัดส่ง	bor-rí-gaan jàt sòng
pharmaceutics	เภสัชกรรม	phay-sàt-cha -gam
printing (industry)	สิ่งพิมพ์	sìng phim
pub	บาร์	baa
publishing house	สำนักพิมพ์	săm-nák phim
radio (~ station)	วิทยุ	wít-thá-yú
real estate	อสังหาริมทรัพย์	a-săng-hăa-rim-má-sáp
restaurant	ร้านอาหาร	ráan aa-hăan
security company	บริษัทรักษา ความปลอดภัย	bor-rí-sàt rák-săa khwaam bplòrt phai
shop	ร้านค้า	ráan kháa
sport	กีฬา	gee-laa
stock exchange	ตลาดหลักทรัพย์	dtà-làat làk sáp
supermarket	ซูเปอร์มาร์เก็ต	soo-bper-maa-gèt
swimming pool (public ~)	สระว่ายน้ำ	sà wâai náam
tailor shop	ร้านตัดเสื้อ	ráan dtàt sêua
television	โทรทัศน์	thoh-rá-thát
theatre	โรงละคร	rohng lá-khon
trade (commerce)	การค้าขาย	gaan kháa kăai
transport companies	การขนส่ง	gaan khŏn sòng
travel	การท่องเที่ยว	gaan thôrng thîeow
undertakers	บริษัทรับจัดงานศพ	bor-rí-sàt ráp jàt ngaan sòp
veterinary surgeon	สัตวแพทย์	sàt phâet
warehouse	โกดังเก็บสินค้า	goh-dang gèp sĭn kháa
waste collection	การเก็บขยะ	gaan gèp khà-yà

Job. Business. Part 2

118. Show. Exhibition

English	Thai	Transcription
exhibition, show	งานแสดง	ngaan sà-daeng
trade show	งานแสดงสินค้า	ngaan sà-daeng sĭn kháa
participation	การเข้าร่วม	gaan khâo rûam
to participate (vi)	เข้ารวมใน	khâo rûam nai
participant (exhibitor)	ผู้เขารวม	phôo khâo rûam
director	ผู้อำนวยการ	phôo am-nuay gaan
organizers' office	สำนักงานผู้จัด	săm-nák ngaan phôo jàt
organizer	ผู้จัด	phôo jàt
to organize (vt)	จัด	jàt
participation form	แบบฟอร์มลงทะเบียน	bàep form long thá-bian
to fill in (vt)	กรอก	gròrk
details	รายละเอียด	raai lá-ìat
information	ขอมูล	khôr moon
price (cost, rate)	ราคา	raa-khaa
including	รวมถึง	ruam thĕung
to include (vt)	รวม	ruam
to pay (vi, vt)	จ่าย	jàai
registration fee	คาลงทะเบียน	khâa long thá-bian
entrance	ทางเข้า	thaang khâo
pavilion, hall	ศาลา	săa-laa
to register (vt)	ลงทะเบียน	long thá-bian
badge (identity tag)	ป้ายชื่อ	bpâai chêu
stand	บูธแสดงสินค้า	bòot sà-daeng sĭn kháa
to reserve, to book	จอง	jorng
display case	ตู้โชว์สินค้า	dtôo choh sĭn kháa
spotlight	ไฟรวมแสงบนเวที	fai ruam săeng bon way-thee
design	การออกแบบ	gaan òrk bàep
to place (put, set)	วาง	waang
to be placed	ถูกตั้ง	thòok dtâng
distributor	ผู้จัดจำหน่าย	phôo jàt jam-nàai
supplier	ผู้จัดหา	phôo jàt hăa
to supply (vt)	จัดหา	jàt hăa
country	ประเทศ	bprà-thâyt
foreign (adj)	ตางชาติ	dtàang châat
product	ผลิตภัณฑ์	phà-lìt-dtà-phan
association	สมาคม	sà-maa khom
conference hall	ห้องประชุม	hôrng bprà-chum

congress	การประชุม	gaan bprà-chum
contest (competition)	การแข่งขัน	gaan khàeng khǎn
visitor (attendee)	ผู้เข้าร่วม	phôo khâo rûam
to visit (attend)	เข้าร่วม	khâo rûam
customer	ลูกค้า	lôok kháa

119. Mass Media

newspaper	หนังสือพิมพ์	nǎng-sěu phim
magazine	นิตยสาร	nít-dtà-yá-sǎan
press (printed media)	สื่อสิ่งพิมพ์	sèu sìng phim
radio	วิทยุ	wít-thá-yú
radio station	สถานีวิทยุ	sà-thǎa-nee wít-thá-yú
television	โทรทัศน์	thoh-rá-thát
presenter, host	ผู้ประกาศข่าว	phôo bprà-gàat khàao
newsreader	ผู้ประกาศข่าว	phôo bprà-gàat khàao
commentator	ผู้อธิบาย	phôo à-thí-baai
journalist	นักข่าว	nák khàao
correspondent (reporter)	ผู้รายงานข่าว	phôo raai ngaan khàao
press photographer	ช่างภาพ หนังสือพิมพ์	châang phâap nǎng-sěu phim
reporter	ผู้รายงาน	phôo raai ngaan
editor	บรรณาธิการ	ban-naa-thí-gaan
editor-in-chief	หัวหน้าบรรณาธิการ	hǔa nâa ban-naa-thí-gaan
to subscribe (to ...)	รับ	ráp
subscription	การรับ	gaan ráp
subscriber	ผู้รับ	phôo ráp
to read (vi, vt)	อ่าน	àan
reader	ผู้อ่าน	phôo àan
circulation (of a newspaper)	การเผยแพร่	gaan phǒie-phrâe
monthly (adj)	รายเดือน	raai deuan
weekly (adj)	รายสัปดาห์	raai sàp-daa
issue (edition)	ฉบับ	chà-bàp
new (~ issue)	ใหม่	mài
headline	ข่าวพาดหัว	khàao phâat hǔa
short article	บทความสั้นๆ	bòt khwaam sân sân
column (regular article)	คอลัมน์	khor lam
article	บทความ	bòt khwaam
page	หน้า	nâa
reportage, report	การรายงานข่าว	gaan raai ngaan khàao
event (happening)	เหตุการณ์	hàyt gaan
sensation (news)	ข่าวดัง	khàao dang
scandal	เรื่องอื้อฉาว	rêuang êu chǎao
scandalous (adj)	อื้อฉาว	êu chǎao
great (~ scandal)	ใหญ่	yài
programme (e.g. cooking ~)	รายการ	raai gaan

interview	การสัมภาษณ์	gaan săm-phâat
live broadcast	ถ่ายทอดสด	thàai thôrt sòt
channel	ช่อง	chôrng

120. Agriculture

agriculture	เกษตรกรรม	gà-sàyt-dtra -gam
peasant (masc.)	ชาวนาผู้ชาย	chaao naa phôo chaai
peasant (fem.)	ชาวนาผู้หญิง	chaao naa phôo yĭng
farmer	ชาวนา	chaao naa

| tractor | รถแทร็คเตอร์ | rót tráek-dtêr |
| combine, harvester | เครื่องเก็บเกี่ยว | khrêuang gèp gìeow |

plough	คันไถ	khan thăi
to plough (vi, vt)	ไถ	thăi
ploughland	ที่ดินที่ไถพรวน	thêe din thêe thăi phruan
furrow (in field)	รองดิน	rôrng din

to sow (vi, vt)	หว่าน	wàan
seeder	เครื่องหว่านเมล็ด	khrêuang wàan má-lét
sowing (process)	การหว่าน	gaan wàan

| scythe | เคียว | khieow |
| to mow, to scythe | ถาง | thăang |

| spade (tool) | พลั่ว | phlûa |
| to till (vt) | ขุด | khùt |

hoe	จอบ	jòrp
to hoe, to weed	ถาก	thàak
weed (plant)	วัชพืช	wát-chá-phêut

watering can	กระป๋องรดน้ำ	grà-bpŏrng rót náam
to water (plants)	รดน้ำ	rót náam
watering (act)	การรดน้ำ	gaan rót nám

| pitchfork | ส้อมเสียบ | sôrm sìap |
| rake | คราด | khrâat |

fertiliser	ปุ๋ย	bpŭi
to fertilise (vt)	ใส่ปุ๋ย	sài bpŭi
manure (fertiliser)	ปุ๋ยคอก	bpŭi khôrk

field	ทุ่งนา	thûng naa
meadow	ทุ่งหญ้า	thûng yâa
vegetable garden	สวนผัก	sŭan phàk
orchard (e.g. apple ~)	สวนผลไม้	sŭan phŏn-lá-máai

to graze (vt)	เล็มหญ้า	lem yâa
herdsman	คนเลี้ยงสัตว์	khon líang sàt
pasture	ทุ่งเลี้ยงสัตว	thûng líang sàt
cattle breeding	การขยายพันธุ์สัตว์	gaan khà-yăai phan sàt
sheep farming	การขยายพันธุ์แกะ	gaan khà-yăai phan gàe

plantation	ที่เพาะปลูก	thêe phór bplòok
row (garden bed ~s)	แถว	thăe
hothouse	เรือนกระจกร้อน	reuan grà-jòk rón
drought (lack of rain)	ภัยแล้ง	phai láeng
dry (~ summer)	แล้ง	láeng
grain	ธัญพืช	than-yá-phêut
cereal crops	ผลผลิตธัญพืช	phŏn phà-lìt than-yá-phêut
to harvest, to gather	เก็บเกี่ยว	gèp gìeow
miller (person)	เจ้าของโรงโม่	jâo khŏrng rohng môh
mill (e.g. gristmill)	โรงสี	rohng sĕe
to grind (grain)	โม่	môh
flour	แป้ง	bpâeng
straw	ฟาง	faang

121. Building. Building process

building site	สถานที่ก่อสร้าง	sà-thăan thêe gòr sâang
to build (vt)	สร้าง	sâang
building worker	คนงานก่อสร้าง	khon ngaan gòr sâang
project	โครงการ	khrohng gaan
architect	สถาปนิก	sà-thăa-bpà-ník
worker	คนงาน	khon ngaan
foundations (of a building)	รากฐาน	râak thăan
roof	หลังคา	lăng khaa
foundation pile	เสาเข็ม	săo khĕm
wall	กำแพง	gam-phaeng
reinforcing bars	เหล็กเส้นเสริมแรง	lèk sên sĕrm raeng
scaffolding	นั่งราน	nâng ráan
concrete	คอนกรีต	khorn-grèet
granite	หินแกรนิต	hĭn grae-nít
stone	หิน	hĭn
brick	อิฐ	ìt
sand	ทราย	saai
cement	ปูนซีเมนต์	bpoon see-mayn
plaster (for walls)	พลาสเตอร์	phláat-dtêr
to plaster (vt)	ฉาบ	chàap
paint	สี	sĕe
to paint (~ a wall)	ทาสี	thaa sĕe
barrel	ถัง	thăng
crane	ปั้นจั่น	bpân jàn
to lift, to hoist (vt)	ยก	yók
to lower (vt)	ลด	lót
bulldozer	รถดันดิน	rót dan din
excavator	รถขุด	rót khùt

scoop, bucket	ช้อนขุด	chórn khùt
to dig (excavate)	ขุด	khùt
hard hat	หมวกนิรภัย	mùak ní-rá-phai

122. Science. Research. Scientists

science	วิทยาศาสตร์	wít-thá-yaa sàat
scientific (adj)	ทางวิทยาศาสตร์	thaang wít-thá-yaa sàat
scientist	นักวิทยาศาสตร	nák wít-thá-yaa sàat
theory	ทฤษฎี	thrít-sà-dee

axiom	สัจพจน์	sàt-jà-phót
analysis	การวิเคราะห์	gaan wí-khrór
to analyse (vt)	วิเคราะห์	wí-khrór
argument (strong ~)	ขอโต้แย้ง	khôr dtôh yáeng
substance (matter)	สาร	sǎan

hypothesis	สมมติฐาน	sǒm-mút thǎan
dilemma	โจทย์	jòht
dissertation	ปริญญานิพนธ์	bpà-rin-yaa ní-phon
dogma	หลัก	làk

doctrine	หลักคำสอน	làk kham sǒrn
research	การวิจัย	gaan wí-jai
to research (vt)	วิจัย	wí-jai
tests (laboratory ~)	การควบคุม	gaan khûap khum
laboratory	หองทดลอง	hôrng thót lorng

method	วิธี	wí-thee
molecule	โมเลกุล	moh-lay-gun
monitoring	การเฝ้าสังเกต	gaan fâo sǎng-gàyt
discovery (act, event)	การคนพบ	gaan khón phóp

postulate	สัจพจน์	sàt-jà-phót
principle	หลักการ	làk gaan
forecast	การคาดการณ์	gaan khâat gaan
to forecast (vt)	คาดการณ์	khâat gaan

synthesis	การสังเคราะห์	gaan sǎng-khrór
trend (tendency)	แนวโน้ม	naew nóhm
theorem	ทฤษฎีบท	thrít-sà-dee bòt

| teachings | คำสอน | kham sǒrn |
| fact | ขอเท็จจริง | khôr thét jing |

| expedition | การสำรวจ | gaan sǎm-rùat |
| experiment | การทดลอง | gaan thót lorng |

academician	นักวิชาการ	nák wí-chaa gaan
bachelor (e.g. ~ of Arts)	บัณฑิต	ban-dìt
doctor (PhD)	ดุษฎีบัณฑิต	dùt-sà-dee ban-dìt
Associate Professor	รองศาสตราจารย์	rorng sàat-sà-dtraa-jaan
Master (e.g. ~ of Arts)	มหาบัณฑิต	má-hǎa ban-dìt
professor	ศาสตราจารย์	sàat-sà-dtraa-jaan

Professions and occupations

job	งาน	ngaan
staff (work force)	พนักงาน	phá-nák ngaan
personnel	พนักงาน	phá-nák ngaan
career	อาชีพ	aa-chêep
prospects (chances)	โอกาส	oh-gàat
skills (mastery)	ทักษะ	thák-sà
selection (screening)	การคัดเลือก	gaan khát lêuak
employment agency	สำนักงานจัดหางาน	sǎm-nák ngaan jàt hǎa ngaan
curriculum vitae, CV	ประวัติย่อ	bprà-wàt yôr
job interview	สัมภาษณ์งาน	sǎm-phâat ngaan
vacancy	ตำแหน่งว่าง	dtam-nàeng wâang
salary, pay	เงินเดือน	ngern deuan
fixed salary	เงินเดือน	ngern deuan
pay, compensation	คาแรง	khâa raeng
position (job)	ตำแหน่ง	dtam-nàeng
duty (of an employee)	หน้าที่	nâa thêe
range of duties	หน้าที่	nâa thêe
busy (I'm ~)	ไม่ว่าง	mâi wâang
to fire (dismiss)	ไล่ออก	lâi òrk
dismissal	การไล่ออก	gaan lâi òrk
unemployment	การว่างงาน	gaan wâang ngaan
unemployed (n)	คนว่างงาน	khon wâang ngaan
retirement	การเกษียณอายุ	gaan gà-sǐan aa-yú
to retire (from job)	เกษียณ	gà-sǐan

director	ผู้อำนวยการ	phôo am-nuay gaan
manager (director)	ผู้จัดการ	phôo jàt gaan
boss	หัวหน้า	hǔa-nâa
superior	ผู้บังคับบัญชา	phôo bang-kháp ban-chaa
superiors	คณะผู้บังคับบัญชา	khá-ná phôo bang-kháp ban-chaa
president	ประธานาธิปดี	bprà-thaa-naa-thí-bor-dee
chairman	ประธาน	bprà-thaan
deputy (substitute)	รอง	rorng

assistant	ผู้ช่วย	phôo chûay
secretary	เลขา	lay-khǎa
personal assistant	ผู้ช่วยส่วนบุคคล	phôo chûay sùan bùk-khon
businessman	นักธุรกิจ	nák thú-rá-gìt
entrepreneur	ผู้ประกอบการ	phôo bprà-gòp gaan
founder	ผู้ก่อตั้ง	phôo gòr dtâng
to found (vt)	ก่อตั้ง	gòr dtâng
founding member	ผู้ก่อตั้ง	phôo gòr dtâng
partner	หุ้นส่วน	hûn sùan
shareholder	ผู้ถือหุ้น	phôo thěu hûn
millionaire	เศรษฐีเงินล้าน	sàyt-thěe ngern láan
billionaire	มหาเศรษฐี	má-hǎa sàyt-thěe
owner, proprietor	เจ้าของ	jâo khǒrng
landowner	เจ้าของที่ดิน	jâo khǒrng thêe din
client	ลูกค้า	lôok kháa
regular client	ลูกค้าประจำ	lôok kháa bprà-jam
buyer (customer)	ลูกค้า	lôok kháa
visitor	ผู้เข้าร่วม	phôo khâo rûam
professional (n)	ผู้เป็นมืออาชีพ	phôo bpen meu aa-chêep
expert	ผู้เชี่ยวชาญ	phôo chîeow-chaan
specialist	ผู้ชำนาญ เฉพาะทาง	phôo cham-naan chà-phó thaang
banker	พนักงาน ธนาคาร	phá-nák ngaan thá-naa-khaan
broker	นายหน้า	naai nâa
cashier	แคชเชียร์	khâet chia
accountant	นักบัญชี	nák ban-chee
security guard	ยาม	yaam
investor	ผู้ลงทุน	phôo long thun
debtor	ลูกหนี้	lôok nêe
creditor	เจ้าหนี้	jâo nêe
borrower	ผู้ยืม	phôo yeum
importer	ผู้นำเข้า	phôo nam khâo
exporter	ผู้ส่งออก	phôo sòng òrk
manufacturer	ผู้ผลิต	phôo phà-lìt
distributor	ผู้จัดจำหน่าย	phôo jàt jam-nàai
middleman	คนกลาง	khon glaang
consultant	ที่ปรึกษา	thêe bprèuk-sǎa
sales representative	พนักงานขาย	phá-nák ngaan khǎai
agent	ตัวแทน	dtua thaen
insurance agent	ตัวแทนประกัน	dtua thaen bprà-gan

125. Service professions

cook	ดูนครัว	khon khrua
chef (kitchen chef)	กุ๊ก	gúk
baker	ช่างอบขนมปัง	châang òp khà-nŏm bpang

barman	บาร์เทนเดอร์	baa-thayn-dêr
waiter	พนักงานเสิร์ฟชาย	phá-nák ngaan sèrf chaai
waitress	พนักงานเสิร์ฟหญิง	phá-nák ngaan sèrf yĭng

lawyer, barrister	ทนายความ	thá-naai khwaam
lawyer (legal expert)	นักกฎหมาย	nák gòt măai
notary public	พนักงานจดทะเบียน	phá-nák ngaan jòt thá-bian

electrician	ช่างไฟฟ้า	châang fai-fáa
plumber	ช่างประปา	châang bprà-bpaa
carpenter	ช่างไม้	châang máai

masseur	หมอนวดชาย	mŏr nûat chaai
masseuse	หมอนวดหญิง	mŏr nûat yĭng
doctor	แพทย์	phâet

taxi driver	คนขับแท็กซี่	khon khàp tháek-sêe
driver	คนขับ	khon khàp
delivery man	คนส่งของ	khon sòng khŏrng

chambermaid	แม่บ้าน	mâe bâan
security guard	ยาม	yaam
flight attendant (fem.)	พนักงานต้อนรับบนเครื่องบิน	phá-nák ngaan dtôrn ráp bon khrêuang bin

schoolteacher	อาจารย์	aa-jaan
librarian	บรรณารักษ์	ban-naa-rák
translator	นักแปล	nák bplae
interpreter	ล่าม	lâam
guide	มัคคุเทศก์	mák-khú-thâyt

hairdresser	ช่างทำผม	châang tham phŏm
postman	บุรุษไปรษณีย์	bù-rùt bprai-sà-nee
salesman (store staff)	คนขายของ	khon khăai khŏrng

gardener	ชาวสวน	chaao sŭan
domestic servant	คนใช้	khon chái
maid (female servant)	สาวใช้	săao chái
cleaner (cleaning lady)	คนทำความสะอาด	khon tham khwaam sà-àat

126. Military professions and ranks

private	พลทหาร	phon-thá-hăan
sergeant	สิบเอก	sìp àyk
lieutenant	ร้อยโท	rói thoh
captain	ร้อยเอก	rói àyk
major	พลตรี	phon-dtree

colonel	พันเอก	phan àyk
general	นายพล	naai phon
marshal	จอมพล	jorm phon
admiral	พลเรือเอก	phon reua àyk
military (n)	ทางทหาร	thaang thá-hǎan
soldier	ทหาร	thá-hǎan
officer	นายทหาร	naai thá-hǎan
commander	ผู้บัญชาการ	phôo ban-chaa gaan
border guard	ยามเฝ้าชายแดน	yaam fâo chaai daen
radio operator	พลวิทยุ	phon wít-thá-yú
scout (searcher)	ทหารพราน	thá-hǎan phraan
pioneer (sapper)	ทหารช่าง	thá-hǎan châang
marksman	พลแมนปืน	phon mâen bpeun
navigator	ตนหน	dtôn hǒn

127. Officials. Priests

king	กษัตริย์	gà-sàt
queen	ราชินี	raa-chí-nee
prince	เจ้าชาย	jâo chaai
princess	เจาหญิง	jâo yǐng
czar	ชาร์	saa
czarina	ชารีนา	saa-ree-naa
president	ประธานาธิบดี	bprà-thaa-naa-thí-bor-dee
Secretary (minister)	รัฐมนตรี	rát-thà-mon-dtree
prime minister	นายกรัฐมนตรี	naa-yók rát-thà-mon-dtree
senator	สมาชิกวุฒิสภา	sà-maa-chík wút-thí sà-phaa
diplomat	นักการทูต	nák gaan thôot
consul	กงสุล	gong-sǔn
ambassador	เอกอัครราชทูต	àyk-gà-àk-krá-râat-chá-tôot
counselor (diplomatic officer)	เจาหนาที่การทูต	jâo nâa-thêe gaan thôot
official, functionary (civil servant)	ข้าราชการ	khâa râat-chá-gaan
prefect	เจาหน้าที่	jâo nâa-thêe
mayor	นายกเทศมนตรี	naa-yók thâyt-sà-mon-dtree
judge	ผู้พิพากษา	phôo phí-phâak-sǎa
prosecutor	อัยการ	ai-yá-gaan
missionary	ผู้สอนศาสนา	phôo sǒrn sàat-sà-nǎa
monk	พระ	phrá
abbot	เจาอาวาส	jâo aa-wâat
rabbi	พระในศาสนายิว	phrá nai sàat-sà-nǎa yiw
vizier	วีซีร์	wee see
shah	กษัตริย์อิหร่าน	gà-sàt i-ràan
sheikh	หัวหน้าเผาอาหรับ	hǔa nâa phào aa-ràp

128. Agricultural professions

beekeeper	คนเลี้ยงผึ้ง	khon líang phêung
shepherd	คนเลี้ยงปศุสัตว์	khon líang bpà-sù-sàt
agronomist	นักปฐพีวิทยา	nák bpà-tà-phee wít-thá-yaa
cattle breeder	ผู้ขยายพันธุ์สัตว์	phôo khà-yǎai phan sàt
veterinary surgeon	สัตวแพทย์	sàt phâet

farmer	ชาวนา	chaao naa
winemaker	ผู้ผลิตไวน์	phôo phà-lìt wai
zoologist	นักสัตววิทยา	nák sàt wít-thá-yaa
cowboy	โคบาล	khoh-baan

129. Art professions

actor	นักแสดงชาย	nák sà-daeng chaai
actress	นักแสดงหญิง	nák sà-daeng yǐng

singer (masc.)	นักร้องชาย	nák rórng chaai
singer (fem.)	นักร้องหญิง	nák rórng yǐng

dancer (masc.)	นักเต้นชาย	nák dtên chaai
dancer (fem.)	นักเต้นหญิง	nák dtên yǐng

performer (masc.)	นักแสดงชาย	nák sà-daeng chaai
performer (fem.)	นักแสดงหญิง	nák sà-daeng yǐng
musician	นักดนตรี	nák don-dtree
pianist	นักเปียโน	nák bpia noh
guitar player	ผู้เล่นกีตาร์	phôo lên gee-dtâa

conductor (orchestra ~)	ผู้ควบคุม วงดนตรี	phôo khûap khum wong don-dtree
composer	นักแต่งเพลง	nák dtàeng phlayng
impresario	ผู้ควบคุม การแสดง	phôo khûap khum gaan sà-daeng

film director	ผู้กำกับ ภาพยนตร์	phôo gam-gàp phâap-phá-yon
producer	ผู้อำนวยการสร้าง	phôo am-nuay gaan sâang
scriptwriter	คนเขียนบท ภาพยนตร์	khon khǐan bòt phâap-phá-yon
critic	นักวิจารณ์	nák wí-jaan

writer	นักเขียน	nák khǐan
poet	นักกวี	nák gà-wee
sculptor	ช่างสลัก	châang sà-làk
artist (painter)	ช่างวาดรูป	châang wâat rôop

juggler	นักมายากล โยนของ	nák maa-yaa gon yohn khǒrng
clown	ตัวตลก	dtua dtà-lòk
acrobat	นักกายกรรม	nák gaai-yá-gam
magician	นักเลนกล	nák lên gon

130. Various professions

doctor	แพทย์	phâet
nurse	พยาบาล	phá-yaa-baan
psychiatrist	จิตแพทย์	jìt-dtà-phâet
dentist	ทันตแพทย์	than-dtà phâet
surgeon	ศัลยแพทย์	săn-yá-phâet
astronaut	นักบินอวกาศ	nák bin a-wá-gàat
astronomer	นักดาราศาสตร์	nák daa-raa sàat
pilot	นักบิน	nák bin
driver (of a taxi, etc.)	คนขับ	khon khàp
train driver	คนขับรถไฟ	khon khàp rót fai
mechanic	ช่างเครื่อง	châang khrêuang
miner	คนงานเหมือง	khon ngaan mĕuang
worker	คนงาน	khon ngaan
locksmith	ช่างโลหะ	châang loh-hà
joiner (carpenter)	ช่างไม้	châang máai
turner (lathe operator)	ช่างกลึง	châang gleung
building worker	คนงานก่อสร้าง	khon ngaan gòr sâang
welder	ช่างเชื่อม	châang chêuam
professor (title)	ศาสตราจารย์	sàat-sà-dtraa-jaan
architect	สถาปนิก	sà-thăa-bpà-ník
historian	นักประวัติศาสตร์	nák bprà-wàt sàat
scientist	นักวิทยาศาสตร	nák wít-thá-yaa sàat
physicist	นักฟิสิกส์	nák fí-sìk
chemist (scientist)	นักเคมี	nák khay-mee
archaeologist	นักโบราณคดี	nák boh-raan-ná-khá-dee
geologist	นักธรณีวิทยา	nák thor-rá-nee wít-thá-yaa
researcher (scientist)	ผู้วิจัย	phôo wí-jai
babysitter	พี่เลี้ยงเด็ก	phêe líang dèk
teacher, educator	อาจารย์	aa-jaan
editor	บรรณาธิการ	ban-naa-thí-gaan
editor-in-chief	หัวหน้าบรรณาธิการ	hŭa nâa ban-naa-thí-gaan
correspondent	ผู้สื่อข่าว	phôo sèu khàao
typist (fem.)	พนักงานพิมพ์ดีด	phá-nák ngaan phim dèet
designer	นักออกแบบ	nák òrk bàep
computer expert	ผู้เชี่ยวชาญด้านคอมพิวเตอร์	pôo chîeow-chaan dâan khorm-piw-dtêr
programmer	นักเขียนโปรแกรม	nák khĭan bproh-graem
engineer (designer)	วิศวกร	wít-sà-wá-gon
sailor	กะลาสี	gà-laa-sĕe
seaman	คนเรือ	khon reua
rescuer	นักกู้ภัย	nák gôo phai
firefighter	เจ้าหน้าที่ดับเพลิง	jâo nâa-thêe dàp phlerng
police officer	เจ้าหน้าที่ตำรวจ	jâo nâa-thêe dtam-rùat

| watchman | คนยาม | khon yaam |
| detective | นักสืบ | nák sèup |

customs officer	เจ้วหน้าที่ศุลกากร	jâo nâa-thêe sǔn-lá-gaa-gon
bodyguard	ผู้คุมกัน	phôo khúm gan
prison officer	ผู้คุม	phôo khum
inspector	ผู้ตรวจการ	phôo dtrùat gaan

sportsman	นักกีฬา	nák gee-laa
trainer, coach	โค้ช	khóht
butcher	คนขายเนื้อ	khon khǎai néua
cobbler (shoe repairer)	คนซ่อมรองเท้า	khon sôrm rorng tháo
merchant	คนค้า	khon kháa
loader (person)	คนงานยกของ	khon ngaan yók khǒrng

| fashion designer | นักออกแบบแฟชั่น | nák òrk bàep fae-chân |
| model (fem.) | นางแบบ | naang bàep |

131. Occupations. Social status

| schoolboy | นักเรียน | nák rian |
| student (college ~) | นักศึกษา | nák sèuk-sǎa |

philosopher	นักปราชญ์	nák bpràat
economist	นักเศรษฐศาสตร์	nák sàyt-thà-sàat
inventor	นักประดิษฐ	nák bprà-dìt

unemployed (n)	คนว่างงาน	khon wâang ngaan
retiree, pensioner	ผู้เกษียณอายุ	phôo gà-sǐan aa-yú
spy, secret agent	สายลับ	sǎai láp

prisoner	นักโทษ	nák thôht
striker	คนนัดหยุดงาน	kon nát yùt ngaan
bureaucrat	อำมาตย์	am-màat
traveller (globetrotter)	นักเดินทาง	nák dern-thaang

gay, homosexual (n)	ผู้รักเพศเดียวกัน	phôo rák phâyt dieow gan
hacker	แฮ็กเกอร	háek-gêr
hippie	ฮิปปี้	híp-bpêe

bandit	โจร	john
hit man, killer	นักฆ่า	nák khâa
drug addict	ผู้ติดยาเสพติด	phôo dtìt yaa-sàyp-dtìt
drug dealer	ผู้ค้ายาเสพติด	phôo kháa yaa-sàyp-dtìt

| prostitute (fem.) | โสเภณี | sǒh-phay-nee |
| pimp | แมงดา | maeng-daa |

sorcerer	พ่อมด	phôr mót
sorceress (evil ~)	แม่มด	mâe mót
pirate	โจรสลัด	john sà-làt
slave	ทาส	thâat
samurai	ซามูไร	saa-moo-rai
savage (primitive)	คนป่าเถื่อน	khon bpàa thèuan

Sports

sportsman	นักกีฬา	nák gee-laa
kind of sport	ประเภทกีฬา	bprà-phâyt gee-laa
basketball	บาสเก็ตบอล	bàat-gèt-bon
basketball player	ผู้เลนบาสเก็ตบอล	phôo lâyn bàat-gèt-bon
baseball	เบสบอล	bàyt-bon
baseball player	ผู้เลนเบสบอล	phôo lâyn bàyt bon
football	ฟุตบอล	fút bon
football player	นักฟุตบอล	nák fút-bon
goalkeeper	ผู้รักษาประตู	phôo rák-sǎa bprà-dtoo
ice hockey	ฮอกกี้	hôk-gêe
ice hockey player	ผู้เลนฮอกกี้	phôo lâyn hôk-gêe
volleyball	วอลเลย์บอล	won-lây-bon
volleyball player	ผู้เลนวอลเลย์บอล	phôo lâyn won-lây-bon
boxing	การชกมวย	gaan chók muay
boxer	นักมวย	nák muay
wrestling	การมวยปล้ำ	gaan muay bplâm
wrestler	นักมวยปล้ำ	nák muay bplâm
karate	คาราเต้	khaa-raa-dtây
karate fighter	นักคาราเต้	nák khaa-raa-dtây
judo	ยูโด	yoo-doh
judo athlete	นักยูโด	nák yoo-doh
tennis	เทนนิส	then-nít
tennis player	นักเทนนิส	nák then-nít
swimming	กีฬาว่ายน้ำ	gee-laa wâai náam
swimmer	นักวายน้ำ	nák wâai náam
fencing	กีฬาฟันดาบ	gee-laa fan dàap
fencer	นักฟันดาบ	nák fan dàap
chess	หมากรุก	màak rúk
chess player	ผู้เลนหมากรุก	phôo lên màak rúk
alpinism	การปีนเขา	gaan bpeen khǎo
alpinist	นักปีนเขา	nák bpeen khǎo
running	การวิ่ง	gaan wîng

runner	นักวิ่ง	nák wîng
athletics	กรีฑา	gree thaa
athlete	นักกรีฑา	nák gree thaa

| horse riding | กีฬาขี่ม้า | gee-laa khèe máa |
| horse rider | นักขี่ม้า | nák khèe máa |

figure skating	สเก็ตลีลา	sà-gèt lee-laa
figure skater (masc.)	นักแสดงสเก็ตลีลา	nák sà-daeng sà-gèt lee-laa
figure skater (fem.)	นักแสดงสเก็ตลีลา	nák sà-daeng sà-gèt lee-laa

powerlifting	กีฬายกน้ำหนัก	gee-laa yók náam nàk
powerlifter	นักยกน้ำหนัก	nák yók nám nàk
car racing	การแข่งรถ	gaan khàeng rót
racer (driver)	นักแข่งรถ	nák khàeng rót

cycling	การแข่งจักรยาน	gaan khàeng jàk-grà-yaan
cyclist	นักแข่งจักรยาน	nák khàeng jàk-grà-yaan
long jump	กีฬากระโดดไกล	gee-laa grà-dòht glai
pole vaulting	กีฬากระโดดค้ำถอ	gee-laa grà dòht khám thòr
jumper	นักกระโดด	nák grà dòht

133. Kinds of sports. Miscellaneous

American football	อเมริกันฟุตบอล	a-may-rí-gan fút bon
badminton	แบดมินตัน	bàet-min-dtân
biathlon	ไบแอธลอน	bpai-oht-lon
billiards	บิลเลียด	bin-lîat

bobsleigh	การขับเลื่อน น้ำแข็ง	gaan khàp lêuan náam khǎeng
bodybuilding	การเพาะกาย	gaan phór gaai
water polo	กีฬาโปโลน้ำ	gee-laa bpoh loh nám
handball	แฮนด์บอล	haen-bon
golf	กอลฟ์	góf

rowing	การพายเรือ	gaan phaai reua
scuba diving	การดำน้ำ	gaan dam náam
cross-country skiing	การแข่งสกี ตามเส้นทาง	gaan khàeng sà-gee dtaam sên thaang
table tennis (ping-pong)	กีฬาปิงปอง	gee-laa bping-bpong

sailing	การแล่นเรือใบ	gaan lâen reua bai
rally	การแข่งแรลลี่	gaan khàeng rae lá-lêe
rugby	รักบี้	rák-bêe
snowboarding	สโนว์บอร์ด	sà-nǒh bòt
archery	การยิงธนู	gaan ying thá-noo

134. Gym

| barbell | บาร์เบลล์ | baa bayn |
| dumbbells | ที่ยกน้ำหนัก | thêe yók nám nàk |

training machine	เครื่องออกกำลังกาย	khrêuang òk gam-lang gaai
exercise bicycle	จักรยานออก	jàk-grà-yaan òk
	กำลังกาย	gam-lang gaai
treadmill	ลู่วิ่งออกกำลังกาย	lôo wîng òk gam-lang gaai
horizontal bar	บาร์เดี่ยว	baa dìeow
parallel bars	บาร์คู่	baa khôo
vault (vaulting horse)	ม้าขวาง	máa khwǎang
mat (exercise ~)	เสื่อออกกำลังกาย	sèua òrk gam-lang gaai
skipping rope	กระโดดเชือก	grà dòht chêuak
aerobics	แอโรบิก	ae-roh-bìk
yoga	โยคะ	yoh-khá

135. Ice hockey

ice hockey	ฮอกกี้	hôk-gêe
ice hockey player	ผู้เล่นฮอกกี้	phôo lâyn hôk-gêe
to play ice hockey	เล่นฮอกกี	lên hók-gêe
ice	น้ำแข็ง	nám khǎeng
puck	ลูกฮอกกี้	lôok hók-gêe
ice hockey stick	ไม้ฮอกกี้	máai hók-gêe
ice skates	รองเท้าสเก็ต	rorng tháo sà-gèt
	น้ำแข็ง	nám khǎeng
board (ice hockey rink ~)	ลานสเก็ตน้ำแข็ง	laan sà-gèt nám khǎeng
shot	การยิง	gaan ying
goaltender	ผู้รักษาประตู	phôo rák-sǎa bprà-dtoo
goal (score)	ประตู	bprà-dtoo
to score a goal	ทำประตู	tham bprà-dtoo
period	ช่วง	chûang
second period	ช่วงที่สอง	chûang thêe sǒrng
substitutes bench	ซุมม้านั่ง	súm máa nâng
	ตัวสำรอง	dtua sǎm-rorng

136. Football

football	ฟุตบอล	fút bon
football player	นักฟุตบอล	nák fút-bon
to play football	เล่นฟุตบอล	lên fút bon
major league	เมเจอร์ลีก	may-jer-lêek
football club	สโมสรฟุตบอล	sà-moh-sǒn fút-bon
coach	โค้ช	khóht
owner, proprietor	เจาของ	jâo khǒrng
team	ทีม	theem
team captain	หัวหน้าทีม	hǔa nâa theem
player	ผู้เล่น	phôo lên

substitute	ผู้เล่นสำรอง	phôo lên săm-rorng
forward	กองหน้า	gorng nâa
centre forward	กองหน้าตัวเป้า	gorng nâa dtua bpâo
scorer	ผู้ทำประตู	phôo tham bprà-dtoo
defender, back	กองหลัง	gorng lăng
midfielder, halfback	กองกลาง	gorng glaang

match	เกมการแข่ง	gaym gaan khàeng
to meet (vi, vt)	พบ	phóp
final	รอบสุดท้าย	rôrp sùt tháai
semi-final	รอบรองชนะเลิศ	rôrp rorng chá-ná lêrt
championship	ชิงแชมป์	ching chaem

period, half	ครึ่ง	khrêung
first period	ครึ่งแรก	khrêung râek
half-time	ช่วงพักครึ่ง	chûang phák khrêung

goal	ประตู	bprà-dtoo
goalkeeper	ผู้รักษาประตู	phôo rák-săa bprà-dtoo
goalpost	เสาประตู	săo bprà-dtoo
crossbar	คานประตู	khaan bprà-dtoo
net	ตาข่าย	dtaa khàai
to concede a goal	เสียประตู	sĭa bprà-dtoo

ball	บอล	bon
pass	การส่ง	gaan sòng
kick	การเตะ	gaan dtè
to kick (~ the ball)	เตะ	dtè
free kick (direct ~)	ฟรีคิก	free khík
corner kick	การเตะมุม	gaan dtè mum

attack	การบุก	gaan bùk
counterattack	การบุกสวนกลับ	gaan bùk sŭan glàp
combination	การผสมผสาน	gaan phà-sŏm phà-săan

referee	ผู้ตัดสิน	phôo dtàt sĭn
to blow the whistle	เป่านกหวีด	bpào nók wèet
whistle (sound)	เสียงนกหวีด	sĭang nók wèet
foul, misconduct	ฟาวล์	faao
to commit a foul	ทำฟาวล์	tham faao
to send off	ไล่ออก	lâi òrk

yellow card	ใบเหลือง	bai lĕuang
red card	ใบแดง	bai daeng
disqualification	การตัดสิทธิ์	gaan dtàt sìt
to disqualify (vt)	ตัดสิทธิ์	dtàt sìt

penalty kick	ลูกโทษ	lôok thôht
wall	กำแพง	gam-phaeng
to score (vi, vt)	ทำประตู	tham bprà-dtoo
goal (score)	ประตู	bprà-dtoo
to score a goal	ทำประตู	tham bprà-dtoo

substitution	ตัวสำรอง	dtua săm-rorng
to replace (a player)	เปลี่ยนตัว	bplìan dtua
rules	กติกา	gà-dtì-gaa

tactics	ยุทธวิธี	yút-thá-wí-thee
stadium	สนาม	sà-năam
terrace	อัฒจันทร์	àt-tá-jan
fan, supporter	แฟน	faen
to shout (vi)	ตะโกน	dtà-gohn

| scoreboard | ป้ายคะแนน | bpâai khá-naen |
| score | คะแนน | khá-naen |

defeat	ความพ่ายแพ้	khwaam phâai pháe
to lose (not win)	แพ้	pháe
draw	เสมอ	sà-měr
to draw (vi)	เสมอ	sà-měr

victory	ชัยชนะ	chai chá-ná
to win (vi, vt)	ชนะ	chá-ná
champion	แชมเปี้ยน	chaem-bpîan
best (adj)	ดีที่สุด	dee têe sùt
to congratulate (vt)	แสดงความยินดี	sà-daeng khwaam yin dee

commentator	ผู้อธิบาย	phôo à-thí-baai
to commentate (vt)	อธิบาย	à-thí-baai
broadcast	การออกอากาศ	gaan òrk aa-gàat

137. Alpine skiing

skis	สกี	sà-gee
to ski (vi)	เล่นสกี	lên sà-gee
mountain-ski resort	รีสอรทสำหรับ	ree sòt săm-ràp
	เล่นสกีบนภูเขา	lên sà-gee bon phoo khăo
ski lift	ลิฟต์สกี	líf sà-gee

ski poles	ไม้ค้ำสกี	máai khám sà-gee
slope	ทางลาด	thaang lâat
slalom	การเล่นสกี	gaan lên sà-gee

138. Tennis. Golf

golf	กอล์ฟ	góf
golf club	กอล์ฟคลับ	góf khláp
golfer	นักกอล์ฟ	nák góf
hole	หลุม	lŭm
club	ไม้ตีกอล์ฟ	mái dtee góf
golf trolley	รถลากถุงกอล์ฟ	rót lâak thŭng góf

tennis	เทนนิส	then-nít
tennis court	สนามเทนนิส	sà-năam then-nít
serve	การเสิรฟ	gaan sèrf
to serve (vt)	เสิรฟ	sèrf
racket	ไม้ตีเทนนิส	mái dtee then-nít
net	ตาข่าย	dtaa khàai
ball	ลูกเทนนิส	lôok then-nít

139. Chess

chess	หมากรุก	màak rúk
chessmen	ตัวหมากรุก	dtua màak rúk
chess player	นักกีฬาหมากรุก	nák gee-laa màak rúk
chessboard	กระดานหมากรุก	grà-daan măak-grùk
chessman	ตัวหมากรุก	dtua màak rúk
White (white pieces)	ขาว	khăao
Black (black pieces)	ดำ	dam
pawn	เบี้ย	bîa
bishop	บิชอป	bì-chôrp
knight	มา	máa
rook	เรือ	reua
queen	ควีน	khween
king	ขุน	khŭn
move	การเดิน	gaan dern
to move (vi, vt)	เดิน	dern
to sacrifice (vt)	สละ	sà-là
castling	การเข้าป้อม	gaan khâo bpôrm
check	รุก	rúk
checkmate	รุกฆาต	rúk khâat
chess tournament	การแข่งขันหมากรุก	gaan khàeng khăn màak rúk
Grand Master	แกรนด์มาสเตอร์	graen maa-sà-dtêr
combination	การเดินหมาก	gaan dern màak
game (in chess)	เกม	gaym
draughts	หมากฮอส	màak-hórt

140. Boxing

boxing	การชกมวย	gaan chók muay
fight (bout)	ชกมวย	chók muay
boxing match	เกมการชกมวย	gaym gaan chók muay
round (in boxing)	ยก	yók
ring	เวที	way-thee
gong	ฆอง	khórng
punch	การต่อย	gaan dtòi
knockdown	การน็อค	gaan nórk
knockout	การน็อคเอาท์	gaan nórk ao
to knock out	น็อคเอาท์	nórk ao
boxing glove	นวมชกมวย	nuam chók muay
referee	กรรมการ	gam-má-gaan
lightweight	ไลท์เวท	lai-wâyt
middleweight	มิดเดิลเวท	mít dêrn wâyt
heavyweight	เฮฟวี่เวท	hay fá-wêe wâyt

141. Sports. Miscellaneous

Olympic Games	กีฬาโอลิมปิก	gee-laa oh-lim-bpìk
winner	ผู้ชนะ	phôo chá-ná
to be winning	ชนะ	chá-ná
to win (vi)	ชนะ	chá-ná
leader	ผู้นำ	phôo nam
to lead (vi)	นำ	nam
first place	อันดับที่หนึ่ง	an-dàp thêe nèung
second place	อันดับที่สอง	an-dàp thêe sŏrng
third place	อันดับที่สาม	an-dàp thêe săam
medal	เหรียญรางวัล	rĭan raang-wan
trophy	ถ้วยรางวัล	thûay raang-wan
prize cup (trophy)	เวท	wâyt
prize (in game)	รางวัล	raang-wan
main prize	รางวัลหลัก	raang-wan làk
record	สถิติ	sà-thì-dtì
to set a record	ทำสถิติ	tham sà-thì-dtì
final	รอบสุดท้าย	rôrp sùt tháai
final (adj)	สุดท้าย	sùt tháai
champion	แชมเปี้ยน	chaem-bpîan
championship	ชิงแชมป์	ching chaem
stadium	สนาม	sà-năam
terrace	อัฒจันทร์	àt-tá-jan
fan, supporter	แฟน	faen
opponent, rival	คู่ต่อสู้	khôo dtòr sôo
start (start line)	เส้นเริ่ม	sên rêrm
finish line	เสนชัย	sên chai
defeat	ความพ่ายแพ้	khwaam phâai pháe
to lose (not win)	แพ้	pháe
referee	กรรมฏาร	gam-má-gaan
jury (judges)	คณะผู้ตัดสิน	khá-ná phôo dtàt sĭn
score	คะแนน	khá-naen
draw	เสมอ	sà-mĕr
to draw (vi)	ได้คะแนนเท่ากัน	dâai khá-naen thâo gan
point	แต้ม	dtâem
result (final score)	ผลลัพธ์	phŏn láp
period	ช่วง	chûang
half-time	ช่วงพักครึ่ง	chûang phák khrêung
doping	การใช้สารต้องห้าม ทางการกีฬา	gaan chái săan dtôrng hâam thaang gaan gee-laa
to penalise (vt)	ทำโทษ	tham thôht
to disqualify (vt)	ตัดสิทธิ์	dtàt sìt

apparatus	อุปกรณ์	ù-bpà-gon
javelin	แหลน	lǎen
shot (metal ball)	ลูกเหล็ก	lôok lèk
ball (snooker, etc.)	ลูก	lôok
aim (target)	เล็งเป้า	leng bpâo
target	เป้านิ่ง	bpâo nîng
to shoot (vi)	ยิง	ying
accurate (~ shot)	แม่นยำ	mâen yam
trainer, coach	โค้ช	khóht
to train (sb)	ฝึก	fèuk
to train (vi)	ฝึกหัด	fèuk hàt
training	การฝึกหัด	gaan fèuk hàt
gym	โรงยิม	rohng-yim
exercise (physical)	การออกกำลัง	gaan òrk gam-lang
warm-up (athlete ~)	การอบอุ่นร่างกาย	gaan òp ùn râang gaai

Education

school	โรงเรียน	rohng rian
headmaster	อาจารย์ใหญ่	aa-jaan yài
student (m)	นักเรียน	nák rian
student (f)	นักเรียน	nák rian
schoolboy	เด็กนักเรียนชาย	dèk nák rian chaai
schoolgirl	เด็กนักเรียนหญิง	dèk nák rian yǐng
to teach (sb)	สอน	sǒrn
to learn (language, etc.)	เรียน	rian
to learn by heart	ท่องจำ	thôrng jam
to learn (~ to count, etc.)	เรียน	rian
to be at school	ไปโรงเรียน	bpai rohng rian
to go to school	ไปโรงเรียน	bpai rohng rian
alphabet	ตัวอักษร	dtua àk-sǒn
subject (at school)	วิชา	wí-chaa
classroom	ห้องเรียน	hôrng rian
lesson	ชั่วโมงเรียน	chûa mohng rian
playtime, break	ช่วงพัก	chûang phák
school bell	สัญญาณหมดเรียน	sǎn-yaan mòt rian
school desk	โต๊ะนักเรียน	dtó nák rian
blackboard	กระดานดำ	grà-daan dam
mark	เกรด	gràyt
good mark	เกรดดี	gràyt dee
bad mark	เกรดแย่	gràyt yâe
to give a mark	ให้เกรด	hâi gràyt
mistake, error	ข้อผิดพลาด	khôr phìt phlâat
to make mistakes	ทำผิดพลาด	tham phìt phlâat
to correct (an error)	แก้ไข	gâe khǎi
crib	โพย	phoi
homework	การบ้าน	gaan bâan
exercise (in education)	แบบฝึกหัด	bàep fèuk hàt
to be present	มาเรียน	maa rian
to be absent	ขาด	khàat
to miss school	ขาดเรียน	khàat rian
to punish (vt)	ลงโทษ	long thôht
punishment	การลงโทษ	gaan long thôht
conduct (behaviour)	ความประพฤติ	khwaam bprà-préut

school report	สมุดพก	sà-mùt phók
pencil	ดินสอ	din-sŏr
rubber	ยางลบ	yaang lóp
chalk	ชอลค	chôrk
pencil case	กล่องดินสอ	glòrng din-sŏr

schoolbag	กระเป๋า	grà-bpǎo
pen	ปากกา	bpàak gaa
exercise book	สมุดจด	sà-mùt jòt
textbook	หนังสือเรียน	nǎng-sěu rian
compasses	วงเวียน	wong wian

| to make technical drawings | ร่างภาพทางเทคนิค | râang phâap thaang thék-nìk |
| technical drawing | ภาพร่างทางเทคนิค | phâap-râang thaang thék-nìk |

poem	กลอน	glorn
by heart (adv)	โดยทองจำ	doi thôrng jam
to learn by heart	ทองจำ	thôrng jam

school holidays	เวลาปิดเทอม	way-laa bpìt therm
to be on holiday	หยุดปิดเทอม	yùt bpìt therm
to spend holidays	ใช้เวลาหยุดปิดเทอม	chái way-laa yùt bpìt therm

test (at school)	การทดสอบ	gaan thót sòrp
essay (composition)	ความเรียง	khwaam riang
dictation	การเขียนตามคำบอก	gaan khĭan dtaam kam bòrk
exam (examination)	การสอบ	gaan sòrp
to do an exam	สอบไล่	sòrp lâi
experiment (e.g., chemistry ~)	การทดลอง	gaan thót lorng

143. College. University

academy	โรงเรียน	rohng rian
university	มหาวิทยาลัย	má-hǎa wít-thá-yaa-lai
faculty (e.g., ~ of Medicine)	คณะ	khá-ná

student (masc.)	นักศึกษา	nák sèuk-sǎa
student (fem.)	นักศึกษา	nák sèuk-sǎa
lecturer (teacher)	อาจารย์	aa-jaan

| lecture hall, room | ห้องบรรยาย | hôrng ban-yaai |
| graduate | บัณฑิต | ban-dìt |

| diploma | อนุปริญญา | a-nú bpà-rin-yaa |
| dissertation | ปริญญานิพนธ์ | bpà-rin-yaa ní-phon |

| study (report) | การวิจัย | gaan wí-jai |
| laboratory | ห้องปฏิบัติการ | hôrng bpà-dtì-bàt gaan |

lecture	การบรรยาย	gaan ban-yaai
coursemate	เพื่อนรวมชั้น	phêuan rûam chán
scholarship, bursary	ทุน	thun
academic degree	วุฒิการศึกษา	wút-thí gaan sèuk-sǎa

144. Sciences. Disciplines

mathematics	คณิตศาสตร์	khá-nít sàat
algebra	พีชคณิต	phee-chá-khá-nít
geometry	เรขาคณิต	ray-khǎa khá-nít
astronomy	ดาราศาสตร์	daa-raa sàat
biology	ชีววิทยา	chee-wá-wít-thá-yaa
geography	ภูมิศาสตร์	phoo-mí-sàat
geology	ธรณีวิทยา	thor-rá-nee wít-thá-yaa
history	ประวัติศาสตร์	bprà-wàt sàat
medicine	แพทยศาสตร์	phâet-tha-ya-sàat
pedagogy	ครุศาสตร์	khrú sàat
law	ธรรมศาสตร์	tham-ma -sàat
physics	ฟิสิกส์	fí-sìk
chemistry	เคมี	khay-mee
philosophy	ปรัชญา	bpràt-yaa
psychology	จิตวิทยา	jìt-wít-thá-yaa

145. Writing system. Orthography

grammar	ไวยากรณ์	wai-yaa-gon
vocabulary	คำศัพท์	kham sàp
phonetics	การออกเสียง	gaan òrk sǐang
noun	นาม	naam
adjective	คำคุณศัพท์	kham khun-ná-sàp
verb	กริยา	grì-yaa
adverb	คำวิเศษณ์	kham wí-sàyt
pronoun	คำสรรพนาม	kham sàp-phá-naam
interjection	คำอุทาน	kham u-thaan
preposition	คำบุพบท	kham bùp-phá-bòt
root	รากศัพท์	râak sàp
ending	คำลงท้าย	kham long tháai
prefix	คำนำหน้า	kham nam nâa
syllable	พยางค์	phá-yaang
suffix	คำเสริมท้าย	kham sěrm tháai
stress mark	เครื่องหมายเน้น	khrêuang mǎai náyn
apostrophe	อะพอสทรอฟี	à-phor-sòt-ror-fee
full stop	จุด	jùt
comma	จุลภาค	jun-lá-phâak
semicolon	อัฒภาค	àt-thá-phâak
colon	ทวิภาค	thá-wí phâak
ellipsis	การละไว้	gaan lá wái
question mark	เครื่องหมายปรัศนี	khrêuang mǎai bpràt-nee
exclamation mark	เครื่องหมายอัศเจรีย์	khrêuang mǎai àt-sà-jay-ree

inverted commas	อัญประกาศ	an-yá-bprà-gàat
in inverted commas	ในอัญประกาศ	nai an-yá-bprà-gàat
parenthesis	วงเล็บ	wong lép
in parenthesis	ในวงเล็บ	nai wong lép

hyphen	ยัติภังค์	yát-dtì-phang
dash	ขีดคั่น	khèet khân
space (between words)	ช่องไฟ	chôrng fai

| letter | ตัวอักษร | dtua àk-sǒn |
| capital letter | อักษรตัวใหญ่ | àk-sǒn dtua yài |

| vowel (n) | สระ | sà-ra |
| consonant (n) | พยัญชนะ | phá-yan-chá-ná |

sentence	ประโยค	bprà-yòhk
subject	ภาคประธาน	phâak bprà-thaan
predicate	ภาคแสดง	phâak sà-daeng

line	บรรทัด	ban-thát
on a new line	ที่บรรทัดใหม่	têe ban-thát mài
paragraph	วรรค	wák

word	คำ	kham
group of words	กลุ่มคำ	glùm kham
expression	วลี	wá-lee
synonym	คำพ้องความหมาย	kham phóng khwaam mǎai
antonym	คำตรงกันข้าม	kham dtrorng gan khâam

rule	กฎ	gòt
exception	ข้อยกเว้น	khôr yok-wâyn
correct (adj)	ถูก	thòok

conjugation	คอนจูเกชัน	khorn joo gay chan
declension	การกระจายคำ	gaan grà-jaai kham
nominal case	การก	gaa-rók
question	คำถาม	kham thǎam
to underline (vt)	ขีดเส้นใต้	khèet sên dtâi
dotted line	เส้นประ	sên bprà

146. Foreign languages

language	ภาษา	phaa-sǎa
foreign (adj)	ต่างชาติ	dtàang châat
foreign language	ภาษาต่างชาติ	phaa-sǎa dtàang châat
to study (vt)	เรียน	rian
to learn (language, etc.)	เรียน	rian

to read (vi, vt)	อ่าน	àan
to speak (vi, vt)	พูด	phôot
to understand (vt)	เข้าใจ	khâo jai
to write (vt)	เขียน	khǐan
fast (adv)	รวดเร็ว	rûat reo
slowly (adv)	อย่างช้า	yàang cháa

fluently (adv)	อย่างคล่อง	yàang khlôrng
rules	กฎ	gòt
grammar	ไวยากรณ์	wai-yaa-gon
vocabulary	คำศัพท์	kham sàp
phonetics	การออกเสียง	gaan òrk sǐang
textbook	หนังสือเรียน	nǎng-sěu rian
dictionary	พจนานุกรม	phót-jà-naa-nú-grom
teach-yourself book	หนังสือแบบเรียนด้วยตนเอง	nǎng-sěu bàep rian dûay dton ayng
phrasebook	เฟรสบุก	frayt bùk
cassette, tape	เทปคาสเซ็ตต์	thâyp khaas-sét
videotape	วิดีโอ	wí-dee-oh
CD, compact disc	CD	see-dee
DVD	DVD	dee-wee-dee
alphabet	ตัวอักษร	dtua àk-sǒn
to spell (vt)	สะกด	sà-gòt
pronunciation	การออกเสียง	gaan òrk sǐang
accent	สำเนียง	sǎm-niang
with an accent	มีสำเนียง	mee sǎm-niang
without an accent	ไม่มีสำเนียง	mâi mee sǎm-niang
word	คำ	kham
meaning	ความหมาย	khwaam mǎai
course (e.g. a French ~)	หลักสูตร	làk sòot
to sign up	สมัคร	sà-màk
teacher	อาจารย์	aa-jaan
translation (process)	การแปล	gaan bplae
translation (text, etc.)	คำแปล	kham bplae
translator	นักแปล	nák bplae
interpreter	ล่าม	lâam
polyglot	ผู้รู้หลายภาษา	phôo róo lǎai paa-sǎa
memory	ความทรงจำ	khwaam song jam

147. Fairy tale characters

Father Christmas	ซานตาคลอส	saan-dtaa-khlôrt
Cinderella	ซินเดอเรลลา	sín-day-rayn-lâa
mermaid	เงือก	ngêuak
Neptune	เนปจูน	nâyp-joon
magician, wizard	พ่อมด	phôr mót
fairy	แม่มด	mâe mót
magic (adj)	วิเศษ	wí-sàyt
magic wand	ไม้กายสิทธิ์	mái gaai-yá-sìt
fairy tale	เทพนิยาย	thâyp ní-yaai
miracle	ปาฏิหาริย์	bpaa dtì-hǎan

dwarf	คนแคระ	khon khráe
to turn into …	กลายเป็น…	glaai bpen…
ghost	ผี	phěe
phantom	ภูตผีปีศาจ	phôot phěe bpee-sàat
monster	สัตว์ประหลาด	sàt bprà-làat
dragon	มังกร	mang-gon
giant	ยักษ์	yák

148. Zodiac Signs

Aries	ราศีเมษ	raa-sěe mâyt
Taurus	ราศีพฤษภ	raa-sěe phréut-sòp
Gemini	ราศีมิถุน	raa-sěe me-thǔn
Cancer	ราศีกรกฎ	raa-sěe gor-rá-gòt
Leo	ราศีสิงห์	raa-sěe-sǐng
Virgo	ราศีกันย์	raa-sěe gan
Libra	ราศีตุล	raa-sěe dtun
Scorpio	ราศีพฤศจิก	raa-sěe phréut-sà-jìk
Sagittarius	ราศีธนู	raa-sěe than
Capricorn	ราศีมังกร	raa-sěe mang-gon
Aquarius	ราศีกุมภ์	raa-sěe gum
Pisces	ราศีมีน	raa-sěe meen
character	บุคลิก	bùk-khá-lík
character traits	ลักษณะบุคลิก	lák-sà-nà bùk-khá-lík
behaviour	พฤติกรรม	phréut-dtì-gam
to tell fortunes	ทำนายชะตา	tham naai chá-dtaa
fortune-teller	หมอดู	mǒr doo
horoscope	ดวงชะตา	duang chá-dtaa

Arts

theatre	โรงละคร	rohng lá-khon
opera	โอเปร่า	oh-bprào
operetta	ละครเพลง	lá-khon phlayng
ballet	บัลเลต์	ban lây
theatre poster	โปสเตอร์ละคร	bpòht-dtêr lá-khon
theatre company	คณะผู้แสดง	khá-ná phôo sà-daeng
tour	การออกแสดง	gaan òrk sà-daeng
to be on tour	ออกแสดง	òrk sà-daeng
to rehearse (vi, vt)	ซ้อม	sórm
rehearsal	การซ้อม	gaan sórm
repertoire	รายการละคร	raai gaan lá-khon
performance	การแสดง	gaan sà-daeng
theatrical show	การแสดง มหรสพ	gaan sà-daeng má-hŏr-rá-sòp
play	ละคร	lá-khon
ticket	ตั๋ว	dtŭa
booking office	ช่องจำหน่ายตั๋ว	chôrng jam-nàai dtŭa
lobby, foyer	ล็อบบี้	lórp-bêe
coat check (cloakroom)	ที่รับฝากเสื้อโค้ท	thêe ráp fàak sêua khóht
cloakroom ticket	ป้ายรับเสื้อ	bpâai ráp sêua
binoculars	กล้องสองสองตา	glôrng sòrng sŏrng dtaa
usher	พนักงานที่นำ ไปยังที่นั่ง	phá-nák ngaan thêe nam bpai yang thêe nâng
stalls (orchestra seats)	ที่นั่งชั้นล่าง	thêe nâng chán lâang
balcony	ที่นั่งชั้นสอง	thêe nâng chán sŏrng
dress circle	ที่นั่งชั้นบน	thêe nâng chán bon
box	ที่นั่งพิเศษ	thêe nâng phí-sàyt
row	แถว	thăe
seat	ที่นั่ง	thêe nâng
audience	ผู้ชม	phôo chom
spectator	ผู้เข้าชม	phôo khâo chom
to clap (vi, vt)	ปรบมือ	bpròp meu
applause	การปรบมือ	gaan bpròp meu
ovation	การปรบมือให้เกียรติ	gaan bpròp meu hâi gìat
stage	เวที	way-thee
curtain	ฉาก	chàak
scenery	ฉาก	chàak
backstage	หลังเวที	lăng way-thee
scene (e.g. the last ~)	ตอน	dtorn
act	องค์	ong
interval	ช่วงหยุดพัก	chûang yùt phák

150. Cinema

actor	นักแสดงชาย	nák sà-daeng chaai
actress	นักแสดงหญิง	nák sà-daeng yĭng
cinema (industry)	ภาพยนตร์	phâap-phá-yon
film	หนัง	năng
episode	ตอน	dtorn
detective film	หนังประโลมโลกสืบสวน	năng sèup sŭan
action film	หนังแอ็คชั่น	năng áek-chân
adventure film	หนังผจญภัย	năng phà-jon phai
science fiction film	หนังนิยายวิทยาศาสตร์	năng ní-yaai wít-thá-yaa sàat
horror film	หนังสยองขวัญ	năng sà-yŏrng khwăn
comedy film	หนังตลก	năng dtà-lòk
melodrama	หนังประโลมโลก	năng bprà-lohm lôhk
drama	หนังดรามา	năng dràa maa
fictional film	หนังเรื่องแต่ง	năng rêuang dtàeng
documentary	หนังสารคดี	năng săa-rá-khá-dee
cartoon	การตูน	gaa-dtoon
silent films	หนังเงียบ	năng ngîap
role (part)	บทบาท	bòt bàat
leading role	บทบาทนำ	bòt bàat nam
to play (vi, vt)	แสดง	sà-daeng
film star	ดาราภาพยนตร์	daa-raa phâap-phá-yon
well-known (adj)	เป็นที่รู้จักดี	bpen thêe róo jàk dee
famous (adj)	ชื่อดัง	chêu dang
popular (adj)	ที่นิยม	thêe ní-yom
script (screenplay)	บท	bòt
scriptwriter	คนเขียนบท	khon khĭan bòt
film director	ผู้กำกับ ภาพยนตร	phôo gam-gàp phâap-phá-yon
producer	ผู้อำนวยการสร้าง	phôo am-nuay gaan sâang
assistant	ผู้ช่วย	phôo chûay
cameraman	ช่างกลอง	châang glôrng
stuntman	นักแสดงแทน	nák sà-daeng thaen
double (body double)	นักแสดงแทน	nák sà-daeng thaen
to shoot a film	ถ่ายทำภาพยนตร์	thàai tham phâap-phá-yon
audition, screen test	การคัดนักแสดง	gaan khát nák sà-daeng
shooting	การถ่ายทำ	gaan thàai tham
film crew	กลุ่มคนถ่าย ภาพยนต	glùm khon thàai phâa-pha-yon
film set	สถานที่ ถ่ายทำภาพยนตร์	sà-thăan thêe thàai tham phâap-phá-yon
camera	กล้อง	glôrng
cinema	โรงภาพยนตร์	rohng phâap-phá-yon
screen (e.g. big ~)	หน้าจอ	nâa jor
to show a film	ฉายภาพยนตร์	chăai phâap-phá-yon

soundtrack	เสียงซาวด์แทร็ก	sĭang saao tráek
special effects	เอฟเฟ็กต์พิเศษ	àyf-fék phí-sàyt
subtitles	ซับ	sáp
credits	เครดิต	khray-dìt
translation	การแปล	gaan bplae

151. Painting

art	ศิลปะ	sĭn-lá-bpà
fine arts	วิจิตรศิลป์	wí-jìt sĭn
art gallery	หอศิลป์	hŏr sĭn
art exhibition	การจัดแสดงศิลปะ	gaan jàt sà-daeng sĭn-lá-bpà

painting (art)	จิตรกรรม	jìt-dtrà-gam
graphic art	เลขนศิลป์	lâyk-ná-sĭn
abstract art	ศิลปะนามธรรม	sĭn-lá-bpà naam-má-tham
impressionism	ลัทธิประทับใจ	lát-thí bprà-tháp jai

picture (painting)	ภาพ	phâap
drawing	ภาพวาด	phâap-wâat
poster	โปสเตอร์	bpòht-dtêr

illustration (picture)	ภาพประกอบ	phâap bprà-gòrp
miniature	รูปปั้นขนาดย่อ	rôop bpân khà-nàat yôr
copy (of painting, etc.)	สำเนา	săm-nao
reproduction	การทำซ้ำ	gaan tham sám

mosaic	โมเสก	moh-sàyk
stained glass window	หน้าต่างกระจกสี	nâa dtàang grà-jòk sĕe
fresco	ภาพผนัง	phâap phà-năng
engraving	การแกะลาย	gaan gàe laai

bust (sculpture)	รูปปั้นครึ่งตัว	rôop bpân khrêung dtua
sculpture	รูปปั้นแกะสลัก	rôop bpân gàe sà-làk
statue	รูปปั้น	rôop bpân
plaster of Paris	ปูนปลาสเตอร์	bpoon bpláat-dtêr
plaster (as adj)	ปูนปลาสเตอร์	bpoon bpláat-dtêr

portrait	ภาพเหมือน	phâap mĕuan
self-portrait	ภาพเหมือนของตนเอง	phâap mĕuan khŏrng dton ayng
landscape painting	ภาพภูมิทัศน์	phâap phoom-mi -thát
still life	ภาพหุ่นนิ่ง	phâap hùn nîng
caricature	ภาพล้อ	phâap-lór
sketch	ภาพสเก็ตช์	phâap sà-gèt

paint	สี	sĕe
watercolor paint	สีน้ำ	sĕe náam
oil (paint)	สีน้ำมัน	sĕe náam man
pencil	ดินสอ	din-sŏr
Indian ink	หมึกสีดำ	mèuk sĕe dam
charcoal	ถ่าน	thàan
to draw (vi, vt)	วาด	wâat
to paint (vi, vt)	ระบายสี	rá-baai sĕe

to pose (vi)	จัดท่า	jàt thâa
artist's model (masc.)	แบบภาพวาด	bàep phâap-wâat
artist's model (fem.)	แบบภาพวาด	bàep phâap-wâat

artist (painter)	ช่างวาดรูป	châang wâat rôop
work of art	งานศิลปะ	ngaan sĭn-lá-bpà
masterpiece	งานชิ้นเอก	ngaan chín àyk
studio (artist's workroom)	สตูดิโอ	sà-dtoo dì oh

canvas (cloth)	ผ้าใบ	phâa bai
easel	ขาตั้งกระดาน	khăa dtâng grà daan
	วาดรูป	wâat rôop
palette	จานสี	jaan sĕe

frame (picture ~, etc.)	กรอบ	gròrp
restoration	การฟื้นฟู	gaan féun foo
to restore (vt)	ฟื้นฟู	féun foo

152. Literature & Poetry

literature	วรรณคดี	wan-ná-khá-dee
author (writer)	ผู้แต่ง	phôo dtàeng
pseudonym	นามปากกา	naam bpàak gaa

book	หนังสือ	năng-sĕu
volume	เล่ม	lêm
table of contents	สารบัญ	săa-rá-ban
page	หน้า	nâa
main character	ตัวละครหลัก	dtua lá-khon làk
autograph	ลายเซ็น	laai sen

short story	เรื่องสั้น	rêuang sân
story (novella)	เรื่องราว	rêuang raao
novel	นิยาย	ní-yaai
work (writing)	งานเขียน	ngaan khĭan
fable	นิทาน	ní-thaan
detective novel	นิยายสืบสวน	ní-yaai sèup sŭan
poem (verse)	กลอน	glorn
poetry	บทกลอน	bòt glorn
poem (epic, ballad)	บทกวี	bòt gà-wee
poet	นักกวี	nák gà-wee

fiction	เรื่องแต่ง	rêuang dtàeng
science fiction	นิยายวิทยาศาสตร์	ní-yaai wít-thá-yaa sàat
adventures	นิยายผจญภัย	ní-yaai phà-jon phai
educational literature	วรรณกรรมการศึกษา	wan-ná-gam gaan sèuk-săa
children's literature	วรรณกรรมสำหรับเด็ก	wan-ná-gam săm-ràp dèk

153. Circus

| circus | ละครสัตว์ | lá-khon sàt |
| travelling circus | ละครสัตว์เร่ร่อน | lá-khon sàt lây rôrn |

| programme | รายการการแสดง | raai gaan gaan sà-daeng |
| performance | การแสดง | gaan sà-daeng |

| act (circus ~) | การแสดง | gaan sà-daeng |
| circus ring | เวทีละครสัตว์ | way-thee lá-kon sàt |

| pantomime (act) | ละครใบ้ | lá-khon bâi |
| clown | ตัวตลก | dtua dtà-lòk |

acrobat	นักกายกรรม	nák gaai-yá-gam
acrobatics	กายกรรม	gaai-yá-gam
gymnast	นักกายกรรม	nák gaai-yá-gam
acrobatic gymnastics	กายกรรม	gaai-yá-gam
somersault	การตีลังกา	gaan dtee lang-gaa

strongman	นักกีฬา	nák gee-laa
tamer (e.g., lion ~)	ผู้ฝึกสัตว์	phôo fèuk sàt
rider (circus horse ~)	นักขี่	nák khèe
assistant	ผู้ช่วย	phôo chûay

stunt	ผาดโผน	phàat phǒhn
magic trick	มายากล	maa-yaa gon
conjurer, magician	นักมายากล	nák maa-yaa gon

juggler	นักมายากล	nák maa-yaa gon
	โยนของ	yohn khǒrng
to juggle (vi, vt)	โยนของ	yohn khǒrng
animal trainer	ผู้ฝึกสัตว์	phôo fèuk sàt
animal training	การฝึกสัตว์	gaan fèuk sàt
to train (animals)	ฝึก	fèuk

154. Music. Pop music

music	ดนตรี	don-dtree
musician	นักดนตรี	nák don-dtree
musical instrument	เครื่องดนตรี	khrêuang don-dtree
to play ...	เล่น	lên

guitar	กีตาร์	gee-dtâa
violin	ไวโอลิน	wai-oh-lin
cello	เชลโล	chayn-lôh
double bass	ดับเบิลเบส	dàp-bern bàyt
harp	พิณ	phin

piano	เปียโน	bpia noh
grand piano	แกรนด์เปียโน	graen bpia-noh
organ	ออร์แกน	or-gaen

wind instruments	เครื่องเป่า	khrêuang bpào
oboe	โอโบ	oh-boh
saxophone	แซ็กโซโฟน	sáek-soh-fohn
clarinet	แคลริเน็ต	khlae-rí-nét
flute	ฟลูต	flút
trumpet	ทรัมเป็ต	thram-bpèt

| accordion | หีบเพลงชัก | hèep phlayng chák |
| drum | กลอง | glorng |

duo	คู่	khôo
trio	วงทริโอ	wong thrí-oh
quartet	กลุมที่มีสี่คน	glùm thêe mee sèe khon
choir	คณะประสานเสียง	khá-ná bprà-săan sĭang
orchestra	วงดุริยางค์	wong dù-rí-yaang

pop music	เพลงป๊อป	phlayng bpòp
rock music	เพลงร็อค	phlayng rók
rock group	วงร็อค	wong rórk
jazz	แจซ	jáet

| idol | ไอดอล | ai-dorn |
| admirer, fan | แฟน | faen |

concert	คอนเสิร์ต	khon-sèrt
symphony	ซิมโฟนี	sím-foh-nee
composition	การแต่งเพลง	gaan dtàeng phlayng
to compose (write)	แต่ง	dtàeng

singing (n)	การร้องเพลง	gaan róng playng
song	เพลง	phlayng
tune (melody)	เสียงเพลง	sĭang phlayng
rhythm	จังหวะ	jang wà
blues	บลูส์	bloo

sheet music	โน้ตเพลง	nóht phlayng
baton	ไม้สั้นของ	máai sân khŏrng
	วาทยากร	wâa-tha-yaa gon
bow	คันชอ	khan sor
string	สาย	săai
case (e.g. guitar ~)	กลอง	glòrng

Rest. Entertainment. Travel

155. Trip. Travel

tourism, travel	การท่องเที่ยว	gaan thôrng thîeow
tourist	นักท่องเที่ยว	nák thôrng thîeow
trip, voyage	การเดินทาง	gaan dern thaang
adventure	การผจญภัย	gaan phà-jon phai
trip, journey	การเดินทาง	gaan dern thaang
holiday	วันหยุดพักผ่อน	wan yùt phák phòrn
to be on holiday	หยุดพักผ่อน	yùt phák phòrn
rest	การพัก	gaan phák
train	รถไฟ	rót fai
by train	โดยรถไฟ	doi rót fai
aeroplane	เครื่องบิน	khrêuang bin
by aeroplane	โดยเครื่องบิน	doi khrêuang bin
by car	โดยรถยนต์	doi rót-yon
by ship	โดยเรือ	doi reua
luggage	สัมภาระ	săm-phaa-rá
suitcase	กระเป๋าเดินทาง	grà-bpăo dern-thaang
luggage trolley	รถขนสัมภาระ	rót khŏn săm-phaa-rá
passport	หนังสือเดินทาง	năng-sĕu dern-thaang
visa	วีซ่า	wee-sâa
ticket	ตั๋ว	dtŭa
air ticket	ตั๋วเครื่องบิน	dtŭa khrêuang bin
guidebook	หนังสือแนะนำ	năng-sĕu náe nam
map (tourist ~)	แผนที่	phăen thêe
area (rural ~)	เขต	khàyt
place, site	สถานที่	sà-thăan thêe
exotica (n)	สิ่งแปลกใหม่	sìng bplàek mài
exotic (adj)	ต่างแดน	dtàang daen
amazing (adj)	น่าประหลาดใจ	nâa bprà-làat jai
group	กลุ่ม	glùm
excursion, sightseeing tour	การเดินทาง ท่องเที่ยว	gaan dern taang thôrng thîeow
guide (person)	มัคคุเทศก์	mák-khú-thâyt

156. Hotel

hotel	โรงแรม	rohng raem
motel	โรงแรม	rohng raem

three-star (~ hotel)	สามดาว	sǎam daao
five-star	หาดาว	hâa daao
to stay (in a hotel, etc.)	พัก	phák

room	ห้อง	hôrng
single room	ห้องเดี่ยว	hôrng dìeow
double room	หองคู	hôrng khôo
to book a room	จองห้อง	jorng hôrng

| half board | พักครึ่งวัน | phák khrêung wan |
| full board | พักเต็มวัน | phák dtem wan |

with bath	มีห้องอาบน้ำ	mee hôrng àap náam
with shower	มีฝักบัว	mee fàk bua
satellite television	โทรทัศน์ดาวเทียม	thoh-rá-thát daao thiam
air-conditioner	เครื่องปรับอากาศ	khrêuang bpràp-aa-gàat
towel	ผาเช็ดตัว	phâa chét dtua
key	กุญแจ	gun-jae

administrator	นักบุริหาร	nák bor-rí-hǎan
chambermaid	แมบาน	mâe bâan
porter	พนักงาน, ขนกระเป๋า	phá-nák ngaan khǒn grà-bpǎo
doorman	พนักงาน เปิดประตู	phá-nák ngaan bpèrt bprà-dtoo

restaurant	ร้านอาหาร	ráan aa-hǎan
pub, bar	บาร์	baa
breakfast	อาหารเช้า	aa-hǎan cháo
dinner	อาหารเย็น	aa-hǎan yen
buffet	บุฟเฟต์	bùf-fây

| lobby | ล็อบบี้ | lórp-bêe |
| lift | ลิฟต์ | líf |

| DO NOT DISTURB | ห้ามรบกวน | hâam róp guan |
| NO SMOKING | หามสูบบุหรี่ | hâam sòop bù rèe |

157. Books. Reading

book	หนังสือ	nǎng-sěu
author	ผู้แตง	phôo dtàeng
writer	นักเขียน	nák khǐan
to write (~ a book)	เขียน	khǐan

reader	ผู้อาน	phôo àan
to read (vi, vt)	อาน	àan
reading (activity)	การอาน	gaan àan

| silently (to oneself) | อย่างเงียบๆ | yàang ngîap ngîap |
| aloud (adv) | ออกเสียงดัง | òrk sǐang dang |

| to publish (vt) | ตีพิมพ์ | dtee phim |
| publishing (process) | การตีพิมพ์ | gaan dtee phim |

publisher	ผู้พิมพ์	phôo phim
publishing house	สำนักพิมพ์	săm-nák phim
to come out (be released)	ออก	òrk
release (of a book)	การออก	gaan òrk
print run	จำนวน	jam-nuan
bookshop	ร้านหนังสือ	ráan năng-sĕu
library	หองสมุด	hôrng sà-mùt
story (novella)	เรื่องราว	rêuang raao
short story	เรื่องสั้น	rêuang sân
novel	นิยาย	ní-yaai
detective novel	นิยายสืบสวน	ní-yaai sèup sŭan
memoirs	บันทึกความทรงจำ	ban-théuk khwaam song jam
legend	ตำนาน	dtam naan
myth	นิทานปรัมปรา	ní-thaan bpram bpraa
poetry, poems	บทกวี	bòt gà-wee
autobiography	อัตชีวประวัติ	àt-chee-wá-bprà-wàt
selected works	งานที่ผาน	ngaan thêe phàan
	การคัดเลือก	gaan khát lêuak
science fiction	นิยายวิทยาศาสตร์	ní-yaai wít-thá-yaa sàat
title	ชื่อเรื่อง	chêu rêuang
introduction	บทนำ	bòt nam
title page	หนาแรก	nâa râek
chapter	บท	bòt
extract	ขอความที่	khôr khwaam thêe
	คัดออกมา	khát òk maa
episode	ตอน	dtorn
plot (storyline)	เค้าเรื่อง	kháo rêuang
contents	เนื้อหา	néua hăa
table of contents	สารบัญ	săa-rá-ban
main character	ตัวละครหลัก	dtua lá-khon làk
volume	เล่ม	lêm
cover	ปก	bpòk
binding	สัน	săn
bookmark	ที่คั่นหนังสือ	thêe khân năng-sĕu
page	หน้า	nâa
to page through	เปิดผานๆ	bpèrt phàan phàan
margins	ระยะขอบ	rá-yá khòrp
annotation	ความเห็นประกอบ	khwaam hĕn bprà-gòp
(marginal note, etc.)		
footnote	เชิงอรรถ	cherng àt-tha
text	บท	bòt
type, fount	ตัวพิมพ์	dtua phim
misprint, typo	ความพิมพ์ผิด	khwaam phim phìt
translation	คำแปล	kham bplae
to translate (vt)	แปล	bplae

original (n)	ต้นฉบับ	dtôn chà-bàp
famous (adj)	โด่งดัง	dòhng dang
unknown (not famous)	ไม่เป็นที่รู้จัก	mâi bpen thêe róo jàk
interesting (adj)	น่าสนใจ	nâa sŏn jai
bestseller	ขายดี	khǎai dee

dictionary	พจนานุกรม	phót-jà-naa-nú-grom
textbook	หนังสือเรียน	nǎng-sěu rian
encyclopedia	สารานุกรม	sǎa-raa-nú-grom

158. Hunting. Fishing

hunting	การล่าสัตว์	gaan lâa sàt
to hunt (vi, vt)	ล่าสัตว์	lâa sàt
hunter	นักล่าสัตว์	nák lâa sàt

to shoot (vi)	ยิง	ying
rifle	ปืนไรเฟิล	bpeun rai-fern
bullet (shell)	กระสุนปืน	grà-sǔn bpeun
shot (lead balls)	กระสุน	grà-sǔn

steel trap	กับดักเหล็ก	gàp dàk lèk
snare (for birds, etc.)	กับดัก	gàp dàk
to fall into the steel trap	ติดกับดัก	dtìt gàp dàk
to lay a steel trap	วางกับดัก	waang gàp dàk

poacher	ผู้ลักลอบล่าสัตว์	phôo lák lôrp lâa sàt
game (in hunting)	สัตว์ที่ถูกล่า	sàt tée thòok lâa
hound dog	หมาล่าเนื้อ	mǎa lâa néua
safari	ซาฟารี	saa-faa-ree
mounted animal	สัตว์สตาฟ	sàt sà-dtàaf

fisherman	คนประมง	khon bprà-mong
fishing (angling)	การจับปลา	gaan jàp bplaa
to fish (vi)	จับปลา	jàp bplaa

fishing rod	คันเบ็ด	khan bèt
fishing line	สายเบ็ด	sǎai bèt
hook	ตะขอ	dtà-khǒr
float	ทุ่น	thûn
bait	เหยื่อ	yèua

to cast a line	เหวี่ยงเบ็ด	wìang bèt
to bite (ab. fish)	งับเหยื่อ	ngáp yèua
catch (of fish)	ปลาจับ	bpla jàp
ice-hole	ช่องน้ำแข็ง	chôrng nám khǎeng

fishing net	แหจับปลา	hǎe jàp bplaa
boat	เรือ	reua
to net (to fish with a net)	จับปลาด้วยแห	jàp bplaa dûay hǎe
to cast[throw] the net	เหวี่ยงแห	wìang hǎe
to haul the net in	ลากอวน	lâak uan
to fall into the net	ติดแห	dtìt hǎe
whaler (person)	นักล่าปลาวาฬ	nák lâa bplaa waan

| whaleboat | เรือล่าปลาวาฬ | reua lâa bplaa waan |
| harpoon | ฉมวก | chà-mùak |

159. Games. Billiards

billiards	บิลเลียด	bin-lîat
billiard room, hall	ห้องบิลเลียด	hôrng bin-lîat
ball (snooker, etc.)	ลูก	lôok

to pocket a ball	แทงลูกลงหลุม	thaeng lôok long lŭm
cue	ไม้คิว	máai khiw
pocket	หลุม	lŭm

160. Games. Playing cards

diamonds	ข้าวหลามตัด	khâao lăam dtàt
spades	โพดำ	phoh dam
hearts	โพแดง	phoh daeng
clubs	ดอกจิก	dòrk jìk

ace	เอส	àyt
king	คิง	king
queen	แหมม	màem
jack, knave	แจค	jáek

playing card	ไพ่	phâi
cards	ไพ	phâi
trump	ไต	dtăi
pack of cards	สำรับไพ่	săm-ráp phâi

point	แต้ม	dtâem
to deal (vi, vt)	แจกไพ่	jàek phâi
to shuffle (cards)	สับไพ	sàp phâi
lead, turn (n)	ที	thee
cardsharp	คนโกงไพ่	khon gohng phâi

161. Casino. Roulette

casino	คาสิโน	khaa-sì-noh
roulette (game)	รูเล็ตต์	roo-lèt
bet	เดิมพัน	derm phan
to place bets	วางเดิมพัน	waang derm phan

red	แดง	daeng
black	ดำ	dam
to bet on red	เดิมพันสีแดง	derm phan sĕe daeng
to bet on black	เดิมพันสีดำ	derm phan sĕe dam

| croupier (dealer) | เจ้ามือ | jâo meu |
| to spin the wheel | หมุนกงล้อ | mŭn gong lór |

| rules (~ of the game) | กติกา | gà-dtì-gaa |
| chip | ชิป | chíp |

| to win (vi, vt) | ชนะ | chá-ná |
| win (winnings) | รางวัล | raang-wan |

| to lose (~ 100 dollars) | เสีย | sĭa |
| loss (losses) | เงินเสียพนัน | ngern sĭa phá-nan |

player	ผู้เล่น	phôo lên
blackjack (card game)	แบล็คแจ๊ค	blàek-jáek
craps (dice game)	เกมลูกเต๋า	gaym lôok dtăo
dice (a pair of ~)	เต๋า	dtăo
fruit machine	ตู้สล็อต	dtôo sà-lòrt

162. Rest. Games. Miscellaneous

to stroll (vi, vt)	เดินเล่น	dern lên
stroll (leisurely walk)	การเดินเล่น	gaan dern lên
car ride	การนั่งรถ	gaan nâng rót
adventure	การผจญภัย	gaan phà-jon phai
picnic	ปิคนิค	bpìk-ník

game (chess, etc.)	เกม	gaym
player	ผู้เล่น	phôo lên
game (one ~ of chess)	เกม	gaym

collector (e.g. philatelist)	นักสะสม	nák sà-sŏm
to collect (stamps, etc.)	สะสม	sà-sŏm
collection	การสะสม	gaan sà-sŏm
crossword puzzle	ปริศนาอักษรไขว้	bprìt-sà-năa àk-sŏn khwâi
racecourse (hippodrome)	ลู่แข่ง	lôo khàeng
disco (discotheque)	ดิสโก้	dít-gôh

sauna	ซาวน่า	saao-nâa
lottery	สลากกินแบ่ง	sà-làak gin bàeng
camping trip	การเดินทาง ตั้งแคมป์	gaan dern thaang dtâng-khaem

camp	แคมป์	khaem
tent (for camping)	เต็นท์	dtáyn
compass	เข็มทิศ	khĕm thít
camper	ผู้เดินทาง ตั้งแคมป์	phôo dern thaang dtâng-khaem

to watch (film, etc.)	ดู	doo
viewer	ผู้ชมทีวี	phôo chom thee wee
TV show (TV program)	รายการทีวี	raai gaan thee wee

163. Photography

| camera (photo) | กล้อง | glôrng |
| photo, picture | ภาพถ่าย | phâap thàai |

photographer	ช่างถ่ายภาพ	châang thàai phâap
photo studio	ห้องถ่ายภาพ	hôrng thàai phâap
photo album	อัลบั้มภาพถ่าย	an-bâm phâap-thàai
camera lens	เลนส์กล้อง	len glôrng
telephoto lens	เลนส์ถ่ายไกล	len thàai glai
filter	ฟิลเตอร์	fin-dtêr
lens	เลนส์	len
optics (high-quality ~)	ออปติก	orp-dtìk
diaphragm (aperture)	รูรับแสง	roo ráp săeng
exposure time (shutter speed)	เวลาในการถ่ายภาพ	way-laa nai gaan thàai phâap
viewfinder	เครื่องจับภาพ	khrêuang jàp phâap
digital camera	กล้องดิจิตอล	glôrng dì-jì-dton
tripod	ขาตั้งกล้อง	khăa dtâng glông
flash	แฟลช	flâet
to photograph (vt)	ถ่ายภาพ	thàai phâap
to take pictures	ถ่ายภาพ	thàai phâap
to have one's picture taken	ได้รับการถ่ายภาพให้	dâai ráp gaan thàai phâap hâi
focus	โฟกัส	foh-gát
to focus	โฟกัส	foh-gát
sharp, in focus (adj)	คมชัด	khom chát
sharpness	ความคมชัด	khwaam khom chát
contrast	ความเปรียบต่าง	khwaam bprìap dtàang
contrast (as adj)	เปรียบต่าง	bprìap dtàang
picture (photo)	ภาพ	phâap
negative (n)	ภาพเนกาทีฟ	phâap nay gaa thêef
film (a roll of ~)	ฟิล์ม	fim
frame (still)	เฟรม	fraym
to print (photos)	พิมพ์	phim

164. Beach. Swimming

beach	ชายหาด	chaai hàat
sand	ทราย	saai
deserted (beach)	ร้าง	ráang
suntan	ผิวคล้ำแดด	phĭw khlám dàet
to get a tan	ตากแดด	dtàak dàet
tanned (adj)	มีผิวคล้ำแดด	mee phĭw khlám dàet
sunscreen	ครีมกันแดด	khreem gan dàet
bikini	บิกินี่	bì-gì-nee
swimsuit, bikini	ชุดว่ายน้ำ	chút wâai náam
swim trunks	กางเกงว่ายน้ำ	gaang-gayng wâai náam
swimming pool	สระว่ายน้ำ	sà wâai náam
to swim (vi)	ว่ายน้ำ	wâai náam

shower	ฝักบัว	fàk bua
to change (one's clothes)	เปลี่ยนชุด	bplìan chút
towel	ผ้าเช็ดตัว	phâa chét dtua
boat	เรือ	reua
motorboat	เรือยนต์	reua yon
water ski	สกีน้ำ	sà-gee nám
pedalo	เรือถีบ	reua thèep
surfing	การโต้คลื่น	gaan dtôh khlêun
surfer	นักโต้คลื่น	nák dtôh khlêun
scuba set	อุปกรณ์ดำน้ำ	u-bpà-gon dam náam
flippers (swim fins)	ตีนกบ	dteen gòp
mask (diving ~)	หน้ากากดำน้ำ	nâa gàak dam náam
diver	นักประดาน้ำ	nák bprà-daa náam
to dive (vi)	ดำน้ำ	dam náam
underwater (adv)	ใต้น้ำ	dtâi nám
beach umbrella	ร่มชายหาด	rôm chaai hàat
beach chair (sun lounger)	เตียงอาบแดด	dtiang àap dàet
sunglasses	แว่นกันแดด	wâen gan dàet
air mattress	ที่นอนเป่าลม	thêe non bpào lom
to play (amuse oneself)	เล่น	lên
to go for a swim	ไปว่ายน้ำ	bpai wâai náam
beach ball	บอล	bon
to inflate (vt)	เติมลม	dterm lom
inflatable, air (adj)	แบบเติมลม	bàep dterm lom
wave	คลื่น	khlêun
buoy (line of ~s)	ทุ่นลอย	thûn loi
to drown (ab. person)	จมน้ำ	jom náam
to save, to rescue	ช่วยชีวิต	chûay chee-wít
life jacket	เสื้อชูชีพ	sêua choo chêep
to observe, to watch	สังเกตการณ์	sǎng-gàyt gaan
lifeguard	ไลฟ์การ์ด	lai-gàat

TECHNICAL EQUIPMENT. TRANSPORT

Technical equipment

165. Computer

computer	คอมพิวเตอร์	khorm-phiw-dtêr
notebook, laptop	โนตบุค	nóht búk
to turn on	เปิด	bpèrt
to turn off	ปิด	bpìt
keyboard	แป้นพิมพ์	bpâen phim
key	ปุ่ม	bpùm
mouse	เมาส์	mao
mouse mat	แผนรองเมาส์	phàen rorng mao
button	ปุ่ม	bpùm
cursor	เคอร์เซอร์	khêr-sêr
monitor	จอมอนิเตอร์	jor mor-ní-dtêr
screen	หนาจอ	nâa jor
hard disk	ฮาร์ดดิสก์	hâat-dìt
hard disk capacity	ความจุฮาร์ดดิสก์	kwaam jù hâat-dìt
memory	หน่วยความจำ	nùay khwaam jam
random access memory	หน่วยความจำ เขาถึงโดยสุม	nùay khwaam jam khâo thĕung doi sùm
file	ไฟล์	fai
folder	โฟลเดอร์	fohl-dêr
to open (vt)	เปิด	bpèrt
to close (vt)	ปิด	bpìt
to save (vt)	บันทึก	ban-théuk
to delete (vt)	ลบ	lóp
to copy (vt)	คัดลอก	khát lôrk
to sort (vt)	จัดเรียง	jàt riang
to transfer (copy)	ทำสำเนา	tham sǎm-nao
programme	โปรแกรม	bproh-graem
software	ซอฟตแวร์	sôf-wae
programmer	นักเขียนโปรแกรม	nák khĭan bproh-graem
to program (vt)	เขียนโปรแกรม	khĭan bproh-graem
hacker	แฮ็กเกอร์	háek-gêr
password	รหัสผาน	rá-hàt phàan
virus	ไวรัส	wai-rát
to find, to detect	ตรวจพบ	dtrùat phóp

| byte | ไบท์ | bai |
| megabyte | เมกะไบท์ | may-gà-bai |

| data | ข้อมูล | khôr moon |
| database | ฐานข้อมูล | thăan khôr moon |

cable (USB, etc.)	สายเคเบิล	săai khay-bêrn
to disconnect (vt)	ตัดการเชื่อมต่อ	dtàt gaan chêuam dtòr
to connect (sth to sth)	เชื่อมต่อ	chêuam dtòr

166. Internet. E-mail

Internet	อินเทอร์เน็ต	in-thêr-nét
browser	เบราว์เซอร์	brao-sêr
search engine	โปรแกรมค้นหา	bproh-graem khón hăa
provider	ผู้ให้บริการ	phôo hâi bor-rí-gaan

webmaster	เว็บมาสเตอร์	wép-mâat-dtêr
website	เว็บไซต์	wép sai
web page	เว็บเพจ	wép phâyt

| address (e-mail ~) | ที่อยู่ | thêe yòo |
| address book | สมุดที่อยู่ | sà-mùt thêe yòo |

postbox	กล่องจดหมายอีเมลล์	glòrng jòt măai ee-mayn
post	จดหมาย	jòt măai
full (adj)	เต็ม	dtem

message	ข้อความ	khôr khwaam
incoming messages	ข้อความขาเข้า	khôr khwaam khăa khâo
outgoing messages	ข้อความขาออก	khôr khwaam khăa òrk

sender	ผู้ส่ง	phôo sòng
to send (vt)	ส่ง	sòng
sending (of mail)	การส่ง	gaan sòng

| receiver | ผู้รับ | phôo ráp |
| to receive (vt) | รับ | ráp |

| correspondence | การติดต่อกันทางจดหมาย | gaan dtìt dtòr gan thaang jòt măai |
| to correspond (vi) | ติดต่อกันทางจดหมาย | dtìt dtòr gan thaang jòt măai |

file	ไฟล์	fai
to download (vt)	ดาวน์โหลด	daao lòht
to create (vt)	สร้าง	sâang
to delete (vt)	ลบ	lóp
deleted (adj)	ถูกลบ	thòok lóp

connection (ADSL, etc.)	การเชื่อมต่อ	gaan chêuam dtòr
speed	ความเร็ว	khwaam reo
modem	โมเด็ม	moh-dem
access	การเข้าถึง	gaan khâo thĕung
port (e.g. input ~)	พอร์ท	phôt

connection (make a ~)	การเชื่อมต่อ	gaan chêuam dtòr
to connect to … (vi)	เชื่อมตอกับ...	chêuam dtòr gàp...
to select (vt)	เลือก	lêuak
to search (for …)	คนหา	khón hǎa

167. Electricity

electricity	ไฟฟ้า	fai fáa
electric, electrical (adj)	ทางไฟฟ้า	thaang fai-fáa
electric power station	โรงไฟฟ้า	rohng fai-fáa
energy	พลังงาน	phá-lang ngaan
electric power	กำลังไฟฟ้า	gam-lang fai-fáa
light bulb	หลอดไฟฟ้า	lòrt fai fáa
torch	ไฟฉาย	fai chǎai
street light	เสาไฟถนน	sǎo fai thà-nǒn
light	ไฟ	fai
to turn on	เปิด	bpèrt
to turn off	ปิด	bpìt
to turn off the light	ปิดไฟ	bpìt fai
to burn out (vi)	ขาด	khàat
short circuit	การลัดวงจร	gaan lát wong-jon
broken wire	สายขาด	sǎai khàat
contact (electrical ~)	สายตอกัน	sǎai dtòr gan
light switch	สวิตช์ไฟ	sà-wít fai
socket outlet	เต๋าเสียบปลั๊กไฟ	dtǎo sìap bplák fai
plug	ปลั๊กไฟ	bplák fai
extension lead	สายพวงไฟ	sǎai phûang fai
fuse	ฟิวส์	fiw
cable, wire	สายไฟ	sǎai fai
wiring	การเดินสายไฟ	gaan dern sǎai fai
ampere	แอมแปร์	aem-bpae
amperage	กำลังไฟฟ้า	gam-lang fai-fáa
volt	โวลต์	wohn
voltage	แรงดันไฟฟ้า	raeng dan fai fáa
electrical device	เครื่องใช้ไฟฟ้า	khrêuang chái fai fáa
indicator	ตัวระบุ	dtua rá-bù
electrician	ช่างไฟฟ้า	châang fai-fáa
to solder (vt)	บัดกรี	bàt-gree
soldering iron	หัวแรงบัดกุรี	hǔa raeng bàt-gree
electric current	กระแสไฟฟ้า	grà-sǎe fai fáa

168. Tools

| tool, instrument | เครื่องมือ | khrêuang meu |
| tools | เครื่องมือ | khrêuang meu |

equipment (factory ~)	อุปกรณ์	ù-bpà-gon
hammer	ค้อน	khórn
screwdriver	ไขควง	khăi khuang
axe	ขวาน	khwăan
saw	เลื่อย	lêuay
to saw (vt)	เลื่อย	lêuay
plane (tool)	กบไสไม้	gòp săi máai
to plane (vt)	ไสกบ	săi gòp
soldering iron	หัวแรงบัดกรี	hŭa ráeng bàt-gree
to solder (vt)	บัดกรี	bàt-gree
file (tool)	ตะไบ	dtà-bai
carpenter pincers	คีม	kheem
combination pliers	คีมปอกสายไฟ	kheem bpòk săai fai
chisel	สิ่ว	sìw
drill bit	หัวสว่าน	hŭa sà-wàan
electric drill	สว่านไฟฟ้า	sà-wàan fai fáa
to drill (vi, vt)	เจาะ	jòr
knife	มีด	mêet
pocket knife	มีดพก	mêet phók
blade	ใบ	bai
sharp (blade, etc.)	คม	khom
dull, blunt (adj)	ทื่อ	thêu
to get blunt (dull)	ทำให้...ทื่อ	tham hâi...thêu
to sharpen (vt)	ลับคม	láp khom
bolt	สลักเกลียว	sà-làk glieow
nut	แหวนสกรู	wăen sà-groo
thread (of a screw)	เกลียว	glieow
wood screw	สกรู	sà-groo
nail	ตะปู	dtà-bpoo
nailhead	หัวตะปู	hŭa dtà-bpoo
ruler (for measuring)	ไม้บรรทัด	máai ban-thát
tape measure	เทปวัดระยะทาง	thâyp wát rá-yá taang
spirit level	เครื่องวัดระดับน้ำ	khrêuang wát rá-dàp náam
magnifying glass	แวนขยาย	wăen khà-yăai
measuring instrument	เครื่องมือวัด	khrêuang meu wát
to measure (vt)	วัด	wát
scale (temperature ~, etc.)	อัตรา	àt-dtraa
readings	คามิเตอร์	khâa mí-dtêr
compressor	เครื่องอัดอากาศ	khrêuang àt aa-gàat
microscope	กลองจุลทัศน์	glôrng jun-la -thát
pump (e.g. water ~)	ปั๊ม	bpám
robot	หุ่นยนต์	hùn yon
laser	เลเซอร์	lay-sêr
spanner	ประแจ	bprà-jae
adhesive tape	เทปกาว	thâyp gaao

glue	กาว	gaao
sandpaper	กระดาษทราย	grà-dàat saai
spring	สปริง	sà-bpring
magnet	แมเหล็ก	mâe lèk
gloves	ถุงมือ	thǔng meu

rope	เชือก	chêuak
cord	สาย	sǎai
wire (e.g. telephone ~)	สายไฟ	sǎai fai
cable	สายเคเบิล	sǎai khay-bêrn

sledgehammer	ค้อนขนาดใหญ่	khón khà-nàat yài
prybar	ชะแลง	chá-laeng
ladder	บันได	ban-dai
stepladder	กระได	grà-dai

to screw (tighten)	ขันเกลียวเข้า	khǎn glieow khâo
to unscrew (lid, filter, etc.)	ขันเกลียวออก	khǎn glieow òk
to tighten (e.g. with a clamp)	ขันให้แน่น	khǎn hâi náen
to glue, to stick	ติดกาว	dtìt gaao
to cut (vt)	ตัด	dtàt

malfunction (fault)	ความผิดพลาด	khwaam phìt phlâat
repair (mending)	การซ่อมแซม	gaan sôrm saem
to repair, to fix (vt)	ซ่อม	sôrm
to adjust (machine, etc.)	ปรับ	bpràp

to check (to examine)	ตรวจ	dtrùat
checking	การตรวจ	gaan dtrùat
readings	คามิเตอร์	khâa mí-dtêr

| reliable, solid (machine) | ไว้วงใจได้ | wái waang jai dâai |
| complex (adj) | ซับซ้อน | sáp són |

to rust (get rusted)	ขึ้นสนิม	khêun sà-nǐm
rusty (adj)	เป็นสนิม	bpen sà-nǐm
rust	สนิม	sà-nǐm

Transport

aeroplane	เครื่องบิน	khrêuang bin
air ticket	ตั๋วเครื่องบิน	dtǔa khrêuang bin
airline	สายการบิน	sǎai gaan bin
airport	สนามบิน	sà-nǎam bin
supersonic (adj)	ความเร็วเหนือเสียง	khwaam reo něua-sǐang

captain	กัปตัน	gàp dtan
crew	ลูกเรือ	lôok reua
pilot	นักบิน	nák bin
stewardess	พนักงวนต้อนรับ บนเครื่องบิน	phá-nák ngaan dtôrn ráp bon khrêuang bin
navigator	ต้นหน	dtôn hǒn

wings	ปีก	bpèek
tail	หาง	hǎang
cockpit	ห้องนักบิน	hôrng nák bin
engine	เครื่องยนต์	khrêuang yon
undercarriage (landing gear)	โครงส่วนล่าง ของเครื่องบิน	khrorng sùan lâang khǒrng khrêuang bin
turbine	กังหัน	gang-hǎn

propeller	ใบพัด	bai phát
black box	กล่องดำ	glòrng dam
yoke (control column)	คันบังคับ	khan bang-kháp
fuel	เชื้อเพลิง	chéua phlerng

safety card	คู่มือความปลอดภัย	khôo meu khwaam bplòt phai
oxygen mask	หน้ากากอ็อกซิเจน	nâa gàak ók sí jayn
uniform	เครื่องแบบ	khrêuang bàep
lifejacket	เสื้อชูชีพ	sêua choo chêep
parachute	รมชูชีพ	rôm choo chêep

takeoff	การบินขึ้น	gaan bin khêun
to take off (vi)	บินขึ้น	bin khêun
runway	ทางวิ่งเครื่องบิน	thaang wîng khrêuang bin

visibility	ทัศนวิสัย	thát sá ná wí-sǎi
flight (act of flying)	การบิน	gaan bin
altitude	ความสูง	khwaam sǒong
air pocket	หลุมอากาศ	lǔm aa-gàat

seat	ที่นั่ง	thêe nâng
headphones	หูฟัง	hǒo fang
folding tray (tray table)	ถาดพับเก็บได้	thàat pháp gèp dâai
airplane window	หน้าตางเครื่องบิน	nâa dtàang khrêuang bin
aisle	ทางเดิน	thaang dern

170. Train

train	รถไฟ	rót fai
commuter train	รถไฟชานเมือง	rót fai chaan meuang
express train	รถไฟด่วน	rót fai dùan
diesel locomotive	รถจักรดีเซล	rót jàk dee-sayn
steam locomotive	รถจักรไอน้ำ	rót jàk ai náam
coach, carriage	ตู้โดยสาร	dtôo doi săan
buffet car	ตูเสบียง	dtôo sà-biang
rails	รางรถไฟ	raang rót fai
railway	ทางรถไฟ	thaang rót fai
sleeper (track support)	หมอนรองราง	mŏrn rorng raang
platform (railway ~)	ชานชลา	chaan-chá-laa
platform (~ 1, 2, etc.)	ราง	raang
semaphore	ไฟสัญญาณรถไฟ	fai săn-yaan rót fai
station	สถานี	sà-thăa-nee
train driver	คนขับรถไฟ	khon khàp rót fai
porter (of luggage)	พนักงานยกกระเป๋า	phá-nák ngaan yók grà-bpăo
carriage attendant	พนักงานรถไฟ	phá-nák ngaan rót fai
passenger	ผู้โดยสาร	phôo doi săan
ticket inspector	พนักงานตรวจตั๋ว	phá-nák ngaan dtrùat dtŭa
corridor (in train)	ทางเดิน	thaang dern
emergency brake	เบรคฉุกเฉิน	bràyk chùk-chĕrn
compartment	ตู้นอน	dtôo norn
berth	เตียง	dtiang
upper berth	เตียงบน	dtiang bon
lower berth	เตียงล่าง	dtiang lâang
bed linen, bedding	ชุดเครื่องนอน	chút khrêuang norn
ticket	ตั๋ว	dtŭa
timetable	ตารางเวลา	dtaa-raang way-laa
information display	กระดานแสดงข้อมูล	grà daan sà-daeng khôr moon
to leave, to depart	ออกเดินทาง	òrk dern thaang
departure (of a train)	การออกเดินทาง	gaan òrk dern thaang
to arrive (ab. train)	มาถึง	maa thĕung
arrival	การมาถึง	gaan maa thĕung
to arrive by train	มาถึงโดยรถไฟ	maa thĕung doi rót fai
to get on the train	ขึ้นรถไฟ	khêun rót fai
to get off the train	ลงจากรถไฟ	long jàak rót fai
train crash	รถไฟตกราง	rót fai dtòk raang
to derail (vi)	ตกราง	dtòk raang
steam locomotive	หัวรถจักรไอน้ำ	hŭa rót jàk ai náam
stoker, fireman	คนควบคุมเตาไฟ	khon khûap khum dtao fai
firebox	เตาไฟ	dtao fai
coal	ถ่านหิน	thàan hĭn

171. Ship

ship	เรือ	reua
vessel	เรือ	reua
steamship	เรือจักรไอน้ำ	reua jàk ai náam
riverboat	เรือลองแมน้ำ	reua lông mâe náam
cruise ship	เรือเดินสมุทร	reua dern sà-mùt
cruiser	เรือลาดตระเวน	reua lâat dtrà-wayn
yacht	เรือยอชต์	reua yôt
tugboat	เรือลากจูง	reua lâak joong
barge	เรือบรรทุก	reua ban-thúk
ferry	เรือขามฟาก	reua khâam fâak
sailing ship	เรือใบ	reua bai
brigantine	เรือใบสองเสากระโดง	reua bai sŏrng săo grà-dohng
ice breaker	เรือตัดน้ำแข็ง	reua dtàt náam khăeng
submarine	เรือดำน้ำ	reua dam náam
boat (flat-bottomed ~)	เรือพาย	reua phaai
dinghy (lifeboat)	เรือบตเล็ก	reua bòt lék
lifeboat	เรือชูชีพ	reua choo chêep
motorboat	เรือยนต์	reua yon
captain	กัปตัน	gàp dtan
seaman	นาวิน	naa-win
sailor	คนเรือ	khon reua
crew	กะลาสี	gà-laa-sĕe
boatswain	สรั่ง	sà-ràng
ship's boy	คนช่วยงานในเรือ	khon chûay ngaan nai reua
cook	กุก	gúk
ship's doctor	แพทย์เรือ	phâet reua
deck	ดาดฟ้าเรือ	dàat-fáa reua
mast	เสากระโดงเรือ	săo grà-dohng reua
sail	ใบเรือ	bai reua
hold	ท้องเรือ	thórng-reua
bow (prow)	หัวเรือ	hŭa-reua
stern	ทวยเรือ	tháai reua
oar	ไม้พาย	máai phaai
screw propeller	ใบจักร	bai jàk
cabin	ห้องพัก	hôrng phák
wardroom	ห้องอาหาร	hôrng aa-hăan
engine room	หองเครื่องยนต์	hôrng khrêuang yon
bridge	สะพานเดินเรือ	sà-phaan dern reua
radio room	หองวิทยุ	hôrng wít-thá-yú
wave (radio)	คลื่นความถี่	khlêun khwaam thèe
logbook	สมุดบันทึก	sà-mùt ban-théuk
spyglass	กลองสองทางไกล	glôrng sòrng thaang glai
bell	ระฆัง	rá-khang

flag	ธง	thorng
hawser (mooring ~)	เชือก	chêuak
knot (bowline, etc.)	ปม	bpom

| deckrails | ราว | raao |
| gangway | ไม้พาดให้
ขึ้นลงเรือ | mái phâat hâi
khêun long reua |

anchor	สมอ	sà-mŏr
to weigh anchor	ถอนสมอ	thŏrn sà-mŏr
to drop anchor	ทอดสมอ	thôrt sà-mŏr
anchor chain	โซ่สมอเรือ	sôh sà-mŏr reua

port (harbour)	ท่าเรือ	thâa reua
quay, wharf	ทา	thâa
to berth (moor)	จอดเทียบท่า	jòt thîap tâa
to cast off	ออกจากทา	òrk jàak tâa

trip, voyage	การเดินทาง	gaan dern thaang
cruise (sea trip)	การล่องเรือ	gaan lôrng reua
course (route)	เส้นทาง	sên thaang
route (itinerary)	เส้นทาง	sên thaang

fairway (safe water channel)	ร่องเรือเดิน	rông reua dern
shallows	โขด	khòht
to run aground	เกยตื้น	goie dtêun

storm	พายุ	phaa-yú
signal	สัญญาณ	săn-yaan
to sink (vi)	ลม	lôm

Man overboard!	คนตกเรือ!	kon dtòk reua
SOS (distress signal)	SOS	es-o-es
ring buoy	ห่วงยาง	hùang yaang

172. Airport

airport	สนามบิน	sà-năam bin
aeroplane	เครื่องบิน	khrêuang bin
airline	สายการบิน	săai gaan bin
air traffic controller	เจ้าหน้าที่ควบคุม จราจรทางอากาศ	jâo nâa-thêe khûap khum jà-raa-jon thaang aa-gàat

departure	การออกเดินทาง	gaan òrk dern thaang
arrival	การมาถึง	gaan maa thĕung
to arrive (by plane)	มาถึง	maa thĕung

| departure time | เวลาขาไป | way-laa khăa bpai |
| arrival time | เวลามาถึง | way-laa maa thĕung |

to be delayed	ถูกเลื่อน	thòok lêuan
flight delay	เลื่อนเที่ยวบิน	lêuan thieow bin
information board	กระดานแสดง ขอมูล	grà daan sà-daeng khôr moon

information	ข้อมูล	khôr moon
to announce (vt)	ประกาศ	bprà-gàat
flight (e.g. next ~)	เที่ยวบิน	thîeow bin

customs	ศุลกากร	sŭn-lá-gaa-gon
customs officer	เจ้าหน้าที่ศุลกากร	jâo nâa-thêe sŭn-lá-gaa-gon

customs declaration	แบบฟอร์มการเสีย ภาษีศุลกากร	bàep form gaan sĭa phaa-sĕe sŭn-lá-gaa-gon
to fill in (vt)	กรอก	gròrk
to fill in the declaration	กรอกแบบฟอร์ม การเสียภาษี	gròrk bàep form gaan sĭa paa-sĕe
passport control	จุดตรวจหนังสือ เดินทาง	jùt dtrùat năng-sĕu dern-thaang

luggage	สัมภาระ	săm-phaa-rá
hand luggage	กระเป๋าถือ	grà-bpăo thĕu
luggage trolley	รถขนสัมภาระ	rót khŏn săm-phaa-rá

landing	การลงจอด	gaan long jòrt
landing strip	ลานบินลงจอด	laan bin long jòrt
to land (vi)	ลงจอด	long jòrt
airstair (passenger stair)	ทางขึ้นลง เครื่องบิน	thaang khêun long khrêuang bin

check-in	การเช็คอิน	gaan chék in
check-in counter	เคาน์เตอร์เช็คอิน	khao-dtêr chék in
to check-in (vi)	เช็คอิน	chék in
boarding card	บัตรที่นั่ง	bàt thêe nâng
departure gate	ช่องเข้า	chôrng khâo

transit	การต่อเที่ยวบิน	gaan tòr thîeow bin
to wait (vt)	รอ	ror
departure lounge	ห้องผู้โดยสารขาออก	hôrng phôo doi săan khăa òk
to see off	ไปส่ง	bpai sòng
to say goodbye	บอกลา	bòrk laa

173. Bicycle. Motorcycle

bicycle	รถจักรยาน	rót jàk-grà-yaan
scooter	สกูตเตอร์	sà-góot-dtêr
motorbike	รถมอเตอร์ไซค์	rót mor-dtêr-sai

to go by bicycle	ขี่จักรยาน	khèe jàk-grà-yaan
handlebars	พวงมาลัยรถ	phuang maa-lai rót
pedal	แป้นเหยียบ	bpâen yìap
brakes	เบรก	bràyk
bicycle seat (saddle)	ที่นั่งจักรยาน	thêe nâng jàk-grà-yaan

pump	ปั๊ม	bpám
pannier rack	ที่วางสัมภาระ	thêe waang săm-phaa-rá
front lamp	ไฟหน้า	fai nâa
helmet	หมวกนิรภัย	mùak ní-rá-phai
wheel	ล้อ	lór

mudguard	บังโคลน	bang khlon
rim	ขอบล้อ	khòp lór
spoke	กำนล้อ	gâan lór

Cars

car	รถยนต์	rót yon
sports car	รถสปอร์ต	rót sà-bpòt
limousine	รถลีมูซีน	rót lee moo seen
off-road vehicle	รถเอสยูวี	rót àyt yoo wee
drophead coupé (convertible)	รถยนต์เปิดประทุน	rót yon bpèrt bprà-thun
minibus	รถบัสเล็ก	rót bàt lék
ambulance	รถพยาบาล	rót phá-yaa-baan
snowplough	รถไถหิมะ	rót thǎi hì-má
lorry	รถบรรทุก	rót ban-thúk
road tanker	รถบรรทุกน้ำมัน	rót ban-thúk nám man
van (small truck)	รถตู้	rót dtôo
tractor unit	รถลาก	rót lâak
trailer	รถพ่วง	rót phûang
comfortable (adj)	สะดวก	sà-dùak
used (adj)	มือสอง	meu sǒrng

bonnet	กระโปรงรถ	grà bprohng rót
wing	บังโคลน	bang khlon
roof	หลังคา	lǎng khaa
windscreen	กระจกหน้ารถ	grà-jòk nâa rót
rear-view mirror	กระจกมองหลัง	grà-jòk morng lǎng
windscreen washer	ที่ฉีดน้ำลวง กระจกหน้ารถ	thêe chèet nám láang grà-jòk nâa rót
windscreen wipers	ที่ปัดล้างกระจก หน้ารถ	thêe bpàt láang grà-jòk nâa rót
side window	กระจกข้าง	grà-jòk khâang
electric window	กระจกไฟฟ้า	grà-jòk fai-fáa
aerial	เสาอากาศ	sǎo aa-gàat
sunroof	หลังคารับแดด	lǎng khaa ráp dàet
bumper	กันชน	gan chon
boot	ท้ายรถ	tháai rót
roof luggage rack	ชั้นวางสัมภาระ	chán waang sǎm-phaa-rá
door	ประตู	bprà-dtoo
door handle	ที่เปิดประตู	thêe bpèrt bprà-dtoo
door lock	ล็อคประตูรถ	lók bprà-dtoo rót

number plate	ป้ายทะเบียน	bpâai thá-bian
silencer	ท่อไอเสีย	thôr ai sǐa
petrol tank	ถังน้ำมัน	thǎng náam man
exhaust pipe	ท่อไอเสีย	thôr ai sǐa

accelerator	เร่ง	râyng
pedal	แป้นเหยียบ	bpâen yìap
accelerator pedal	คันเร่ง	khan râyng

brake	เบรก	bràyk
brake pedal	แป้นเบรค	bpâen bràyk
to brake (use the brake)	เบรก	bràyk
handbrake	เบรกมือ	bràyk meu

clutch	คลัตช์	khlát
clutch pedal	แป้นคลัตช์	bpâen khlát
clutch disc	จานคลัตช์	jaan khlát
shock absorber	โช้คอัพ	chóhk-àp

wheel	ล้อ	lór
spare tyre	ล้อสำรอง	lór sǎm-rorng
tyre	ยางรถ	yaang rót
wheel cover (hubcap)	ล้อแม็ก	lór-máek

driving wheels	ล้อพวงมาลัย	lór phuang maa-lai
front-wheel drive (as adj)	ขับเคลื่อนล้อหน้า	khàp khlêuan lór nâa
rear-wheel drive (as adj)	ขับเคลื่อนล้อหลัง	khàp khlêuan lór lǎng
all-wheel drive (as adj)	ขับเคลื่อนสี่ล้อ	khàp khlêuan sèe lór

gearbox	กระปุกเกียร์	grà-bpùk gia
automatic (adj)	อัตโนมัติ	àt-noh-mát
mechanical (adj)	กลไก	gon-gai
gear lever	คันเกียร์	khan gia

| headlamp | ไฟหน้า | fai nâa |
| headlights | ไฟหน้า | fai nâa |

dipped headlights	ไฟต่ำ	fai dtàm
full headlights	ไฟสูง	fai sǒong
brake light	ไฟเบรก	fai bràyk

sidelights	ไฟจอดรถ	fai jòt rót
hazard lights	ไฟฉุกเฉิน	fai chùk-chěrn
fog lights	ไฟตัดหมอก	fai dtàt mòk
turn indicator	ไฟเลี้ยว	fai líeow
reversing light	ไฟรถถอย	fai rót thǒi

176. Cars. Passenger compartment

car interior	ภายในรถ	phaai nai rót
leather (as adj)	หนัง	nǎng
velour (as adj)	กำมะหยี่	gam-má-yèe
upholstery	เครื่องเบาะ	khrêuang bòr
instrument (gage)	อุปกรณ์	ù-bpà-gon

dashboard	แผงหน้าปัด	phǎeng nâa bpàt
speedometer	มาตรวัดความเร็ว	mâat wát khwaam reo
needle (pointer)	เข็มชี้วัด	khěm chée wát

mileometer	มิเตอร์วัดระยะทาง	mí-dtêr wát rá-yá thaang
indicator (sensor)	มิเตอร์วัด	mí-dtêr wát
level	ระดับ	rá-dàp
warning light	ไฟเตือน	fai dteuan

steering wheel	พวงมาลัยรถ	phuang maa-lai rót
horn	แตร	dtrae
button	ปุ่ม	bpùm
switch	สวิตช์	sà-wít

seat	ที่นั่ง	thêe nâng
backrest	พนักพิง	phá-nák phing
headrest	ที่พิงศีรษะ	thêe phing sěe-sà
seat belt	เข็มขัดนิรภัย	khěm khàt ní-rá-phai
to fasten the belt	คาดเข็มขัดนิรภัย	khâat khěm khàt ní-rá-phai
adjustment (of seats)	การปรับ	gaan bpràp

| airbag | ถุงลมนิรภัย | thǔng lom ní-rá-phai |
| air-conditioner | เครื่องปรับอากาศ | khrêuang bpràp-aa-gàat |

radio	วิทยุ	wít-thá-yú
CD player	เครื่องเล่น CD	khrêuang lên see-dee
to turn on	เปิด	bpèrt
aerial	เสาอากาศ	sǎo aa-gàat
glove box	ซองเก็บของ ข้างคนขับ	chôrng gèp khǒrng khâang khon khàp
ashtray	ที่เขี่ยบุหรี่	thêe khìa bù rèe

177. Cars. Engine

engine	เครื่องยนต์	khrêuang yon
motor	มอเตอร์	mor-dtêr
diesel (as adj)	ดีเซล	dee-sayn
petrol (as adj)	น้ำมันเบนซิน	nám man bayn-sin

engine volume	ขนาดเครื่องยนต์	khà-nàat khrêuang yon
power	กำลัง	gam-lang
horsepower	แรงม้า	raeng máa
piston	ก้านลูกสูบ	gâan lôok sòop
cylinder	กระบอกสูบ	grà-bòrk sòop
valve	วาล์ว	waao

injector	หัวฉีด	hǔa chèet
generator (alternator)	เครื่องกำเนิดไฟฟ้า	khrêuang gam-nèrt fai fáa
carburettor	คาร์บูเรเตอร์	khaa-boo-ray-dtêr
motor oil	น้ำมันเครื่อง	nám man khrêuang

radiator	หม้อน้ำ	môr náam
coolant	สารทำความเย็น	sǎan tham khwaam yen
cooling fan	พัดลมระบายความร้อน	phát lom rá-baai khwaam rón

battery (accumulator)	แบตเตอรี่	bàet-dter-rêe
starter	มอเตอรสตาร์ต	mor-dtêr sà-dtàat
ignition	การจุดระเบิด	gaan jùt rá-bèrt
sparking plug	หัวเทียน	hŭa thian

terminal (battery ~)	ขั้วแบตเตอรี่	khŭa bàet-dter-rêe
positive terminal	ขั้วบวก	khŭa bùak
negative terminal	ขั้วลบ	khŭa lóp
fuse	ฟิวส์	fiw

air filter	เครื่องกรองอากาศ	khrêuang grorng aa-gàat
oil filter	ไส้กรองน้ำมัน	sâi grorng nám man
fuel filter	ไส้กรองน้ำมัน เชื้อเพลิง	sâi grorng nám man chéua phlerng

178. Cars. Crash. Repair

car crash	อุบัติเหตุรถชน	u-bàt hàyt rót chon
traffic accident	อุบัติเหตุจราจร	u-bàt hàyt jà-raa-jon
to crash (into the wall, etc.)	ชน	chon
to get smashed up	ชนโครม	chon khrohm
damage	ความเสียหาย	khwaam sǐa hǎi
intact (unscathed)	ไม่มีความเสียหาย	mâi mee khwaam sǐa hǎi

breakdown	การเสีย	gaan sǐa
to break down (vi)	ตาย	dtaai
towrope	เชือกลากรถยนต์	chêuak lâak rót yon

puncture	ยางรั่ว	yaang rûa
to have a puncture	ทำให้ยางแบน	tham hâi yaang baen
to pump up	เติมลมยาง	dterm lom yaang
pressure	แรงดัน	raeng dan
to check (to examine)	ตรวจสอบ	dtrùat sòrp

repair	การซ่อม	gaan sôrm
garage (auto service shop)	ร้านซ่อมรถยนต์	ráan sôrm rót yon
spare part	อะไหล่	a lài
part	ชิ้นส่วน	chín sùan

bolt (with nut)	สลักเกลียว	sà-làk glieow
screw (fastener)	สกรู	sà-groo
nut	แหวนสกรู	wǎen sà-groo
washer	แหวนเล็ก	wǎen lék
bearing (e.g. ball ~)	แบริง	bae-ring

tube	ท่อ	thôr
gasket (head ~)	ปะเก็น	bpà gen
cable, wire	สายไฟ	sǎai fai

jack	แม่แรง	mâe raeng
spanner	ประแจ	bprà-jae
hammer	ค้อน	khórn
pump	ปั๊ม	bpám
screwdriver	ไขควง	khǎi khuang

| fire extinguisher | ถังดับเพลิง | thăng dàp phlerng |
| warning triangle | ป้ายเตือน | bpâai dteuan |

to stall (vi)	มีเครื่องดับ	mee khrêuang dàp
stall (n)	การดับ	gaan dàp
to be broken	เสีย	sĭa

to overheat (vi)	ร้อนเกิน	rórn gern
to be clogged up	อุดตัน	ùt dtan
to freeze up (pipes, etc.)	เยือกแข็ง	yêuak khăeng
to burst (vi, ab. tube)	แตก	dtàek

pressure	แรงดัน	raeng dan
level	ระดับ	rá-dàp
slack (~ belt)	อ่อน	òrn

dent	รอยบุบ	roi bùp
knocking noise (engine)	เสียงเครื่องยนต์ดับ	sĭang khrêuang yon dàp
crack	รอยแตก	roi dtàek
scratch	รอยขูด	roi khòot

179. Cars. Road

road	ถนน	thà-nŏn
motorway	ทางหลวง	thaang lŭang
highway	ทางด่วน	thaang dùan
direction (way)	ทิศทาง	thít thaang
distance	ระยะทาง	rá-yá thaang

bridge	สะพาน	sà-phaan
car park	ลานจอดรถ	laan jòrt rót
square	จัตุรัส	jàt-dtù-ràt
road junction	ทางแยกต่างระดับ	thaang yâek dtàang rá-dàp
tunnel	อุโมงค์	u-mohng

petrol station	ปั๊มน้ำมัน	bpám náam man
car park	ลานจอดรถ	laan jòrt rót
petrol pump	ที่เติมน้ำมัน	thêe dterm náam man
auto repair shop	ร้านซ่อมรถยนต์	ráan sôrm rót yon
to fill up	เติมน้ำมัน	dterm náam man
fuel	น้ำมันเชื้อเพลิง	nám man chéua phlerng
jerrycan	ถังน้ำมัน	thăng náam man

asphalt, tarmac	ถนนลาดยาง	thà-nŏn lâat yaang
road markings	เครื่องหมายจราจร บนพื้นทาง	khrêuang măai jà-raa-jon bon phéun thaang
kerb	ขอบถนน	khòrp thà-nŏn
crash barrier	รั้วกั้น	rúa gân
ditch	คู	khoo
roadside (shoulder)	ข้างถนน	khâang thà-nŏn
lamppost	เสาไฟ	săo fai

| to drive (a car) | ขับ | khàp |
| to turn (e.g., ~ left) | เลี้ยว | líeow |

| to make a U-turn | กลับรถ | glàp rót |
| reverse (~ gear) | ถอยรถ | thŏri rót |

to honk (vi)	บีบแตร	bèep dtrae
honk (sound)	เสียงบีบแตร	sĭang bèep dtrae
to get stuck (in the mud, etc.)	ติด	dtìt
to spin the wheels	หมุนล้อ	mŭn lór
to cut, to turn off (vt)	ปิด	bpìt

speed	ความเร็ว	khwaam reo
to exceed the speed limit	ขับเร็วเกิน	khàp reo gern
to give a ticket	ให้ใบสั่ง	hâi bai sàng
traffic lights	ไฟสัญญาณจราจร	fai săn-yaan jà-raa-jon
driving licence	ใบขับขี่	bai khàp khèe

level crossing	ทางข้ามรถไฟ	thaang khâam rót fai
crossroads	สี่แยก	sèe yâek
zebra crossing	ทางม้าลาย	thaang máa laai
bend, curve	ทางโค้ง	thaang khóhng
pedestrian precinct	ถนนคนเดิน	thà-nŏn khon dern

180. Signs

Highway Code	กฎจราจร	gòt jà-raa-jon
road sign (traffic sign)	ป้ายสัญญาณจราจร	bpâai săn-yaan jà-raa-jon
overtaking	การแซง	gaan saeng
curve	การโค้ง	gaan khóhng
U-turn	การกลับรถ	gaan glàp rót
roundabout	วงเวียน	wong wian

No entry	ห้ามเข้า	hâam khâo
All vehicles prohibited	ห้ามรถเข้า	hâam rót khâo
No overtaking	ห้ามแซง	hâam saeng
No parking	ห้ามจอดรถ	hâam jòrt rót
No stopping	ห้ามหยุด	hâam yùt

dangerous curve	โค้งอันตราย	khóhng an-dtà-raai
steep descent	ทางลงลาดชัน	thaang long lâat chan
one-way traffic	การจราจรทางเดียว	gaan jà-raa-jon thaang dieow
zebra crossing	ทางม้าลาย	thaang máa laai
slippery road	ทางลื่น	thaang lêun
GIVE WAY	ให้ทาง	hâi taang

PEOPLE. LIFE EVENTS

181. Holidays. Event

celebration, holiday	วันหยุดเฉลิมฉลอง	wan yùt chà-lěrm chà-lŏng
national day	วันชาติ	wan châat
public holiday	วันหยุดนักขัตฤกษ์	wan yùt nák-kàt-rêrk
to commemorate (vt)	เฉลิมฉลอง	chà-lěrm chà-lŏrng

event (happening)	เหตุการณ์	hàyt gaan
event (organized activity)	งานอีเวนต์	ngaan ee wayn
banquet (party)	งานเลี้ยง	ngaan líang
reception (formal party)	งานเลี้ยง	ngaan líang
feast	งานฉลอง	ngaan chà-lŏrng

anniversary	วันครบรอบ	wan khróp rôrp
jubilee	วันครบรอบปี	wan khróp rôrp bpee
to celebrate (vt)	ฉลอง	chà-lŏrng

New Year	ปีใหม่	bpee mài
Happy New Year!	สวัสดีปีใหม่!	sà-wàt-dee bpee mài
Father Christmas	ซานตาคลอส	saan-dtaa-khlôrt

Christmas	คริสต์มาส	khrít-mâat
Merry Christmas!	สุขสันต์วันคริสต์มาส	sùk-săn wan khrít-mâat
Christmas tree	ต้นคริสต์มาส	dtôn khrít-mâat
fireworks (fireworks show)	ดอกไม้ไฟ	dòrk máai fai

wedding	งานแต่งงาน	ngaan dtàeng ngaan
groom	เจ้าบ่าว	jâo bàao
bride	เจ้าสาว	jâo săao

to invite (vt)	เชิญ	chern
invitation card	บัตรเชิญ	bàt chern

guest	แขก	khàek
to visit (~ your parents, etc.)	ไปเยี่ยม	bpai yîam
to meet the guests	ต้อนรับแขก	dton ráp khàek

gift, present	ของขวัญ	khŏrng khwăn
to give (sth as present)	ให้	hâi
to receive gifts	รับของขวัญ	ráp khŏrng khwăn
bouquet (of flowers)	ช่อดอกไม้	chôr dòrk máai

congratulations	คำแสดงความยินดี	kham sà-daeng khwaam yin-dee
to congratulate (vt)	แสดงความยินดี	sà-daeng khwaam yin dee

greetings card	บัตรอวยพร	bàt uay phon
to send a postcard	ส่งโปสการ์ด	sòng bpòht-gàat

to get a postcard	รับโปสการ์ด	ráp bpòht-gàat
toast	ดื่มอวยพร	dèum uay phon
to offer (a drink, etc.)	เลี้ยงเครื่องดื่ม	líang khrêuang dèum
champagne	แชมเปญ	chaem-bpayn

to enjoy oneself	มีความสุข	mee khwaam sùk
merriment (gaiety)	ความรื่นเริง	khwaam rêun-rerng
joy (emotion)	ความสุขสันต์	khwaam sùk-sǎn

| dance | การเต้น | gaan dtên |
| to dance (vi, vt) | เต้น | dtên |

| waltz | วอลทูซ์ | wɔ:lts |
| tango | แทงโก | thaeng-gôh |

182. Funerals. Burial

cemetery	สุสาน	sù-sǎan
grave, tomb	หลุมศพ	lǔm sòp
cross	ไม้กางเขน	mái gaang khǎyn
gravestone	ป้ายหลุมศพ	bpâai lǔm sòp
fence	รั้ว	rúa
chapel	โรงสวด	rohng sùat

death	ความตาย	khwaam dtaai
to die (vi)	ตาย	dtaai
the deceased	ผู้เสียชีวิต	phôo sǐa chee-wít
mourning	การไว้อาลัย	gaan wái aa-lai

to bury (vt)	ฝังศพ	fǎng sòp
undertakers	บริษัทรับจัดงานศพ	bor-rí-sàt ráp jàt ngaan sòp
funeral	งานศพ	ngaan sòp

wreath	พวงหรีด	phuang rèet
coffin	โลงศพ	lohng sòp
hearse	รถขนศพ	rót khǒn sòp
shroud	ผ้าห่อศพ	phâa hòr sòp

funeral procession	พิธีศพ	phí-tee sòp
funerary urn	โกศ	gòht
crematorium	เมรุ	mayn

obituary	ข่าวมรณกรรม	khàao mor-rá-ná-gam
to cry (weep)	ร้องไห้	rórng hâi
to sob (vi)	สะอื้น	sà-êun

183. War. Soldiers

platoon	หมวด	mùat
company	กองร้อย	gorng rói
regiment	กรม	grom
army	กองทัพ	gorng tháp

division	กองพล	gorng phon-la
section, squad	หมู่	mòo
host (army)	กองทัพ	gorng tháp

| soldier | ทหาร | thá-hăan |
| officer | นายทหาร | naai thá-hăan |

private	พลทหาร	phon-thá-hăan
sergeant	สิบเอก	sìp àyk
lieutenant	ร้อยโท	rói thoh
captain	ร้อยเอก	rói àyk
major	พลตรี	phon-dtree

| colonel | พันเอก | phan àyk |
| general | นายพล | naai phon |

sailor	กะลาสี	gà-laa-sĕe
captain	กัปตัน	gàp dtan
boatswain	สรั่งเรือ	sà-ràng reua

artilleryman	ทหารปืนใหญ่	thá-hăan bpeun yài
paratrooper	พลรม	phon-rôm
pilot	นักบิน	nák bin

| navigator | ต้นหน | dtôn hŏn |
| mechanic | ช่างเครื่อง | châang khrêuang |

| pioneer (sapper) | ทหารช่าง | thá-hăan châang |
| parachutist | ทหารราบอากาศ | thá-hăan râap aa-gàat |

| reconnaissance scout | ทหารพราน | thá-hăan phraan |
| sniper | พลซุ่มยิง | phon sûm ying |

patrol (group)	หน่วยลาดตระเวน	nùay lâat dtrà-wayn
to patrol (vt)	ลาดตระเวน	lâat dtrà-wayn
sentry, guard	ทหารยาม	tá-hăan yaam

| warrior | นักรบ | nàk róp |
| patriot | ผู้รักชาติ | phôo rák châat |

| hero | วีรบุรุษ | wee-rá-bù-rùt |
| heroine | วีรสตรี | wee rá-sot dtree |

| traitor | ผู้ทรยศ | phôo thor-rá-yót |
| to betray (vt) | ทรยศ | thor-rá-yót |

| deserter | ทหารหนีทัพ | thá-hăan nĕe tháp |
| to desert (vi) | หนีทัพ | nĕe tháp |

mercenary	ทหารรับจ้าง	thá-hăan ráp jâang
recruit	เกณฑ์ทหาร	gayn thá-hăan
volunteer	อาสาสมัคร	aa-săa sà-màk

dead (n)	คนถูกฆ่า	khon thòok khâa
wounded (n)	ผู้ได้รับบาดเจ็บ	phôo dâai ráp bàat jèp
prisoner of war	เชลยศึก	chá-loie sèuk

184. War. Military actions. Part 1

war	สงคราม	sŏng-khraam
to be at war	ทำสงคราม	tham sŏng-khraam
civil war	สงครามกลางเมือง	sŏng-khraam glaang-meuang
treacherously (adv)	ตลบตะแลง	dtà-lòp-dtà-laeng
declaration of war	การประกาศสงคราม	gaan bprà-gàat sŏng-khraam
to declare (~ war)	ประกาศสงคราม	bprà-gàat sŏng-khraam
aggression	การรุกราน	gaan rúk-raan
to attack (invade)	บุกรุก	bùk rúk
to invade (vt)	บุกรุก	bùk rúk
invader	ผู้บุกรุก	phôo bùk rúk
conqueror	ผู้ยึดครอง	phôo yéut khrorng
defence	การป้องกัน	gaan bpôrng gan
to defend (a country, etc.)	ปกป้อง	bpòk bpôrng
to defend (against …)	ป้องกัน	bpôrng gan
enemy	ศัตรู	sàt-dtroo
foe, adversary	ข้าศึก	khâa sèuk
enemy (as adj)	ศัตรู	sàt-dtroo
strategy	ยุทธศาสตร์	yút-thá-sàat
tactics	ยุทธวิธี	yút-thá-wí-thee
order	คำสั่ง	kham sàng
command (order)	คำบัญชาการ	kham ban-chaa gaan
to order (vt)	สั่ง	sàng
mission	ภารกิจ	phaa-rá-gìt
secret (adj)	อย่างลับ	yàang láp
battle, combat	การรบ	gaan róp
attack	การจู่โจม	gaan jòo johm
charge (assault)	การเข้าจู่โจม	gaan khâo jòo johm
to storm (vt)	บุกจู่โจม	bùk jòo johm
siege (to be under ~)	การโอบล้อมโจมตี	gaan òhp lóm johm dtee
offensive (n)	การโจมตี	gaan johm dtee
to go on the offensive	โจมตี	johm dtee
retreat	การถอย	gaan thŏi
to retreat (vi)	ถอย	thŏi
encirclement	การปิดล้อม	gaan bpìt lórm
to encircle (vt)	ปิดล้อม	bpìt lórm
bombing (by aircraft)	การทิ้งระเบิด	gaan thíng rá-bèrt
to drop a bomb	ทิ้งระเบิด	thíng rá-bèrt
to bomb (vt)	ทิ้งระเบิด	thíng rá-bèrt
explosion	การระเบิด	gaan rá-bèrt
shot	การยิง	gaan ying
to fire (~ a shot)	ยิง	ying

firing (burst of ~)	การยิง	gaan ying
to aim (to point a weapon)	เล็ง	leng
to point (a gun)	ชี้	chée
to hit (the target)	ถูกเป้าหมาย	thòok bpâo măai

to sink (~ a ship)	จม	jom
hole (in a ship)	รู	roo
to founder, to sink (vi)	จม	jom

front (war ~)	แนวหน้า	naew nâa
evacuation	การอพยพ	gaan òp-phá-yóp
to evacuate (vt)	อพยพ	òp-phá-yóp

trench	สนามเพลาะ	sà-năam phlór
barbed wire	ลวดหนาม	lûat năam
barrier (anti tank ~)	สิ่งกีดขวาง	sìng gèet-khwăang
watchtower	หอสังเกตการณ์	hŏr săng-gàyt gaan

military hospital	โรงพยาบาล ทหาร	rohng phá-yaa-baan thá-hăan
to wound (vt)	ทำให้บาดเจ็บ	tham hâi bàat jèp
wound	แผล	phlăe
wounded (n)	ผู้ได้รับบาดเจ็บ	phôo dâai ráp bàat jèp
to be wounded	ได้รับบาดเจ็บ	dâai ráp bàat jèp
serious (wound)	รายแรง	ráai raeng

185. War. Military actions. Part 2

captivity	การเป็นเชลย	gaan bpen chá-loie
to take captive	จับเชลย	jàp chá-loie
to be held captive	เป็นเชลย	bpen chá-loie
to be taken captive	ถูกจับเป็นเชลย	thòok jàp bpen chá-loie

concentration camp	ค่ายกักกัน	khâai gàk gan
prisoner of war	เชลยศึก	chá-loie sèuk
to escape (vi)	หนี	nĕe

to betray (vt)	ทูรยศ	thor-rá-yót
betrayer	ผู้ทรยศ	phôo thor-rá-yót
betrayal	การทรยศ	gaan thor-rá-yót

| to execute (by firing squad) | ประหาร | bprà-hăan |
| execution (by firing squad) | การประหาร | gaan bprà-hăan |

equipment (military gear)	ชุดเสื้อผ้าทหาร	chút sêua phâa thá-hăan
shoulder board	บั้ง	bâng
gas mask	หน้ากากกันแก๊ส	nâa gàak gan gàet

field radio	วิทยุสนาม	wít-thá-yú sà-năam
cipher, code	รหัส	rá-hàt
secrecy	ความลับ	khwaam láp
password	รหัสผาน	rá-hàt phàan
land mine	กับระเบิด	gàp rá-bèrt
to mine (road, etc.)	วางกับระเบิด	waang gàp rá-bèrt

minefield	เขตทุ่นระเบิด	khàyt thûn rá-bèrt
air-raid warning	สัญญาณเตือนภัย ทางอากาศ	săn-yaan dteuan phai thaang aa-gàat
alarm (alert signal)	สัญญาณเตือนภัย	săn-yaan dteuan phai
signal	สัญญาณ	săn-yaan
signal flare	พลุสัญญาณ	phlú săn-yaan
headquarters	กองบัญชาการ	gorng ban-chaa gaan
reconnaissance	การลาดตระเวน	gaan lâat dtrà-wayn
situation	สถานการณ์	sà-thăan gaan
report	การรายงาน	gaan raai ngaan
ambush	การซุ่มโจมตี	gaan sûm johm dtee
reinforcement (army)	กำลังเสริม	gam-lang sěrm
target	เป้าหมาย	bpâo măai
training area	สถานที่ทดลอง	sà-tăan thêe thót long
military exercise	การซ้อมรบ	gaan sórm róp
panic	ความตื่นตระหนก	khwaam dtèun dtrà-nòk
devastation	การทำลายล้าง	gaan tham-laai láang
destruction, ruins	ซาก	sâak
to destroy (vt)	ทำลาย	tham laai
to survive (vi, vt)	รอดชีวิต	rôt chee-wít
to disarm (vt)	ปลดอาวุธ	bplòt aa-wút
to handle (~ a gun)	ใช้	chái
Attention!	หยุด	yùt
At ease!	พัก	phák
feat, act of courage	การแสดงความ กล้าหาญ	gaan sà-daeng khwaam glâa hăan
oath (vow)	คำสาบาน	kham săa-baan
to swear (an oath)	สาบาน	săa baan
decoration (medal, etc.)	รางวัล	raang-wan
to award (give a medal to)	มอบรางวัล	môrp raang-wan
medal	เหรียญรางวัล	rĭan raang-wan
order (e.g. ~ of Merit)	เครื่องอิสริยาภรณ์	khrêuang ìt-sà-rí-yaa-phon
victory	ชัยชนะ	chai chá-ná
defeat	ความพ่ายแพ้	khwaam phâai pháe
armistice	การพักรบ	gaan phák róp
standard (battle flag)	ธงรบ	thorng róp
glory (honour, fame)	ความรุ่งโรจน์	khwaam rûng-rôht
parade	ขบวนสวนสนาม	khà-buan sŭan sà-năam
to march (on parade)	เดินสวนสนาม	dern sŭan sà-năam

186. Weapons

weapons	อาวุธ	aa-wút
firearms	อาวุธปืน	aa-wút bpeun
cold weapons (knives, etc.)	อาวุธเย็น	aa-wút yen

chemical weapons	อาวุธเคมี	aa-wút khay-mee
nuclear (adj)	นิวเคลียร์	niw-khlia
nuclear weapons	อาวุธนิวเคลียร์	aa-wút niw-khlia
bomb	ลูกระเบิด	lôok rá-bèrt
atomic bomb	ลูกระเบิดปรมาณู	lôok rá-bèrt bpà-rá-maa-noo
pistol (gun)	ปืนพก	bpeun phók
rifle	ปืนไรเฟิล	bpeun rai-fern
submachine gun	ปืนกลมือ	bpeun gon meu
machine gun	ปืนกล	bpeun gon
muzzle	ปากปะบอกปืน	bpàak bprà bòrk bpeun
barrel	ลำกลอง	lam glôrng
calibre	ขนาดลำกลอง	khà-nàat lam glôrng
trigger	ไกปืน	gai bpeun
sight (aiming device)	ศูนย์เล็ง	sŏon leng
magazine	แม็กกาซีน	máek-gaa-seen
butt (shoulder stock)	พานท้ายปืน	phaan tháai bpeun
hand grenade	ระเบิดมือ	rá-bèrt meu
explosive	วัตถุระเบิด	wát-thù rá-bèrt
bullet	ลูกกระสุน	lôok grà-sǔn
cartridge	ตลับกระสุน	dtà-làp grà-sǔn
charge	กระสุน	grà-sǔn
ammunition	อาวุธยุทธภัณฑ์	aa-wút yút-thá-phan
bomber (aircraft)	เครื่องบินทิ้งระเบิด	khrêuang bin thíng rá-bèrt
fighter	เครื่องบินขับไล่	khrêuang bin khàp lâi
helicopter	เฮลิคอปเตอร์	hay-lí-khôrp-dtêr
anti-aircraft gun	ปืนต่อสู้อากาศยาน	bpeun dtòr sôo aa-gàat-sà-yaan
tank	รถถัง	rót thăng
tank gun	ปืนรถถัง	bpeun rót thăng
artillery	ปืนใหญ่	bpeun yài
gun (cannon, howitzer)	ปืน	bpeun
to lay (a gun)	เล็งเป้าปืน	leng bpâo bpeun
shell (projectile)	กระสุน	grà-sǔn
mortar bomb	กระสุนปืนครก	grà-sǔn bpeun khrók
mortar	ปืนครก	bpeun khrók
splinter (shell fragment)	สะเก็ดระเบิด	sà-gèt rá-bèrt
submarine	เรือดำน้ำ	reua dam náam
torpedo	ตอร์ปิโด	dtor-bpì-doh
missile	ขีปนาวุธ	khĕe-bpà-naa-wút
to load (gun)	ใส่กระสุน	sài grà-sǔn
to shoot (vi)	ยิง	ying
to point at (the cannon)	เล็ง	leng
bayonet	ดาบปลายปืน	dàap bplaai bpeun
rapier	เรเปียร์	ray-bpia

sabre (e.g. cavalry ~)	ดาบโค้ง	dàap khóhng
spear (weapon)	หอก	hòrk
bow	ธนู	thá-noo
arrow	ลูกธนู	lôok-thá-noo
musket	ปืนคาบศิลา	bpeun khâap sì-laa
crossbow	หน้าไม้	nâa máai

187. Ancient people

primitive (prehistoric)	แบบดั้งเดิม	bàep dâng derm
prehistoric (adj)	ยุคก่อนประวัติศาสตร์	yúk gòn bprà-wàt sàat
ancient (~ civilization)	โบราณ	boh-raan

Stone Age	ยุคหิน	yúk hĭn
Bronze Age	ยุคสำริด	yúk săm-rít
Ice Age	ยุคน้ำแข็ง	yúk nám khăeng

tribe	เผ่า	phào
cannibal	ผู้ที่กินเนื้อคน	phôo thêe gin néua khon
hunter	นักล่าสัตว์	nák lâa sàt
to hunt (vi, vt)	ล่าสัตว์	lâa sàt
mammoth	ช้างแมมมอธ	cháang-maem-môt

cave	ถ้ำ	thâm
fire	ไฟ	fai
campfire	กองไฟ	gorng fai
cave painting	ภาพวาดในถ้ำ	phâap-wâat nai thâm

tool (e.g. stone axe)	เครื่องมือ	khrêuang meu
spear	หอก	hòrk
stone axe	ขวานหิน	khwăan hĭn
to be at war	ทำสงคราม	tham sŏng-khraam
to domesticate (vt)	เชื่อง	chêuang

| idol | เทวรูป | theu-rôop |
| to worship (vt) | บูชา | boo-chaa |

| superstition | ความเชื่องมงาย | khwaam chêua ngom-ngaai |
| rite | พิธีกรรม | phí-thee gam |

| evolution | วิวัฒนาการ | wí-wát-thá-naa-gaan |
| development | การพัฒนา | gaan phát-thá-naa |

| disappearance (extinction) | การสูญพันธุ์ | gaan sŏon phan |
| to adapt oneself | ปรับตัว | bpràp dtua |

archaeology	โบราณคดี	boh-raan khá-dee
archaeologist	นักโบราณคดี	nák boh-raan-ná-khá-dee
archaeological (adj)	ทางโบราณคดี	thaang boh-raan khá-dee

excavation site	แหล่งขุดค้น	làeng khùt khón
excavations	การขุดค้น	gaan khùt khón
find (object)	สิ่งที่ค้นพบ	sìng thêe khón phóp
fragment	เศษชิ้นส่วน	sàyt chín sùan

188. Middle Ages

people (ethnic group)	ชาติพันธุ์	châat-dtì-phan
peoples	ชุติพันธุ	châat-dtì-phan
tribe	เผ่า	phào
tribes	เผ่า	phào
barbarians	อนารยชน	à-naa-rá-yá-chon
Gauls	ชาวโกล	chaao gloh
Goths	ชาวกอธ	chaao gòt
Slavs	ชาวสลาฟ	chaao sà-làaf
Vikings	ชาวไวกิ้ง	chaao wai-gîng
Romans	ชาวโรมัน	chaao roh-man
Roman (adj)	โรมัน	roh-man
Byzantines	ชาวไบแซนไทน์	chaao bai-saen-tpai
Byzantium	ไบแซนเทียม	bai-saen-thiam
Byzantine (adj)	ไบแซนไทน์	bai-saen-thai
emperor	จักรพรรดิ	jàk-grà-phát
leader, chief (tribal ~)	ผู้นำ	phôo nam
powerful (~ king)	ทรงพลัง	song phá-lang
king	มูหากษัตริย์	má-hǎa gà-sàt
ruler (sovereign)	ผู้ปกครอง	phôo bpòk khrorng
knight	อัศวิน	àt-sà-win
feudal lord	เจ้าครองนคร	jâo khrorng ná-khon
feudal (adj)	ระบบศักดินา	rá-bòp sàk-gà-dì naa
vassal	เจ้าของที่ดิน	jâo khǒrng thêe din
duke	ดยุค	dà-yúk
earl	เอิร์ล	ern
baron	บารอน	baa-rorn
bishop	พระบิชอป	phrá bì-chôp
armour	เกราะ	gròr
shield	โล	lôh
sword	ดาบ	dàap
visor	กระบังหน้าของหมวก	gà-bang nâa khǒrng mùak
chainmail	เสื้อเกราะถัก	sêua gròr thàk
Crusade	สงครามครูเสด	sǒng-khraam khroo-sàyt
crusader	ผู้ทำสงคราม ศาสนา	phôo tham sǒng-kraam sàat-sà-nǎa
territory	อาณาเขต	aa-naa khàyt
to attack (invade)	โจมตี	johm dtee
to conquer (vt)	ยึดครอง	yéut khrorng
to occupy (invade)	บุกยึด	bùk yéut
siege (to be under ~)	การโอบล้อมโจมตี	gaan òhp lóm johm dtee
besieged (adj)	ถูกล้อมกรอบ	thòok lóm gròp
to besiege (vt)	ล้อมโจมตี	lóm johm dtee
inquisition	การไต่สวน	gaan dtài sǔan

inquisitor	ผู้ไต่สวน	phôo dtài sŭan
torture	การทูรมาน	gaan thor-rá-maan
cruel (adj)	โหดร้าย	hòht ráai
heretic	ผู้นอกรีต	phôo nôrk rêet
heresy	ความนอกรีต	khwaam nôrk rêet

seafaring	การเดินเรือทะเล	gaan dern reua thá-lay
pirate	โจรสลัด	john sà-làt
piracy	การปล้นสะดม ในนานน้ำทะเล	gaan bplôn-sà-dom nai nâan náam thá-lay
boarding (attack)	การบุกขึ้นเรือ	gaan bùk khêun reua
loot, booty	ของที่ปล้น สะดมมา	khŏrng têe bplôn- sà-dom maa
treasure	สมบัติ	sŏm-bàt

discovery	การค้นพบ	gaan khón phóp
to discover (new land, etc.)	ค้นพบ	khón phóp
expedition	การสำรวจ	gaan săm-rùat

musketeer	ทหารถือ ปืนคาบศิลา	thá-hăan thĕu bpeun khâap sì-laa
cardinal	พระคาร์ดินัล	phrá khaa-dì-nan
heraldry	มุทราศาสตร์	mút-raa sàat
heraldic (adj)	ทางมุทราศาสตร์	thaang mút-raa sàat

189. Leader. Chief. Authorities

king	ราชา	raa-chaa
queen	ราชินี	raa-chí-nee
royal (adj)	เกี่ยวกับราชวงศ์	gleow gàp râat-cha-wong
kingdom	ราชอาณาจักร	râat aa-naa jàk

prince	เจ้าชาย	jâo chaai
princess	เจ้าหญิง	jâo yĭng

president	ประธานาธิบดี	bprà-thaa-naa-thí-bor-dee
vice-president	รองประธา นาธิบดี	rorng bprà-thaa- naa-thí-bor-dee
senator	สมาชิกวุฒิสภา	sà-maa-chík wút-thí sà-phaa

monarch	กษัตริย์	gà-sàt
ruler (sovereign)	ผู้ปกครอง	phôo bpòk khrorng
dictator	เผด็จการ	phà-dèt gaan
tyrant	ทูรราช	thor-rá-râat
magnate	ผู้มีอิทธิพลสูง	phôo mee ìt-thí phon sŏong

director	ผู้อำนวยการ	phôo am-nuay gaan
chief	หัวหน้า	hŭa-nâa
manager (director)	ผู้จัดการ	phôo jàt gaan
boss	หัวหน้า	hŭa-nâa
owner	เจ้าของ	jâo khŏrng

leader	ผู้นำ	phôo nam
head (~ of delegation)	หัวหน้า	hŭa-nâa

| authorities | เจ้าหน้าที่ | jâo nâa-thêe |
| superiors | ผู้บังคับบัญชา | phôo bang-kháp ban-chaa |

governor	ผู้ว่าการ	phôo wâa gaan
consul	กงสุล	gong-sŭn
diplomat	นักการทูต	nák gaan thôot
mayor	นายกเทศมนตรี	naa-yók thâyt-sà-mon-dtree
sheriff	นายอำเภอ	naai am-pher

emperor	จักรพรรดิ	jàk-grà-phát
tsar, czar	ซาร์	saa
pharaoh	ฟาโรห์	faa-roh
khan	ขาน	khàan

190. Road. Way. Directions

| road | ถนน | thà-nŏn |
| way (direction) | ทิศทาง | thít thaang |

highway	ทางด่วน	thaang dùan
motorway	ทางหลวง	thaang lŭang
trunk road	ทางหลวงอินเตอร์สเตต	thaang lŭang in-dtèrt-dtàyt

| main road | ถนนใหญ่ | thà-nŏn yài |
| dirt road | ถนนลูกรัง | thà-nŏn loo-grang |

| pathway | ทางเดิน | thaang dern |
| footpath (troddenpath) | ทางเดิน | thaang dern |

Where?	ที่ไหน?	thêe nǎi
Where (to)?	ที่ไหน?	thêe nǎi
From where?	จากที่ไหน?	jàak thêe nǎi

| direction (way) | ทิศทาง | thít thaang |
| to point (~ the way) | ชี้ | chée |

to the left	ทางซ้าย	thaang sáai
to the right	ทางขวา	thaang khwǎa
straight ahead (adv)	ตรงไป	dtrorng bpai
back (e.g. to turn ~)	กลับ	glàp

bend, curve	ทางโค้ง	thaang khóhng
to turn (e.g., ~ left)	เลี้ยว	líeow
to make a U-turn	กลับรถ	glàp rót

to be visible	มองเห็นได้	morng hěn dâai
(mountains, castle, etc.)		
to appear (come into view)	ปรากฏ	bpraa-gòt

stop, halt (e.g., during a trip)	การหยุด	gaan yùt
to rest, to pause (vi)	พัก	phák
rest (pause)	การหยุดพัก	gaan yùt phák
to lose one's way	หลงทาง	lŏng thaang
to lead to ... (ab. road)	ไปสู่	bpai sòo

to came out (e.g., on the highway)	ออกมาถึง	òrk maa thěung
stretch (of the road)	ส่วน	sùan
asphalt	ถนนลาดยาง	thà-nǒn lâat yaang
kerb	ขอบถนน	khòrp thà-nǒn
ditch	คูน้ำ	khoo náam
manhole	ฝาทอระบายน้ำ	fǎa thôr rá-baai nám
roadside (shoulder)	ขางถนน	khâang thà-nǒn
pit, pothole	หลุม	lǔm
to go (on foot)	ไป	bpai
to overtake (vt)	แซง	saeng
step (footstep)	ก้าวเดิน	gâao dern
on foot (adv)	เดินเทา	dern tháo
to block (road)	กีดขวาง	gèet khwǎang
boom gate	แขนกั้นรถ	khǎen gân rót
dead end	ทางตัน	thaang dtan

191. Breaking the law. Criminals. Part 1

bandit	โจร	john
crime	อาชญากรรม	àat-yaa-gam
criminal (person)	อาชญากร	àat-yaa-gon
thief	ขโมย	khà-moi
to steal (vi, vt)	ขโมย	khà-moi
stealing (larceny)	การลักขโมย	gaan lák khà-moi
theft	การลักทรัพย์	gaan lák sáp
to kidnap (vt)	ลักพาตัว	lák phaa dtua
kidnapping	การลักพาตัว	gaan lák phaa dtua
kidnapper	ผู้ลักพาตัว	phôo lák phaa dtua
ransom	ค่าไถ่	khâa thài
to demand ransom	เรียกเงินค่าไถ่	rîak ngern khâa thài
to rob (vt)	ปล้น	bplôn
robbery	การปล้น	gaan bplôn
robber	ขโมยขโจร	khà-moi khà-john
to extort (vt)	รีดไถ	rêet thǎi
extortionist	ผู้รีดไถ	phôo rêet thǎi
extortion	การรีดไถ	gaan rêet thǎi
to murder, to kill	ฆ่า	khâa
murder	ฆาตกรรม	khâat-dtà-gaam
murderer	ฆาตกร	khâat-dtà-gon
gunshot	การยิงปืน	gaan ying bpeun
to fire (~ a shot)	ยิง	ying
to shoot to death	ยิงให้ตาย	ying hâi dtaai

| to shoot (vi) | ยิง | ying |
| shooting | การยิง | gaan ying |

incident (fight, etc.)	เหตุการณ์	hàyt gaan
fight, brawl	การต่อสู้	gaan dtòr sôo
Help!	ขอช่วย	khŏr chûay
victim	เหยื่อ	yèua

to damage (vt)	ทำความเสียหาย	tham khwaam sĭa hăai
damage	ความเสียหาย	khwaam sĭa hăai
dead body, corpse	ศพ	sòp
grave (~ crime)	รายแรง	ráai raeng

to attack (vt)	จู่โจม	jòo johm
to beat (to hit)	ตี	dtee
to beat up	ซ้อม	sórm
to take (rob of sth)	ปล้น	bplôn
to stab to death	แทงให้ตาย	thaeng hâi dtaai
to maim (vt)	ทำให้บาดเจ็บสาหัส	tham hâi bàat jèp săa hàt
to wound (vt)	บาด	bàat

blackmail	การกรรโชก	gaan-gan-chôhk
to blackmail (vt)	กรรโชก	gan-chôhk
blackmailer	ผู้กรรโชก	phôo khòo gan-chôhk

| protection racket | การคุมครอง
ผิดกฎหมาย | gaan khum khrorng
phìt gòt măai |
| racketeer | ผู้ที่หาเงิน
จากกิจกรรมที่
ผิดกฎหมาย | phôo thêe hăa ngern
jàak gìt-jà-gam thêe
phìt gòt măai |

| gangster | เหล่าร้าย | lào ráai |
| mafia | มาเฟีย | maa-fia |

pickpocket	ขโมยล้วงกระเป๋า	khà-moi lúang grà-bpăo
burglar	ขโมยย่องเบา	khà-moi yông bao
smuggling	การลักลอบ	gaan lák-lôrp
smuggler	ผู้ลักลอบ	phôo lák lôrp

forgery	การปลอมแปลง	gaan bplorm bplaeng
to forge (counterfeit)	ปลอมแปลง	bplorm bplaeng
fake (forged)	ปลอม	bplorm

192. Breaking the law. Criminals. Part 2

rape	การข่มขืน	gaan khòm khĕun
to rape (vt)	ข่มขืน	khòm khĕun
rapist	โจรขุมขืน	john khòm khĕun
maniac	คนบ้า	khon bâa

prostitute (fem.)	โสเภณี	sŏh-phay-nee
prostitution	การค้าประเวณี	gaan kháa bprà-way-nee
pimp	แมงดา	maeng-daa
drug addict	ผู้ติดยาเสพติด	phôo dtìt yaa-sàyp-dtìt
drug dealer	พอคายาเสพติด	phôr kháa yaa-sàyp-dtìt

to blow up (bomb)	ระเบิด	rá-bèrt
explosion	การระเบิด	gaan rá-bèrt
to set fire	เผา	phǎo
arsonist	ผู้ลอบวางเพลิง	phôo lôp waang phlerng

terrorism	การก่อการร้าย	gaan gòr gaan ráai
terrorist	ผู้ก่อการราย	phôo gòr gaan ráai
hostage	ตัวประกัน	dtua bprà-gan

to swindle (deceive)	ลอลวง	lôr luang
swindle, deception	การลอลวง	gaan lôr luang
swindler	นักตมตุน	nák dtôm dtǔn

to bribe (vt)	ติดสินบน	dtìt sǐn-bon
bribery	การติดสินบน	gaan dtìt sǐn-bon
bribe	สินบน	sǐn bon

poison	ยาพิษ	yaa phít
to poison (vt)	วางยาพิษ	waang-yaa phít
to poison oneself	กินยาตาย	gin yaa dtaai

| suicide (act) | การฆ่าตัวตาย | gaan khâa dtua dtaai |
| suicide (person) | ผู้ฆ่าตัวตาย | phôo khâa dtua dtaai |

to threaten (vt)	ขู่	khòo
threat	คำขู่	kham khòo
to make an attempt	พยายามฆ่า	phá-yaa-yaam khâa
attempt (attack)	การพยายามฆ่า	gaan phá-yaa-yaam khâa

| to steal (a car) | จี้ | jêe |
| to hijack (a plane) | จี้ | jêe |

| revenge | การแก้แค้น | gaan gâe kháen |
| to avenge (get revenge) | แกแคน | gâe kháen |

to torture (vt)	ทรมาณ	thon-maan
torture	การทรมาน	gaan thor-rá-maan
to torment (vt)	ทำทารุณ	tam taa-run

pirate	โจรสลัด	john sà-làt
hooligan	นักเลง	nák-layng
armed (adj)	มีอาวุธ	mee aa-wút
violence	ความรุนแรง	khwaam run raeng
illegal (unlawful)	ผิดกฎหมาย	phìt gòt mǎai

| spying (espionage) | จารกรรม | jaa-rá-gam |
| to spy (vi) | ลวงความลับ | lúang khwaam láp |

193. Police. Law. Part 1

justice	ยุติธรรม	yút-dtì-tham
court (see you in ~)	ศาล	sǎan
judge	ผู้พิพากษา	phôo phí-phâak-sǎa
jurors	ลูกขุน	lôok khǔn

jury trial	การไต่สวนคดี แบบมีลูกขุน	gaan dtài sŭan khá-dee bàep mee lôok khŭn
to judge, to try (vt)	พิพากษา	phí-phâak-săa
lawyer, barrister	ทนายความ	thá-naai khwaam
defendant	จำเลย	jam loie
dock	คอกจำเลย	khôrk jam loie
charge	ข้อกล่าวหา	khôr glàao hăa
accused	ถูกกล่าวหา	thòok glàao hăa
sentence	การลงโทษ	gaan long thôht
to sentence (vt)	พิพากษา	phí-phâak-săa
guilty (culprit)	ผู้กระทำความผิด	phôo grà-tham khwaam phìt
to punish (vt)	ลงโทษ	long thôht
punishment	การลงโทษ	gaan long thôht
fine (penalty)	ปรับ	bpràp
life imprisonment	การจำคุก ตลอดชีวิต	gaan jam khúk dtà-lòt chee-wít
death penalty	โทษประหาร	thôht-bprà-hăan
electric chair	เก้าอี้ไฟฟ้า	gâo-êe fai-fáa
gallows	ตะแลงแกง	dtà-laeng-gaeng
to execute (vt)	ประหาร	bprà-hăan
execution	การประหาร	gaan bprà-hăan
prison	คุก	khúk
cell	ห้องขัง	hôrng khăng
escort (convoy)	ผู้ควบคุมตัว	phôo khûap khum dtua
prison officer	ผู้คุม	phôo khum
prisoner	นักโทษ	nák thôht
handcuffs	กุญแจมือ	gun-jae meu
to handcuff (vt)	ใส่กุญแจมือ	sài gun-jae meu
prison break	การแหกคุก	gaan hàek khúk
to break out (vi)	แหก	hàek
to disappear (vi)	หายตัวไป	hăai dtua bpai
to release (from prison)	ถูกปล่อยตัว	thòok bplòi dtua
amnesty	การนิรโทษกรรม	gaan ní-rá-thôht gam
police	ตำรวจ	dtam-rùat
police officer	เจ้าหน้าที่ตำรวจ	jâo nâa-thêe dtam-rùat
police station	สถานีตำรวจ	sà-thăa-nee dtam-rùat
truncheon	กระบองตำรวจ	grà-bong dtam-rùat
megaphone (loudhailer)	โทรโข่ง	toh-ra -khòhng
patrol car	รถลาดตระเวน	rót lâat dtrà-wayn
siren	หวอ	wŏr
to turn on the siren	เปิดหวอ	bpèrt wŏr
siren call	เสียงหวอ	sĭang wŏr
crime scene	ที่เกิดเหตุ	thêe gèrt hàyt
witness	พยาน	phá-yaan

freedom	อิสระ	ìt-sà-rà
accomplice	ผู้รวมกระทำผิด	phôo rûam grà-tham phìt
to flee (vi)	หนี	něe
trace (to leave a ~)	รองรอย	rông roi

194. Police. Law. Part 2

search (investigation)	การสืบสวน	gaan sèup sǔan
to look for ...	หาตัว	hǎa dtua
suspicion	ความสงสัย	khwaam sǒng-sǎi
suspicious (e.g., ~ vehicle)	น่าสงสัย	nâa sǒng-sǎi
to stop (cause to halt)	เรียกให้หยุด	rîak hâi yùt
to detain (keep in custody)	กักตัว	gàk dtua

case (lawsuit)	คดี	khá-dee
investigation	การสืบสวน	gaan sèup sǔan
detective	นักสืบ	nák sèup
investigator	นักสอบสวน	nák sòrp sǔan
hypothesis	สันนิษฐาน	sǎn-nít-thǎan

motive	เหตุจูงใจ	hàyt joong jai
interrogation	การสอบปากคำ	gaan sòp bpàak kham
to interrogate (vt)	สอบสวน	sòrp sǔan
to question	ไต่ถาม	thài thǎam
(~ neighbors, etc.)		
check (identity ~)	การตรวจสอบ	gaan dtrùat sòp

round-up (raid)	การรวบตัว	gaan rûap dtua
search (~ warrant)	การตรวจค้น	gaan dtrùat khón
chase (pursuit)	การไล่ล่า	gaan lâi lâa
to pursue, to chase	ไล่ล่า	lâi lâa
to track (a criminal)	สืบ	sèup

arrest	การจับกุม	gaan jàp gum
to arrest (sb)	จับกุม	jàp gum
to catch (thief, etc.)	จับ	jàp
capture	การจับ	gaan jàp

document	เอกสาร	àyk sǎan
proof (evidence)	หลักฐาน	làk thǎan
to prove (vt)	พิสูจน์	phí-sòot
footprint	รอยเท้า	roi tháo
fingerprints	รอยนิ้วมือ	roi níw meu
piece of evidence	หลักฐาน	làk thǎan

alibi	ข้อแก้ตัว	khôr gâe dtua
innocent (not guilty)	พ้นผิด	phón phìt
injustice	ความอยุติธรรม	khwaam a-yút-dtì-tam
unjust, unfair (adj)	ไม่เป็นธรรม	mâi bpen-tham

criminal (adj)	อาชญากร	àat-yaa-gon
to confiscate (vt)	ยึด	yéut
drug (illegal substance)	ยาเสพติด	yaa sàyp dtìt
weapon, gun	อาวุธ	aa-wút

to disarm (vt)	ปลดอาวุธ	bplòt aa-wút
to order (command)	ออกคำสั่ง	òrk kham sàng
to disappear (vi)	หายตัวไป	hăai dtua bpai

law	กฎหมาย	gòt măai
legal, lawful (adj)	ตามกฎหมาย	dtaam gòt măai
illegal, illicit (adj)	ผิดกฎหมาย	phìt gòt măai

responsibility (blame)	ความรับผิดชอบ	khwaam ráp phìt chôp
responsible (adj)	รับผิดชอบ	ráp phìt chôp

NATURE

The Earth. Part 1

195. Outer space

space	อวกาศ	a-wá-gàat
space (as adj)	ทางอวกาศ	thang a-wá-gàat
outer space	อวกาศ	a-wá-gàat
world	โลก	lôhk
universe	จักรวาล	jàk-grà-waan
galaxy	ดาราจักร	daa-raa jàk
star	ดาว	daao
constellation	กลุ่มดาว	glùm daao
planet	ดาวเคราะห์	daao khrór
satellite	ดาวเทียม	daao thiam
meteorite	ดาวตก	daao dtòk
comet	ดาวหาง	daao hăang
asteroid	ดาวเคราะห์น้อย	daao khrór nói
orbit	วงโคจร	wong khoh-jon
to revolve	เวียน	wian
(~ around the Earth)		
atmosphere	บรรยากาศ	ban-yaa-gàat
the Sun	ดวงอาทิตย์	duang aa-thít
solar system	ระบบสุริยะ	rá-bòp sù-rí-yá
solar eclipse	สุริยุปราคา	sù-rí-yú-bpà-raa-kaa
the Earth	โลก	lôhk
the Moon	ดวงจันทร์	duang jan
Mars	ดาวอังคาร	daao ang-khaan
Venus	ดาวศุกร์	daao sùk
Jupiter	ดาวพฤหัส	daao phá-réu-hàt
Saturn	ดาวเสาร์	daao săo
Mercury	ดาวพุธ	daao phút
Uranus	ดาวยูเรนัส	daao-yoo-ray-nát
Neptune	ดาวเนปจูน	daao-nâyp-joon
Pluto	ดาวพลูโต	daao phloo-dtoh
Milky Way	ทางช้างเผือก	thaang cháang phèuak
Great Bear (Ursa Major)	กลุ่มดาวหมีใหญ่	glùm daao měe yài
North Star	ดาวเหนือ	daao něua
Martian	ชาวดาวอังคาร	chaao daao ang-khaan

extraterrestrial (n)	มนุษย์ต่างดาว	má-nút dtàang daao
alien	มนุษย์ตางดาว	má-nút dtàang daao
flying saucer	จานบิน	jaan bin

spaceship	ยานอวกาศ	yaan a-wá-gàat
space station	สถานีอวกาศ	sà-thăa-nee a-wá-gàat
blast-off	การปล่อยจรวด	gaan bplòi jà-rùat

engine	เครื่องยนต์	khrêuang yon
nozzle	ท่อไอพ่น	thôr ai phôn
fuel	เชื้อเพลิง	chéua phlerng

cockpit, flight deck	ที่นั่งคนขับ	thêe nâng khon khàp
aerial	เสาอากาศ	săo aa-gàat
porthole	ช่อง	chôrng
solar panel	อุปกรณ์พลังงานแสงอาทิตย์	ù-bpà-gon phá-lang ngaan săeng aa-thít
spacesuit	ชุดอวกาศ	chút a-wá-gàat

| weightlessness | สภาพไร้น้ำหนัก | sà-phâap rái nám nàk |
| oxygen | อ็อกซิเจน | ók sí jayn |

| docking (in space) | การเทียบท่า | gaan thîap thâa |
| to dock (vi, vt) | เทียบทา | thîap thâa |

observatory	หอดูดาว	hŏr doo daao
telescope	กล้องโทรทรรศน์	glôrng thoh-rá-thát
to observe (vt)	เฝ้าสังเกต	fâo săng-gàyt
to explore (vt)	สำรวจ	săm-rùat

196. The Earth

the Earth	โลก	lôhk
the globe (the Earth)	ลูกโลก	lôok lôhk
planet	ดาวเคราะห์	daao khrór

atmosphere	บรรยากาศ	ban-yaa-gàat
geography	ภูมิศาสตร์	phoo-mí-sàat
nature	ธรรมชาติ	tham-má-châat

globe (table ~)	ลูกโลก	lôok lôhk
map	แผนที่	phăen thêe
atlas	หนังสือแผนที่โลก	năng-sĕu phăen thêe lôhk

Europe	ยุโรป	yú-ròhp
Asia	เอเชีย	ay-chia
Africa	แอฟริกา	àef-rí-gaa
Australia	ออสเตรเลีย	òrt-dtray-lia

America	อเมริกา	a-may-rí-gaa
North America	อเมริกาเหนือ	a-may-rí-gaa nĕua
South America	อเมริกาใต้	a-may-rí-gaa dtâi
Antarctica	แอนตาร์กติกา	aen-dtàak-dtì-gaa
the Arctic	อาร์กติค	àak-dtìk

197. Cardinal directions

north	เหนือ	nĕua
to the north	ทิศเหนือ	thít nĕua
in the north	ที่ภาคเหนือ	thêe phâak nĕua
northern (adj)	ทางเหนือ	thaang nĕua

south	ใต้	dtâi
to the south	ทิศใต้	thít dtâi
in the south	ที่ภาคใต้	thêe phâak dtâi
southern (adj)	ทางใต้	thaang dtâi

west	ตะวันตก	dtà-wan dtòk
to the west	ทิศตะวันตก	thít dtà-wan dtòk
in the west	ที่ภาคตะวันตก	thêe phâak dtà-wan dtòk
western (adj)	ทางตะวันตก	thaang dtà-wan dtòk

east	ตะวันออก	dtà-wan òrk
to the east	ทิศตะวันออก	thít dtà-wan òrk
in the east	ที่ภาคตะวันออก	thêe phâak dtà-wan òrk
eastern (adj)	ทางตะวันออก	thaang dtà-wan òrk

198. Sea. Ocean

sea	ทะเล	thá-lay
ocean	มหาสมุทร	má-hăa sà-mùt
gulf (bay)	อ่าว	àao
straits	ช่องแคบ	chôrng khâep

| land (solid ground) | พื้นดิน | phéun din |
| continent (mainland) | ทวีป | thá-wêep |

island	เกาะ	gòr
peninsula	คาบสมุทร	khâap sà-mùt
archipelago	หมู่เกาะ	mòo gòr

bay, cove	อ่าว	àao
harbour	ท่าเรือ	thâa reua
lagoon	ลากูน	laa-goon
cape	แหลม	lăem

atoll	อะทอลล์	à-thorn
reef	แนวปะการัง	naew bpà-gaa-rang
coral	ปะการัง	bpà gaa-rang
coral reef	แนวปะการัง	naew bpà-gaa-rang

deep (adj)	ลึก	léuk
depth (deep water)	ความลึก	khwaam léuk
abyss	หุบเหวลึก	hùp wăy léuk
trench (e.g. Mariana ~)	ร่องลึกก้นสมุทร	rông léuk gôn sà-mùt

| current (Ocean ~) | กระแสน้ำ | grà-săe náam |
| to surround (bathe) | ล้อมรอบ | lórm rôrp |

| shore | ชายฝั่ง | chaai fàng |
| coast | ชายฝั่ง | chaai fàng |

flow (flood tide)	น้ำขึ้น	náam khêun
ebb (ebb tide)	น้ำลง	náam long
shoal	หาดตื้น	hàat dtêun
bottom (~ of the sea)	กนทะเล	gôn thá-lay

wave	คลื่น	khlêun
crest (~ of a wave)	มวนคลื่น	múan khlêun
spume (sea foam)	ฟองคลื่น	forng khlêun

storm (sea storm)	พายุ	phaa-yú
hurricane	พายุเฮอร์ริเคน	phaa-yú her-rí-khayn
tsunami	คลื่นยักษ์	khlêun yák
calm (dead ~)	ภาวะไร้ลมพัด	phaa-wá rái lom phát
quiet, calm (adj)	สงบ	sà-ngòp

| pole | ขั้วโลก | khûa lôhk |
| polar (adj) | ขั้วโลก | khûa lôhk |

latitude	เส้นรุ้ง	sên rúng
longitude	เส้นแวง	sên waeng
parallel	เส้นขนาน	sên khà-nǎan
equator	เส้นศูนย์สูตร	sên sǒon sòot

sky	ท้องฟ้า	thórng fáa
horizon	ขอบฟ้า	khòrp fáa
air	อากาศ	aa-gàat

lighthouse	ประภาคาร	bprà-phaa-khaan
to dive (vi)	ดำ	dam
to sink (ab. boat)	จม	jom
treasure	สมบัติ	sǒm-bàt

199. Seas & Oceans names

Atlantic Ocean	มหาสมุทรแอตแลนติก	má-hǎa sà-mùt àet-laen-dtìk
Indian Ocean	มหาสมุทรอินเดีย	má-hǎa sà-mùt in-dia
Pacific Ocean	มหาสมุทรแปซิฟิก	má-hǎa sà-mùt bpae-sí-fík
Arctic Ocean	มหาสมุทรอารคติก	má-hǎa sà-mùt aa-ká-dtìk

Black Sea	ทะเลดำ	thá-lay dam
Red Sea	ทะเลแดง	thá-lay daeng
Yellow Sea	ทะเลเหลือง	thá-lay lěuang
White Sea	ทะเลขาว	thá-lay khǎao

Caspian Sea	ทะเลแคสเปียน	thá-lay khâet-bpian
Dead Sea	ทะเลเดดซี	thá-lay dàyt-see
Mediterranean Sea	ทะเลเมดิเตอร์เรเนียน	thá-lay may-dì-dtêr-ray-nian

Aegean Sea	ทะเลเอเจี้ยน	thá-lay ay-jîan
Adriatic Sea	ทะเลเอเดรียติก	thá-lay ay-day-ree-yá-dtìk
Arabian Sea	ทะเลอาหรับ	thá-lay aa-ràp

Sea of Japan	ทะเลญี่ปุ่น	thá-lay yêe-bpùn
Bering Sea	ทะเลเบริง	thá-lay bae-rîng
South China Sea	ทะเลจีนใต้	thá-lay jeen-dtâi
Coral Sea	ทะเลคอรัล	thá-lay khor-ran
Tasman Sea	ทะเลแทสมัน	thá-lay thâet man
Caribbean Sea	ทะเลแคริบเบียน	thá-lay khae-ríp-bian
Barents Sea	ทะเลบาเรนท์	thá-lay baa-rayn
Kara Sea	ทะเลคารา	thá-lay khaa-raa
North Sea	ทะเลเหนือ	thá-lay něua
Baltic Sea	ทะเลบอลติก	thá-lay bon-dtìk
Norwegian Sea	ทะเลนอรเวย์	thá-lay nor-rá-way

200. Mountains

mountain	ภูเขา	phoo khǎo
mountain range	ทิวเขา	thiw khǎo
mountain ridge	สันเขา	sǎn khǎo
summit, top	ยอดเขา	yôrt khǎo
peak	ยอด	yôrt
foot (~ of the mountain)	ตีนเขา	dteun khǎo
slope (mountainside)	ไหลเขา	lài khǎo
volcano	ภูเขาไฟ	phoo khǎo fai
active volcano	ภูเขาไฟมีพลัง	phoo khǎo fai mee phá-lang
dormant volcano	ภูเขาไฟที่ดับแล้ว	phoo khǎo fai thêe dàp láew
eruption	ภูเขาไฟระเบิด	phoo khǎo fai rá-bèrt
crater	ปล่องภูเขาไฟ	bplòng phoo khǎo fai
magma	หินหนืด	hǐn nèut
lava	ลาวา	laa-waa
molten (~ lava)	หลอมเหลว	lǒrm lěo
canyon	หุบเขาลึก	hùp khǎo léuk
gorge	ช่องเขา	chôrng khǎo
crevice	รอยแตกภูเขา	roi dtàek phoo khǎo
abyss (chasm)	หุบเหวลึก	hùp wǎy léuk
pass, col	ทางผ่าน	thaang phàan
plateau	ที่ราบสูง	thêe râap sǒong
cliff	หน้าผา	nâa phǎa
hill	เนินเขา	nern khǎo
glacier	ธารน้ำแข็ง	thaan náam khǎeng
waterfall	น้ำตก	nám dtòk
geyser	น้ำพุร้อน	nám phú rórn
lake	ทะเลสาบ	thá-lay sàap
plain	ที่ราบ	thêe râap
landscape	ภูมิทัศน์	phoom thát
echo	เสียงสะท้อน	sǐang sà-thón

alpinist	นักปีนเขา	nák bpeen khǎo
rock climber	นักไต่เขา	nák dtài khǎo
to conquer (in climbing)	ไต่เขาถึงยอด	dtài khǎo thěung yôt
climb (an easy ~)	การปีนเขา	gaan bpeen khǎo

201. Mountains names

The Alps	เทือกเขาแอลป์	thêuak-khǎo-aen
Mont Blanc	ยอดเขามงบล็อง	yôt khǎo mong-bà-lǒng
The Pyrenees	เทือกเขาไพรีนีส	thêuak khǎo pai-ree-nêet
The Carpathians	เทือกเขาคาร์เพเทียน	thêuak khǎo khaa-phay-thian
The Ural Mountains	เทือกเขายูรัล	thêuak khǎo yoo-ran
The Caucasus Mountains	เทือกเขาคอเคซัส	thêuak khǎo khor-khay-sát
Mount Elbrus	ยอดเขาเอลบรุส	yôt khǎo ayn-brùt
The Altai Mountains	เทือกเขาอัลไต	thêuak khǎo an-dtai
The Tian Shan	เทือกเขาเทียนชาน	thêuak khǎo thian-chaan
The Pamirs	เทือกเขาพาเมียร์	thêuak khǎo paa-mia
The Himalayas	เทือกเขาหิมาลัย	thêuak khǎo hì-maa-lai
Mount Everest	ยอดเขาเอเวอเรสต์	yôt khǎo ay-wer-râyt
The Andes	เทือกเขาแอนดีส	thêuak-khǎo-aen-dèet
Mount Kilimanjaro	ยอดเขาคิลิมันจาโร	yôt khǎo khí-lí-man-jaa-roh

202. Rivers

river	แม่น้ำ	mâe náam
spring (natural source)	แหล่งน้ำแร่	làeng náam râe
riverbed (river channel)	เส้นทางแม่น้ำ	sên thaang mâe náam
basin (river valley)	ลุ่มน้ำ	lûm náam
to flow into ...	ไหลไปสู่...	lǎi bpai sòo...
tributary	สาขา	sǎa-khǎa
bank (river ~)	ฝั่งแม่น้ำ	fàng mâe náam
current (stream)	กระแสน้ำ	grà-sǎe náam
downstream (adv)	ตามกระแสน้ำ	dtaam grà-sǎe náam
upstream (adv)	ทวนน้ำ	thuan náam
inundation	น้ำท่วม	nám thûam
flooding	น้ำทวม	nám thûam
to overflow (vi)	เออล้น	èr lón
to flood (vt)	ทวม	thûam
shallow (shoal)	บริเวณน้ำตื้น	bor-rí-wayn nám dtêun
rapids	กระแสน้ำเชี่ยว	grà-sǎe nám-chîeow
dam	เขื่อน	khèuan
canal	คลอง	khlorng
reservoir (artificial lake)	ที่เก็บกักน้ำ	thêe gèp gàk náam
sluice, lock	ประตูระบายน้ำ	bprà-dtoo rá-baai náam

water body (pond, etc.)	พื้นน้ำ	phéun náam
swamp (marshland)	บึง	beung
bog, marsh	หวย	hûay
whirlpool	น้ำวน	nám won
stream (brook)	ลำธาร	lam thaan
drinking (ab. water)	น้ำดื่มได้	nám dèum dâai
fresh (~ water)	น้ำจืด	nám jèut
ice	น้ำแข็ง	nám khǎeng
to freeze over (ab. river, etc.)	แชแข็ง	châe khǎeng

203. Rivers names

Seine	แม่น้ำเซน	mâe náam sayn
Loire	แม่น้ำลัวร์	mâe-náam lua
Thames	แม่น้ำเทมส์	mâe-náam them
Rhine	แม่น้ำไรน์	mâe-náam rai
Danube	แม่น้ำดานูบ	mâe-náam daa-nôop
Volga	แม่น้ำวอลกา	mâe-náam won-gaa
Don	แม่น้ำดอน	mâe-náam don
Lena	แม่น้ำลีนา	mâe-náam lee-naa
Yellow River	แม่น้ำหวง	mâe-náam hǔang
Yangtze	แม่น้ำแยงซี	mâe-náam yaeng-see
Mekong	แม่น้ำโขง	mâe-náam khǒhng
Ganges	แม่น้ำคงคา	mâe-náam khong-khaa
Nile River	แม่น้ำไนล์	mâe-náam nai
Congo River	แม่น้ำคองโก	mâe-náam khong-goh
Okavango River	แม่น้ำโอคาวังโก	mâe-náam oh-khaa wang goh
Zambezi River	แม่น้ำแซมบีซี	mâe-náam saem bee see
Limpopo River	แม่น้ำลิมโปโป	mâe-náam lim-bpoh-bpoh
Mississippi River	แม่น้ำมิสซิสซิปปี	mâe-náam mít-sít-síp-bpee

204. Forest

forest, wood	ป่าไม้	bpàa máai
forest (as adj)	ป่า	bpàa
thick forest	ป่าทึบ	bpàa théup
grove	ป่าละเมาะ	bpàa lá-mór
forest clearing	ทุ่งโล่ง	thûng lôhng
thicket	ป่าละเมาะ	bpàa lá-mór
scrubland	ป่าละเมาะ	bpàa lá-mór
footpath (troddenpath)	ทางเดิน	thaang dern
gully	รองธาร	rông thaan

tree	ต้นไม้	dtôn máai
leaf	ใบไม้	bai máai
leaves (foliage)	ใบไม้	bai máai
fall of leaves	ใบไม้ร่วง	bai máai rûang
to fall (ab. leaves)	ร่วง	rûang
top (of the tree)	ยอด	yôrt
branch	กิ่ง	gìng
bough	กานไม้	gâan mái
bud (on shrub, tree)	ยอดอ่อน	yôrt òrn
needle (of the pine tree)	เข็ม	khěm
fir cone	ลูกสน	lôok sŏn
tree hollow	โพรงไม้	phrohng máai
nest	รัง	rang
burrow (animal hole)	โพรง	phrohng
trunk	ลำต้น	lam dtôn
root	ราก	râak
bark	เปลือกไม้	bplèuak máai
moss	มอส	môt
to uproot (remove trees or tree stumps)	ถอนราก	thŏrn râak
to chop down	โค่น	khôhn
to deforest (vt)	ตัดไม้ทำลายป่า	dtàt mái tham laai bpàa
tree stump	ตอไม้	dtor máai
campfire	กองไฟ	gorng fai
forest fire	ไฟป่า	fai bpàa
to extinguish (vt)	ดับไฟ	dàp fai
forest ranger	เจ้าหน้าที่ดูแลป่า	jâo nâa-thêe doo lae bpàa
protection	การปกป้อง	gaan bpòk bpôrng
to protect (~ nature)	ปกป้อง	bpòk bpôrng
poacher	นักลอบล่าสัตว์	nák lôrp lâa sàt
steel trap	กับดักเหล็ก	gàp dàk lèk
to gather, to pick (vt)	เก็บ	gèp
to lose one's way	หลงทาง	lŏng thaang

205. Natural resources

natural resources	ทรัพยากร ธรรมชาติ	sáp-pá-yaa-gon tham-má-châat
minerals	แร่	râe
deposits	ตะกอน	dtà-gorn
field (e.g. oilfield)	บ่อ	bòr
to mine (extract)	ขุดแร่	khùt râe
mining (extraction)	การขุดแร่	gaan khùt râe
ore	แร่	râe
mine (e.g. for coal)	เหมืองแร่	mĕuang râe

| shaft (mine ~) | ช่องเหมือง | chôrng mĕuang |
| miner | คนงานเหมือง | khon ngaan mĕuang |

| gas (natural ~) | แก๊ส | gáet |
| gas pipeline | ทอแก๊ส | thôr gáet |

oil (petroleum)	น้ำมัน	nám man
oil pipeline	ทอน้ำมัน	thôr náam man
oil well	บ่อน้ำมัน	bòr náam man
derrick (tower)	ปั้นจั่นขนาดใหญ่	bpân jàn khà-nàat yài
tanker	เรือบรรทุกน้ำมัน	reua ban-thúk nám man

sand	ทราย	saai
limestone	หินปูน	hĭn bpoon
gravel	กรวด	grùat
peat	พีต	phêet
clay	ดินเหนียว	din nĭeow
coal	ถ่านหิน	thàan hĭn

iron (ore)	เหล็ก	lèk
gold	ทอง	thorng
silver	เงิน	ngern
nickel	นิเกิล	ní-gêrn
copper	ทองแดง	thorng daeng

zinc	สังกะสี	săng-gà-sĕe
manganese	แมงกานีส	maeng-gaa-nêet
mercury	ปรอท	bpa -ròrt
lead	ตะกั่ว	dtà-gùa

mineral	แร่	râe
crystal	ผลึก	phà-lèuk
marble	หินอ่อน	hĭn òrn
uranium	ยูเรเนียม	yoo-ray-niam

The Earth. Part 2

weather	สภาพอากาศ	sà-phâap aa-gàat
weather forecast	พยากรณ์	phá-yaa-gon
	สภาพอากาศ	sà-phâap aa-gàat
temperature	อุณหภูมิ	un-hà-phoom
thermometer	ปรอทวัดอุณหภูมิ	bpà-ròrt wát un-hà-phoom
barometer	เครื่องวัดความดัน	khrêuang wát khwaam dan
	บรรยากาศ	ban-yaa-gàat
humid (adj)	ชื้น	chéun
humidity	ความชื้น	khwaam chéun
heat (extreme ~)	ความร้อน	khwaam rórn
hot (torrid)	ร้อน	rórn
it's hot	มันร้อน	man rórn
it's warm	มันอุ่น	man ùn
warm (moderately hot)	อุ่น	ùn
it's cold	อากาศเย็น	aa-gàat yen
cold (adj)	เย็น	yen
sun	ดวงอาทิตย์	duang aa-thít
to shine (vi)	สองแสง	sòrng săeng
sunny (day)	มีแสงแดด	mee săeng dàet
to come up (vi)	ขึ้น	khêun
to set (vi)	ตก	dtòk
cloud	เมฆ	mâyk
cloudy (adj)	มีเมฆมาก	mee mâyk mâak
rain cloud	เมฆฝน	mâyk fŏn
somber (gloomy)	มืดครึ้ม	mêut khréum
rain	ฝน	fŏn
it's raining	ฝนตก	fŏn dtòk
rainy (~ day, weather)	ฝนตก	fŏn dtòk
to drizzle (vi)	ฝนปรอย	fòn bproi
pouring rain	ฝนตกหนัก	fŏn dtòk nàk
downpour	ฝนห่าใหญ่	fŏn hàa yài
heavy (e.g. ~ rain)	หนัก	nàk
puddle	หลมน้ำ	lòm nám
to get wet (in rain)	เปียก	bpìak
fog (mist)	หมอก	mòrk
foggy	หมอกจัด	mòrk jàt
snow	หิมะ	hì-má
it's snowing	หิมะตก	hì-má dtòk

207. Severe weather. Natural disasters

thunderstorm	พายุฟ้าคะนอง	phaa-yú fáa khá-nong
lightning (~ strike)	ฟ้าผ่า	fáa phàa
to flash (vi)	แลบ	lâep
thunder	ฟ้าคะนอง	fáa khá-norng
to thunder (vi)	มีฟ้าคะนอง	mee fáa khá-norng
it's thundering	มีฟ้าร้อง	mee fáa rórng
hail	ลูกเห็บ	lôok hèp
it's hailing	มีลูกเห็บตก	mee lôok hèp dtòk
to flood (vt)	ท่วม	thûam
flood, inundation	น้ำท่วม	nám thûam
earthquake	แผ่นดินไหว	phàen din wǎi
tremor, shoke	ไหว	wǎi
epicentre	จุดเหนือศูนย์แผ่นดินไหว	jùt nɛ̌ua sǒon phàen din wǎi
eruption	ภูเขาไฟระเบิด	phoo khǎo fai rá-bèrt
lava	ลาวา	laa-waa
twister	พายุหมุน	phaa-yú mǔn
tornado	พายุทอร์เนโด	phaa-yú thor-nay-doh
typhoon	พายุไต้ฝุ่น	phaa-yú dtâi fùn
hurricane	พายุเฮอร์ริเคน	phaa-yú her-rí-khayn
storm	พายุ	phaa-yú
tsunami	คลื่นสึนามิ	khlêun sèu-naa-mí
cyclone	พายุไซโคลน	phaa-yú sai-khlohn
bad weather	อากาศไม่ดี	aa-gàat mâi dee
fire (accident)	ไฟไหม้	fai mâi
disaster	ความหายนะ	khwaam hǎa-yá-ná
meteorite	อุกกาบาต	ùk-gaa-bàat
avalanche	หิมะถล่ม	hì-má thà-lòm
snowslide	หิมะถล่ม	hì-má thà-lòm
blizzard	พายุหิมะ	phaa-yú hì-má
snowstorm	พายุหิมะ	phaa-yú hì-má

208. Noises. Sounds

silence (quiet)	ความเงียบ	khwaam ngîap
sound	เสียง	sǐang
noise	เสียงรบกวน	sǐang róp guan
to make noise	ทำเสียง	tam sǐang
noisy (adj)	หนวกหู	nùak hǒo
loudly (to speak, etc.)	เสียงดัง	sǐang dang
loud (voice, etc.)	ดัง	dang
constant (e.g., ~ noise)	ต่อเนื่อง	dtòr nêuang

cry, shout (n)	เสียงตะโกน	sĭang dtà-gohn
to cry, to shout (vi)	ตะโกน	dtà-gohn
whisper	เสียงกระซิบ	sĭang grà síp
to whisper (vi, vt)	กระซิบ	grà síp
barking (dog's ~)	เสียงเห่า	sĭang hào
to bark (vi)	เห่า	hào
groan (of pain, etc.)	เสียงคราง	sĭang khraang
to groan (vi)	คราง	khraang
cough	เสียงไอ	sĭang ai
to cough (vi)	ไอ	ai
whistle	เสียงผิวปาก	sĭang phĭw bpàak
to whistle (vi)	ผิวปาก	phĭw bpàak
knock (at the door)	เสียงเคาะ	sĭang khór
to knock (on the door)	เคาะ	khór
to crack (vi)	เปรี๊ยะ	bpría
crack (cracking sound)	เสียงเปรี๊ยะ	sĭang bpría
siren	เสียงสัญญาณเตือน	sĭang săn-yaan dteuan
whistle (factory ~, etc.)	เสียงนกหวีด	sĭang nók wèet
to whistle (ab. train)	เป่านกหวีด	bpào nók wèet
honk (car horn sound)	เสียงแตร	sĭang dtrae
to honk (vi)	บีบแตร	bèep dtrae

209. Winter

winter (n)	ฤดูหนาว	réu-doo năao
winter (as adj)	ฤดูหนาว	réu-doo năao
in winter	ช่วงฤดูหนาว	chûang réu-doo năao
snow	หิมะ	hì-má
it's snowing	มีหิมะตก	mee hì-má dtòk
snowfall	หิมะตก	hì-má dtòk
snowdrift	กองหิมะ	gong hì-má
snowflake	เกล็ดหิมะ	glèt hì-má
snowball	ก้อนหิมะ	gôn hì-má
snowman	ตุ๊กตาหิมะ	dtúk-gà-dtaa hì-má
icicle	แท่งน้ำแข็ง	thâeng nám khăeng
December	ธันวาคม	than-waa khom
January	มกราคม	mók-gà-raa khom
February	กุมภาพันธ์	gum-phaa phan
frost (severe ~, freezing cold)	ความหนาวๆ	kwaam năao năao
frosty (weather, air)	หนาวจัด	năao jàt
below zero (adv)	ต่ำกว่าศูนย์องศา	dtàm gwàa sŏon ong-săa
first frost	ลมหนาวแรก	lom năao râek
hoarfrost	น้ำค้างแข็ง	náam kháang khăeng
cold (cold weather)	ความหนาว	khwaam năao

it's cold	อากาศหนาว	aa-gàat nǎao
fur coat	เสื้อโค้ทขนสัตว์	sêua khóht khǒn sàt
mittens	ถุงมือ	thǔng meu

to fall ill	เป็นหวัด	bpen wàt
cold (illness)	หวัด	wàt
to catch a cold	เป็นหวัด	bpen wàt

ice	น้ำแข็ง	nám khǎeng
black ice	น้ำแข็งบาง บนพื้นถนน	nám khǎeng baang bon phéun thà-nǒn
to freeze over (ab. river, etc.)	แช่แข็ง	châe khǎeng
ice floe	แพน้ำแข็ง	phae nám khǎeng

skis	สกี	sà-gee
skier	นักสกี	nák sà-gee
to ski (vi)	เล่นสกี	lên sà-gee
to skate (vi)	เลนสเก็ต	lên sà-gèt

Fauna

210. Mammals. Predators

predator	สัตว์กินเนื้อ	sàt gin néua
tiger	เสือ	sĕua
lion	สิงโต	sĭng dtoh
wolf	หมาป่า	mǎa bpàa
fox	หมาจิ้งจอก	mǎa jîng-jòk
jaguar	เสือจากัวร์	sĕua jaa-gua
leopard	เสือดาว	sĕua daao
cheetah	เสือชีตาห์	sĕua chee-dtaa
black panther	เสือดำ	sĕua dam
puma	สิงโตภูเขา	sĭng-dtoh phoo khǎo
snow leopard	เสือดาวหิมะ	sĕua daao hì-má
lynx	แมวป่า	maew bpàa
coyote	โคโยตี้	khoh-yoh-dtêe
jackal	หมาจิ้งจอกทอง	mǎa jîng-jòk thorng
hyena	ไฮยีนา	hai-yee-naa

211. Wild animals

animal	สัตว์	sàt
beast (animal)	สัตว	sàt
squirrel	กระรอก	grà rôk
hedgehog	เมน	mâyn
hare	กระต่ายป่า	grà-dtàai bpàa
rabbit	กระต่าย	grà-dtàai
badger	แบดเจอร์	baet-jer
raccoon	แร็คคูน	ráek khoon
hamster	หนูแฮมสเตอร์	nǒo haem-sà-dtêr
marmot	มารมอต	maa-môt
mole	ตุ่น	dtùn
mouse	หนู	nǒo
rat	หนู	nǒo
bat	คางคาว	kháang khaao
ermine	เออร์มิน	er-min
sable	เซเบิล	say bern
marten	มารเทิน	maa thern
weasel	เพียงพอนสีน้ำตาล	phiang phon sĕe nám dtaan
mink	เพียงพอน	phiang phorn

| beaver | บีเวอร์ | bee-wer |
| otter | นาก | nâak |

horse	ม้า	máa
moose	กวางมูส	gwaang môot
deer	กวาง	gwaang
camel	อูฐ	òot

bison	วัวป่า	wua bpàa
wisent	วัวป่าออรอช	wua bpàa or rôt
buffalo	ควาย	khwaai

zebra	ม้าลาย	máa laai
antelope	แอนทีโลป	aen-thi-lòp
roe deer	กวางโรเดียร์	gwaang roh-dia
fallow deer	กวางแฟลโลว์	gwaang flae-loh
chamois	เลียงผา	liang-phǎa
wild boar	หมูป่า	mǒo bpàa

whale	วาฬ	waan
seal	แมวน้ำ	maew náam
walrus	ช้างน้ำ	cháang náam
fur seal	แมวน้ำมีขน	maew náam mee khǒn
dolphin	โลมา	loh-maa

bear	หมี	mǐe
polar bear	หมีขั้วโลก	mǐe khûa lôhk
panda	หมีแพนดา	mǐe phaen-dâa

monkey	ลิง	ling
chimpanzee	ลิงชิมแปนซี	ling chim-bpaen-see
orangutan	ลิงอุรังอุตัง	ling u-rang-u-dtang
gorilla	ลิงกอริลลา	ling gor-rin-lâa
macaque	ลิงแม็กแคก	ling mâk-khâk
gibbon	ชะนี	chá-nee

elephant	ช้าง	cháang
rhinoceros	แรด	râet
giraffe	ยีราฟ	yee-râaf
hippopotamus	ฮิปโปโปเตมัส	híp-bpoh-bpoh-dtay-mát

| kangaroo | จิงโจ้ | jing-jôh |
| koala (bear) | หมีโคอาล่า | mǐe khoh aa lâa |

mongoose	พังพอน	phang phon
chinchilla	ชินชิลลา	khin-khin laa
skunk	สกังก์	sà-gang
porcupine	เมน	mâyn

212. Domestic animals

cat	แมวตัวเมีย	maew dtua mia
tomcat	แมวตัวผู้	maew dtua phôo
dog	สุนัข	sù-nák

horse	ม้า	máa
stallion (male horse)	ม้าตัวผู้	máa dtua phôo
mare	ม้าตัวเมีย	máa dtua mia

cow	วัว	wua
bull	กระทิง	grà-thing
ox	วัว	wua

sheep (ewe)	แกะตัวเมีย	gàe dtua mia
ram	แกะตัวผู้	gàe dtua phôo
goat	แพะตัวเมีย	pháe dtua mia
billy goat, he-goat	แพะตัวผู้	pháe dtua phôo

| donkey | ลา | laa |
| mule | ลอ | lôr |

pig	หมู	mŏo
piglet	ลูกหมู	lôok mŏo
rabbit	กระต่าย	grà-dtàai

| hen (chicken) | ไก่ตัวเมีย | gài dtua mia |
| cock | ไก่ตัวผู้ | gài dtua phôo |

duck	เป็ดตัวเมีย	bpèt dtua mia
drake	เป็ดตัวผู้	bpèt dtua phôo
goose	ห่าน	hàan

| tom turkey, gobbler | ไก่งวงตัวผู้ | gài nguang dtua phôo |
| turkey (hen) | ไก่งวงตัวเมีย | gài nguang dtua mia |

domestic animals	สัตว์เลี้ยง	sàt líang
tame (e.g. ~ hamster)	เลี้ยง	líang
to tame (vt)	เชื่อง	chêuang
to breed (vt)	ขยายพันธุ์	khà-yăai phan

farm	ฟาร์ม	faam
poultry	สัตว์ปีก	sàt bpèek
cattle	วัวควาย	wua khwaai
herd (cattle)	ฝูง	fŏong

stable	คอกม้า	khôrk máa
pigsty	คอกหมู	khôrk mŏo
cowshed	คอกวัว	khôrk wua
rabbit hutch	คอกกระต่าย	khôrk grà-dtàai
hen house	เล้าไก่	láo gài

213. Dogs. Dog breeds

dog	สุนัข	sù-nák
sheepdog	สุนัขเลี้ยงแกะ	sù-nák líang gàe
German shepherd	เยอรมันเชฟเฟิร์ด	yer-rá-man chayf-fêrt
poodle	พูเดิ้ล	phoo dêrn
dachshund	ดัชชุน	dàt chun
bulldog	บูลด็อก	boon dòrk

boxer	บ็อกเชอร์	bòk-sêr
mastiff	มัสตีฟ	mát-dtèef
Rottweiler	ร็อตไวเลอร์	rót-wai-ler
Doberman	โดเบอรแมน	doh-ber-maen
basset	บาสเช็ต	bàat-sét
bobtail	บ็อบเทล	bòp-thayn
Dalmatian	ดัลเมเชียน	dan-may-chian
cocker spaniel	ค็อกเกอรสเปเนียล	khórk-gêr sà-bpay-nian
Newfoundland	นิวฟาวนด์ฮาวน์ดแลนด์	niw-faao-dà-haao-dà-lǎen
Saint Bernard	เชนตเบอรนารด	sayn ber nâat
husky	ฮัสกี้	hát-gêe
Chow Chow	เชาเชา	chao chao
spitz	สปิตช์	sà-bpìt
pug	ปั๊ก	bpák

214. Sounds made by animals

barking (n)	เสี่ยงเห่า	sìang hào
to bark (vi)	เห่า	hào
to miaow (vi)	รองเหมียว	rórng mǐeow
to purr (vi)	ทำเสี่ยงคราง	tham sìang khraang
to moo (vi)	ร้องมอๆ	rórng mor mor
to bellow (bull)	สงเสี่ยงคำราม	sòng sǐang kham-raam
to growl (vi)	โฮก	hôhk
howl (n)	เสียงหอน	sǐang hǒn
to howl (vi)	หอน	hǒrn
to whine (vi)	ครางหงิงๆ	khraang ngǐng ngǐng
to bleat (sheep)	ร้องแบะๆ	rórng bàe bàe
to oink, to grunt (pig)	รองอูดๆ	rórng ùùt ùùt
to squeal (vi)	รองเสียงแหลม	rórng sǐang lǎem
to croak (vi)	ร้องอ๊บๆ	rórng ôp ôp
to buzz (insect)	หึ่ง	hèung
to chirp (crickets, grasshopper)	ทำเสียงจ๊อกแจ๊ก	tham sǐang jòrk jáek

215. Young animals

cub	ลูกสัตว์	lôok sàt
kitten	ลูกแมว	lôok maew
baby mouse	ลูกหนู	lôok nǒo
puppy	ลูกหมา	lôok mǎa
leveret	ลูกกระต่ายป่า	lôok grà-dtàai bpàa
baby rabbit	ลูกกระตาย	lôok grà-dtàai
wolf cub	ลูกหมาป่า	lôok mǎa bpàa

| fox cub | ลูกหมาจิ้งจอก | lôok măa jîng-jòk |
| bear cub | ลูกหมี | lôok mĕe |

lion cub	ลูกสิงโต	lôok sĭng dtoh
tiger cub	ลูกเสือ	lôok sĕua
elephant calf	ลูกช้าง	lôok cháang

piglet	ลูกหมู	lôok mŏo
calf (young cow, bull)	ลูกวัว	lôok wua
kid (young goat)	ลูกแพะ	lôok pháe
lamb	ลูกแกะ	lôok gàe
fawn (young deer)	ลูกกวาง	lôok gwaang
young camel	ลูกอูฐ	lôok òot

| snakelet (baby snake) | ลูกงู | lôok ngoo |
| froglet (baby frog) | ลูกกบ | lôok gòp |

baby bird	ลูกนก	lôok nók
chick (of chicken)	ลูกไก่	lôok gài
duckling	ลูกเป็ด	lôok bpèt

216. Birds

bird	นก	nók
pigeon	นกพิราบ	nók phí-râap
sparrow	นกกระจิบ	nók grà-jìp
tit (great tit)	นกติ๊ด	nók dtít
magpie	นกสาลิกา	nók săa-lí gaa

raven	นกอีกา	nók ee-gaa
crow	นกกา	nók gaa
jackdaw	นกจำพวกกา	nók jam phûak gaa
rook	นกการูด	nók gaa róok

duck	เป็ด	bpèt
goose	ห่าน	hàan
pheasant	ไก่ฟ้า	gài fáa

eagle	นกอินทรี	nók in-see
hawk	นกเหยี่ยว	nók yìeow
falcon	นกเหยี่ยว	nók yìeow
vulture	นกแร้ง	nók ráeng
condor (Andean ~)	นกแร้งขนาดใหญ่	nók ráeng kà-nàat yài

swan	นกหงส์	nók hŏng
crane	นกกระเรียน	nók grà rian
stork	นกกระสา	nók grà-săa

parrot	นกแก้ว	nók gâew
hummingbird	นกฮัมมิ่งเบิร์ด	nók ham-mîng-bèrt
peacock	นกยูง	nók yoong

| ostrich | นกกระจอกเทศ | nók grà-jòrk-thâyt |
| heron | นกยาง | nók yaang |

flamingo	นกฟลามิงโก	nók flaa-ming-goh
pelican	นกกระทุง	nók-grà-thung
nightingale	นกไนติงเกล	nók-nai-dting-gayn
swallow	นกนางแอ่น	nók naang-àen
thrush	นกเดินดง	nók dern dong
song thrush	นกเดินดงร้องเพลง	nók dern dong rórng phlayng
blackbird	นกเดินดงสีดำ	nók-dern-dong sĕe dam
swift	นกแอ่น	nók àen
lark	นกลาร์ค	nók lâak
quail	นกคุ่ม	nók khûm
woodpecker	นกหัวขวาน	nók hŭa khwǎan
cuckoo	นกดุเหว่า	nók dù hǎy wâa
owl	นกฮูก	nók hôok
eagle owl	นกเค้าใหญ่	nók kháo yài
wood grouse	ไก่ป่า	gài bpàa
black grouse	ไก่ดำ	gài dam
partridge	นกกระทา	nók-grà-thaa
starling	นกกิ้งโครง	nók-gîng-khrohng
canary	นกขุนมิน	nók khà-mîn
hazel grouse	ไก่น้ำตาล	gài nám dtaan
chaffinch	นกจาบ	nók-jàap
bullfinch	นกบูลฟินช์	nók boon-fin
seagull	นกนางนวล	nók naang-nuan
albatross	นกอัลบาทรอส	nók an-baa-thrôt
penguin	นกเพนกวิน	nók phayn-gwin

217. Birds. Singing and sounds

to sing (vi)	ร้องเพลง	rórng phlayng
to call (animal, bird)	ร้อง	rórng
to crow (cock)	ร้องขัน	rórng khǎn
cock-a-doodle-doo	เสียงขัน	sǐang khǎn
to cluck (hen)	ร้องกุ๊กๆ	rórng gúk gúk
to caw (crow call)	ร้องเสียงกาๆ	rórng sǐang gaa gaa
to quack (duck call)	ร้องกาบๆ	rórng gâap gâap
to cheep (vi)	ร้องเสียงจิ๊บ ๆ	rórng sǐang jíp jíp
to chirp, to twitter	ร้องจอกแจก	rórng jòk jáek

218. Fish. Marine animals

bream	ปลาบรีม	bplaa bpreem
carp	ปลาคาร์ป	bplaa khâap
perch	ปลาเพิร์ช	bplaa phêrt
catfish	ปลาดุก	bplaa-dùk
pike	ปลาไพค์	bplaa phai

salmon	ปลาแซลมอน	bplaa saen-morn
sturgeon	ปลาสเตอร์เจียน	bpláa sà-dtêr jian
herring	ปลาเฮอร์ริง	bplaa her-ring
Atlantic salmon	ปลาแซลมอนแอตแลนติก	bplaa saen-mon àet-laen-dtìk
mackerel	ปลาซาบะ	bplaa saa-bà
flatfish	ปลาลิ้นหมา	bplaa lín-măa
zander, pike perch	ปลาไพค์เพิร์ช	bplaa phái phert
cod	ปลาค็อด	bplaa khót
tuna	ปลาทูน่า	bplaa thoo-nâa
trout	ปลาเทราท์	bplaa thrau
eel	ปลาไหล	bplaa lăi
electric ray	ปลากระเบนไฟฟ้า	bplaa grà-bayn-fai-fáa
moray eel	ปลาไหลมอเรย์	bplaa lăi mor-ray
piranha	ปลาปิรันยา	bplaa bpì-ran-yâa
shark	ปลาฉลาม	bplaa chà-lăam
dolphin	โลมา	loh-maa
whale	วาฬ	waan
crab	ปู	bpoo
jellyfish	แมงกะพรุน	maeng gà-phrun
octopus	ปลาหมึก	bplaa mèuk
starfish	ปลาดาว	bplaa daao
sea urchin	หอยเม่น	hŏi mâyn
seahorse	ม้าน้ำ	máa nám
oyster	หอยนางรม	hŏi naang rom
prawn	กุ้ง	gûng
lobster	กุ้งมังกร	gûng mang-gon
spiny lobster	กุ้งมังกร	gûng mang-gon

219. Amphibians. Reptiles

snake	งู	ngoo
venomous (snake)	พิษ	phít
viper	งูแมวเซา	ngoo maew sao
cobra	งูเห่า	ngoo hào
python	งูเหลือม	ngoo lĕuam
boa	งูโบอา	ngoo boh-aa
grass snake	งูเล็กที่ไม่เป็น อันตราย	ngoo lék thêe mâi bpen an-dtà-raai
rattle snake	งูหางกระดิ่ง	ngoo hăang grà-dìng
anaconda	งูอนาคอนดา	ngoo a -naa-khon-daa
lizard	กิ้งก่า	gîng-gàa
iguana	อีกัวน่า	ee gua naa
monitor lizard	กิ้งกามอนิเตอร์	gîng-gàa mor-ní-dtêr
salamander	ซาลาแมนเดอร์	saa-laa-maen-dêr

| chameleon | กิ้งก่าคามิเลียน | gîng-gàa khaa-mí-lian |
| scorpion | แมงป่อง | maeng bpòrng |

turtle	เต่า	dtào
frog	กบ	gòp
toad	คางคก	khaang-kók
crocodile	จระเข้	jor-rá-khây

220. Insects

insect	แมลง	má-laeng
butterfly	ผีเสื้อ	phěe sêua
ant	มด	mót
fly	แมลงวัน	má-laeng wan
mosquito	ยุง	yung
beetle	แมลงปีกแข็ง	má-laeng bpèek khǎeng

wasp	ตัวต่อ	dtòr
bee	ผึ้ง	phêung
bumblebee	ผึ้งบัมเบิลบี	phêung bam-bern bee
gadfly (botfly)	เหลือบ	lèuap

| spider | แมงมุม | maeng mum |
| spider's web | ใยแมงมุม | yai maeng mum |

dragonfly	แมลงปอ	má-laeng bpor
grasshopper	ตั๊กแตน	dták-gà-dtaen
moth (night butterfly)	ผีเสื้อกลางคืน	phěe sêua glaang kheun

cockroach	แมลงสาบ	má-laeng sàap
tick	เห็บ	hèp
flea	หมัด	màt
midge	ริ้น	rín

locust	ตั๊กแตน	dták-gà-dtaen
snail	หอยทาก	hǒi thâak
cricket	จิ้งหรีด	jîng-rèet
firefly	หิงห้อย	hìng-hôi
ladybird	แมลงเต่าทอง	má-laeng dtào thorng
cockchafer	แมงอีนูน	maeng ee noon

leech	ปูลิง	bpling
caterpillar	บุ้ง	bûng
earthworm	ไส้เดือน	sâi deuan
larva	ตัวอ่อน	dtua òrn

221. Animals. Body parts

beak	จงอยปาก	ja-ngoi bpàak
wings	ปีก	bpèek
foot (of the bird)	เท้า	tháo
feathers (plumage)	ขนนก	khǒn nók

| feather | ขนนก | khŏn nók |
| crest | ขนหัว | khŏn hǔa |

gills	เหงือก	ngèuak
spawn	ไข่ปลา	khài-bplaa
larva	ตัวอ่อน	dtua òrn
fin	ครีบ	khrêep
scales (of fish, reptile)	เกล็ด	glèt

fang (canine)	เขี้ยว	khîeow
paw (e.g. cat's ~)	เท้า	tháo
muzzle (snout)	จมูกและปาก	jà-mòok láe bpàak
mouth (cat's ~)	ปาก	bpàak
tail	หาง	hǎang
whiskers	หนวด	nùat

| hoof | กีบ | gèep |
| horn | เขา | khǎo |

carapace	กระดอง	grà dorng
shell (mollusk ~)	เปลือก	bplèuak
eggshell	เปลือกไข่	bplèuak khài

| animal's hair (pelage) | ขน | khŏn |
| pelt (hide) | หนัง | nǎng |

222. Actions of animals

to fly (vi)	บิน	bin
to fly in circles	บินวน	bin-won
to fly away	บินไป	bin bpai
to flap (~ the wings)	กระพือ	grà-pheu

to peck (vi)	จิก	jìk
to sit on eggs	กกไข่	gòk khài
to hatch out (vi)	ฟักตัวออกจากไข่	fák dtua òrk jàak kài
to build a nest	สร้างรัง	sâang rang

to slither, to crawl	เลื้อย	léuay
to sting, to bite (insect)	ต่อย	dtòi
to bite (ab. animal)	กัด	gàt

to sniff (vt)	ดม	dom
to bark (vi)	เห่า	hào
to hiss (snake)	ออกเสียงฟ่อ	òrk sǐang fôr
to scare (vt)	ทำให้...กลัว	tham hâi...glua
to attack (vt)	จู่โจม	jòo johm

to gnaw (bone, etc.)	ขุบ	khòp
to scratch (with claws)	ข่วน	khùan
to hide (vi)	ซ่อน	sôrn

| to play (kittens, etc.) | เล่น | lên |
| to hunt (vi, vt) | ล่า | lâa |

to hibernate (vi)	จำศีล	jam sĕen
to go extinct	สูญพันธุ์	sŏon phan

223. Animals. Habitats

habitat	ที่อยู่อาศัย	thêe yòo aa-săi
migration	การอพยพ	gaan òp-phá-yóp
mountain	ภูเขา	phoo khăo
reef	แนวปะการัง	naew bpà-gaa-rang
cliff	หน้าผา	nâa phăa
forest	ป่า	bpàa
jungle	ป่าดิบชื้น	bpàa dìp chéun
savanna	สะวันนา	sà wan naa
tundra	ทันดรา	than-draa
steppe	ทุ่งหญ้าสเตปป์	thûng yâa sà-dtàyp
desert	ทะเลทราย	thá-lay saai
oasis	โอเอซิส	oh-ay-sít
sea	ทะเล	thá-lay
lake	ทะเลสาบ	thá-lay sàap
ocean	มหาสมุทร	má-hăa sà-mùt
swamp (marshland)	บึง	beung
freshwater (adj)	น้ำจืด	nám jèut
pond	บ่อน้ำ	bòr náam
river	แม่น้ำ	mâe náam
den (bear's ~)	ถ้ำสัตว์	thâm sàt
nest	รัง	rang
tree hollow	โพรงไม้	phrohng máai
burrow (animal hole)	โพรง	phrohng
anthill	รังมด	rang mót

224. Animal care

zoo	สวนสัตว์	sŭan sàt
nature reserve	เขตสงวน ธรรมชาติ	khàyt sà-ngŭan tham-má-châat
breeder (cattery, kennel, etc.)	ที่ขยายพันธุ์	thêe khà-yăi phan
open-air cage	กรง	grorng
cage	กรง	grorng
kennel	บ้านสุนัข	baan sù-nák
dovecot	บ้านนกพิราบ	bâan nók phí-râap
aquarium (fish tank)	ตู้ปลา	dtôo bplaa
dolphinarium	บ่อโลมา	bòr loh-maa
to breed (animals)	ขยายพันธุ์	khà-yăi phan
brood, litter	ลูกสัตว์	lôok sàt

to tame (vt)	เชื่อง	chêuang
to train (animals)	ฝึก	fèuk
feed (fodder, etc.)	อาหาร	aa-hǎan
to feed (vt)	ให้อาหาร	hâi aa-hǎan

pet shop	ร้านสัตว์เลี้ยง	ráan sàt líang
muzzle (for dog)	ตะกร้อปาก	dtà-grôr bpàak
collar (e.g., dog ~)	ปลอกคอ	bplòrk kor
name (of an animal)	ชื่อ	chêu
pedigree (dog's ~)	สายพันธุ์	sǎai phan

225. Animals. Miscellaneous

pack (wolves)	ฝูง	fǒong
flock (birds)	ฝูง	fǒong
shoal, school (fish)	ฝูง	fǒong
herd (horses)	ฝูง	fǒong

| male (n) | ตัวผู้ | dtua phôo |
| female (n) | ตัวเมีย | dtua mia |

hungry (adj)	หิว	hǐw
wild (adj)	ป่า	bpàa
dangerous (adj)	อันตราย	an-dtà-raai

226. Horses

| horse | ม้า | máa |
| breed (race) | พันธุ์ | phan |

| foal | ลูกม้า | lôok máa |
| mare | มาตัวเมีย | máa dtua mia |

mustang	ม้าป่า	máa bpàa
pony	ม้าพันธุ์เล็ก	máa phan lék
draught horse	มางาน	máa ngaan

| mane | แผงคอ | phǎeng khor |
| tail | หาง | hǎang |

hoof	กีบ	gèep
horseshoe	เกือก	gèuak
to shoe (vt)	ใส่เกือก	sài gèuak
blacksmith	ช่างเหล็ก	châang lèk

saddle	อานม้า	aan máa
stirrup	โกลน	glohn
bridle	บังเหียน	bang hǐan
reins	สายบังเหียน	sǎai bang hǐan
whip (for riding)	แส่	sâe
rider	นักขี่ม้า	nák khèe máa
to saddle up (vt)	ใส่อานม้า	sài aan máa

to mount a horse	ขึ้นขี่ม้า	khêun khèe máa
gallop	การควบม้า	gaan khûap máa
to gallop (vi)	ควบม้า	khûap máa
trot (n)	การเหยาะย่าง	gaan yòr yâang
at a trot (adv)	แบบเหยาะย่าง	bàep yòr yâang
to go at a trot	เหยาะย่าง	yòr yâang

| racehorse | ม้าแข่ง | máa khàeng |
| horse racing | การแข่งม้า | gaan khàeng máa |

stable	คอกม้า	khôrk máa
to feed (vt)	ให้อาหาร	hâi aa-hǎan
hay	หญ้าแห้ง	yâa hâeng
to water (animals)	ให้น้ำ	hâi nám
to wash (horse)	ทำความสะอาด	tham khwaam sà-àat

horse-drawn cart	รถเทียมม้า	rót thiam máa
to graze (vi)	เล็มหญ้า	lem yâa
to neigh (vi)	ร้องฮี่ๆ	rórng híí híí
to kick (to buck)	ถีบ	thèep

Flora

tree	ต้นไม้	dtôn máai
deciduous (adj)	ผลัดใบ	phlàt bai
coniferous (adj)	สน	sǒn
evergreen (adj)	ซึ่งเขียวชอุ่ม	sêung khǐeow chá-ùm
	ตลอดปี	dtà-lòrt bpee
apple tree	ต้นแอปเปิ้ล	dtôn àep-bpêrn
pear tree	ตูนแพร	dtôn phae
sweet cherry tree	ตูนเชอรี่ป่า	dtôn cher-rêe bpàa
sour cherry tree	ตูนเชอรี่	dtôn cher-rêe
plum tree	ตนพลัม	dtôn phlam
birch	ตูนเบิร์ช	dtôn bèrt
oak	ตูนโอ๊ค	dtôn óhk
linden tree	ตนไมดอกเหลือง	dtôn máai dòrk lěuang
aspen	ตูนแอสเพน	dtôn ae sà-phayn
maple	ตนเมเปิล	dtôn may bpêrn
spruce	ตูนเฟอร์	dtôn fer
pine	ตูนเกี๊ยะ	dtôn gía
larch	ตนลารช	dtôn lâat
fir tree	ตูนเฟอร์	dtôn fer
cedar	ตนซีดาร์	dtôn-see-daa
poplar	ตูนปอปลาร์	dtôn bpor-bplaa
rowan	ตนโรแวน	dtôn-roh-waen
willow	ตูนวิลโลว์	dtôn win-loh
alder	ตนอัลเดอร์	dtôn an-dêr
beech	ตูนบีช	dtôn bèet
elm	ตนเอลม	dtôn elm
ash (tree)	ตูนแอช	dtôn aesh
chestnut	ตนเกาลัด	dtôn gao lát
magnolia	ตูนแมกูโนเลีย	dtôn mâek-noh-lia
palm tree	ตูนปาลม	dtôn bpaam
cypress	ตนไซเปรส	dtôn-sai-bpràyt
mangrove	ตูนโกงกาง	dtôn gohng gaang
baobab	ตูนเบาบับ	dtôn bao-bàp
eucalyptus	ตูนยูคาลิปตัส	dtôn yoo-khaa-líp-dtàt
sequoia	ตนสนซีค้วยา	dtôn sǒn see kua yaa

228. Shrubs

bush	พุ่มไม้	phûm máai
shrub	ต้นไม้พุ่ม	dtôn máai phûm
grapevine	ต้นองุ่น	dtôn a-ngùn
vineyard	ไร่องุ่น	râi a-ngùn
raspberry bush	พุ่มราสเบอร์รี่	phûm râat-ber-rêe
blackcurrant bush	พุ่มแบล็คเคอร์แรนท์	phûm blàek-khêr-raen
redcurrant bush	พุ่มเรดเคอร์แรนท	phûm râyt-khêr-raen
gooseberry bush	พุ่มกูสเบอร์รี	phûm gòot-ber-rêe
acacia	ต้นอาเคเชีย	dtôn aa-khay-chia
barberry	ต้นบาร์เบอร์รี่	dtôn baa-ber-rêe
jasmine	มะลิ	má-lí
juniper	ต้นจูนิเปอร์	dtôn joo-ní-bper
rosebush	พุ่มกุหลาบ	phûm gù làap
dog rose	พุ่มดอกโรส	phûm dòrk-rôht

229. Mushrooms

mushroom	เห็ด	hèt
edible mushroom	เห็ดกินได้	hèt gin dâai
poisonous mushroom	เห็ดมีพิษ	hèt mee pít
cap	ดอกเห็ด	dòrk hèt
stipe	ต้นเห็ด	dtôn hèt
cep, penny bun	เห็ดพอร์ชินี	hèt phor chí nee
orange-cap boletus	เห็ดพอร์ชินีดอกเหลือง	hèt phor chí nee dòrk lěuang
birch bolete	เห็ดตับเตาที่ขึ้นบนต้นเบิร์ช	hèt dtàp dtào thêe khêun bon dtôn-bèrt
chanterelle	เห็ดก๋อเหลือง	hèt gòr lěuang
russula	เห็ดตะไค	hèt dtà khai
morel	เห็ดมอเรล	hèt mor rayn
fly agaric	เห็ดพิษหมวกแดง	hèt phít mùak daeng
death cap	เห็ดระโงกหิน	hèt rá ngôhk hǐn

230. Fruits. Berries

fruit	ผลไม้	phǒn-lá-máai
fruits	ผลไม	phǒn-lá-máai
apple	แอปเปิ้ล	àep-bpêrn
pear	ลูกแพร	lôok phae
plum	พลัม	phlam
strawberry (garden ~)	สตรอว์เบอร์รี่	sà-dtror-ber-rêe
sour cherry	เชอรรี่	cher-rêe

| sweet cherry | เชอรรี่ป่า | cher-rêe bpàa |
| grape | องุ่น | a-ngùn |

raspberry	ราสเบอรร์รี่	râat-ber-rêe
blackcurrant	แบล็คเคอรแรนท์	blàek khêr-raen
redcurrant	เรดเคอรแรนท์	râyt-khêr-raen
gooseberry	กูสเบอรี่	gòot-ber-rêe
cranberry	แครนเบอรรี่	khraen-ber-rêe

orange	ส้ม	sôm
tangerine	สมแมนดาริน	sôm maen daa rin
pineapple	สับปะรด	sàp-bpà-rót
banana	กล้วย	glûay
date	อินทผลัม	in-thá-phâ-lam

lemon	เลมอน	lay-mon
apricot	แอปริคอท	ae-bprì-khôrt
peach	ลูกทอ	lôok thór
kiwi	กีวี	gee wee
grapefruit	สมโอ	sôm oh

berry	เบอรรี่	ber-rêe
berries	เบอรรี่	ber-rêe
cowberry	คาวเบอรรี่	khaao-ber-rêe
wild strawberry	สตรอวเบอรรี่ป่า	sá-dtrorw ber-rêe bpàa
bilberry	บิลเบอรรี่	bil-ber-rêe

231. Flowers. Plants

| flower | ดอกไม้ | dòrk máai |
| bouquet (of flowers) | ชอดอกไม้ | chôr dòrk máai |

rose (flower)	ดอกกุหลาบ	dòrk gù làap
tulip	ดอกทิวลิป	dòrk thiw-líp
carnation	ดอกคารเนชั่น	dòrk khaa-nay-chân
gladiolus	ดอกแกลดิโอลัส	dòrk gaen-dì-oh-lát

cornflower	ดอกคอรน์ฟลาววเวอร์	dòrk khon-flaao-wer
harebell	ดอกกระฆัง	dòrk rá-khang
dandelion	ดอกแดนดิไลออน	dòrk daen-dì-lai-on
camomile	ดอกคาโมมายล	dòrk khaa-moh maai

aloe	ว่านหางจระเข้	wâan-hăang-jor-rá-khây
cactus	ตะบองเพชร	dtà-bong-phét
rubber plant, ficus	ตนเลียบ	dtôn lîap

lily	ดอกลิลี่	dòrk lí-lêe
geranium	ดอกเจอราเนียม	dòrk jer-raa-niam
hyacinth	ดอกไฮอะซินท์	dòrk hai-a-sin

mimosa	ดอกไมยราบ	dòrk mai râap
narcissus	ดอกนารซิสซัส	dòrk naa-sít-sát
nasturtium	ดอกแนสเตอรชัม	dòrk nâet-dtêr-cham
orchid	ดอกกล้วยไม	dòrk glûay máai

| peony | ดอกโบตั๋น | dòrk boh-dtǎn |
| violet | ดอกไวโอเล็ต | dòrk wai-oh-lét |

pansy	ดอกแพนซี	dòrk phaen-see
forget-me-not	ดอกฟอรเก็ตมีน็อต	dòrk for-gèt-mee-nót
daisy	ดอกเดซี	dòrk day see

poppy	ดอกป๊อปปี้	dòrk bpóp-bpêe
hemp	กัญชา	gan chaa
mint	สะระแหน่	sà-rá-nàe

| lily of the valley | ดอกลิลลี่แห่งหุบเขา | dòrk lí-lá-lêe hàeng hùp khǎo |
| snowdrop | ดอกหยาดหิมะ | dòrk yàat hì-má |

nettle	ตำแย	dtam-yae
sorrel	ซอรเรล	sor-rayn
water lily	บัว	bua
fern	เฟิร์น	fern
lichen	ไลเคน	lai-khayn

conservatory (greenhouse)	เรือนกระจก	reuan grà-jòk
lawn	สนามหญ้า	sà-nǎam yâa
flowerbed	สนามดอกไม้	sà-nǎam-dòrk-máai

plant	พืช	phêut
grass	หญ้า	yâa
blade of grass	ใบหญ้า	bai yâa

leaf	ใบไม้	bai máai
petal	กลีบดอก	glèep dòrk
stem	ลำตัน	lam dtôn
tuber	หัวใต้ดิน	hǔa dtâi din

| young plant (shoot) | ต้นอ่อน | dtôn òrn |
| thorn | หนาม | nǎam |

to blossom (vi)	บาน	baan
to fade, to wither	เหี่ยว	hìeow
smell (odour)	กลิ่น	glìn
to cut (flowers)	ตัด	dtàt
to pick (a flower)	เด็ด	dèt

232. Cereals, grains

grain	เมล็ด	má-lét
cereal crops	ธัญพืช	than-yá-phêut
ear (of barley, etc.)	รวงขาว	ruang khâao

wheat	ข้าวสาลี	khâao sǎa-lee
rye	ข้าวไรย์	khâao rai
oats	ข้าวโอต	khâao óht
millet	ข้าวฟาง	khâao fâang
barley	ข้าวบาร์เลย์	khâao baa-lây
maize	ข้าวโพด	khâao-phôht

| rice | ข้าว | khâao |
| buckwheat | บัควีท | bàk-wêet |

pea plant	ถั่วลันเตา	thùa-lan-dtao
kidney bean	ถั่วรูปไต	thùa rôop dtai
soya	ถั่วเหลือง	thùa lěuang
lentil	ถั่วเลนทิล	thùa layn thin
beans (pulse crops)	ถั่ว	thùa

233. Vegetables. Greens

| vegetables | ผัก | phàk |
| greens | ผักใบเขียว | phàk bai khǐeow |

tomato	มะเขือเทศ	má-khěua thâyt
cucumber	แตงกวา	dtaeng-gwaa
carrot	แครอท	khae-rót
potato	มันฝรั่ง	man fà-ràng
onion	หัวหอม	hǔa hǒrm
garlic	กระเทียม	grà-thiam

cabbage	กะหล่ำปลี	gà-làm bplee
cauliflower	ดอกกะหล่ำ	dòrk gà-làm
Brussels sprouts	กะหล่ำดาว	gà-làm-daao
broccoli	บร็อคโคลี่	bròrk-khoh-lêe

beetroot	บีท	beet
aubergine	มะเขือยาว	má-khěua-yaao
marrow	ซูกินี	soo-gi -nee
pumpkin	ฟักทอง	fák-thorng
turnip	หัวผักกาด	hǔa-phàk-gàat

parsley	ผักชีฝรั่ง	phàk chee fà-ràng
dill	ผักชีลาว	phàk-chee-laao
lettuce	ผักกาดหอม	phàk gàat hǒrm
celery	คื่นช่าย	khêun-châai
asparagus	หน่อไม้ฝรั่ง	nòr máai fà-ràng
spinach	ผักโขม	phàk khǒm

pea	ถั่วลันเตา	thùa-lan-dtao
beans	ถั่ว	thùa
maize	ข้าวโพด	khâao-phôht
kidney bean	ถั่วรูปไต	thùa rôop dtai

pepper	พริกหยวก	phrík-yùak
radish	หัวผักกาดแดง	hǔa-phàk-gàat daeng
artichoke	อาร์ติโชค	aa dtì chôhk

REGIONAL GEOGRAPHY

234. Western Europe

Europe	ยุโรป	yú-ròhp
European Union	สหภาพยุโรป	sà-hà phâap yú-rôhp
European (n)	คนยุโรป	khon yú-rôhp
European (adj)	ยุโรป	yú-ròhp
Austria	ประเทศออสเตรีย	bprà-thâyt òt-dtria
Austrian (masc.)	คนออสเตรีย	khon òt-dtria
Austrian (fem.)	คนออสเตรีย	khon òt-dtria
Austrian (adj)	ออสเตรีย	òrt-dtria
Great Britain	บริเตนใหญ่	brì-dtayn yài
England	ประเทศอังกฤษ	bprà-thâyt ang-grìt
British (masc.)	คนอังกฤษ	khon ang-grìt
British (fem.)	คนอังกฤษ	khon ang-grìt
English, British (adj)	อังกฤษ	ang-grìt
Belgium	ประเทศเบลเยียม	bprà-thâyt bayn-yiam
Belgian (masc.)	คนเบลเยียม	khon bayn-yiam
Belgian (fem.)	คนเบลเยียม	khon bayn-yiam
Belgian (adj)	เบลเยียม	bayn-yiam
Germany	ประเทศเยอรมนี	bprà-thâyt yer-rá-ma-nee
German (masc.)	คนเยอรมัน	khon yer-rá-man
German (fem.)	คนเยอรมัน	khon yer-rá-man
German (adj)	เยอรมัน	yer-rá-man
Netherlands	ประเทศเนเธอร์แลนด์	bprà-thâyt nay-ther-laen
Holland	ประเทศฮอลแลนด์	bprà-thâyt hon-laen
Dutch (masc.)	คนเนเธอร์แลนด์	khon nay-ther-laen
Dutch (fem.)	คนเนเธอร์แลนด์	khon nay-ther-laen
Dutch (adj)	เนเธอร์แลนด์	nay-ter-laen
Greece	ประเทศกรีซ	bprà-thâyt grèet
Greek (masc.)	คนกรีก	khon grèek
Greek (fem.)	คนกรีก	khon grèek
Greek (adj)	กรีซ	grèet
Denmark	ประเทศเดนมาร์ก	bprà-thâyt dayn-màak
Dane (masc.)	คนเดนมาร์ก	khon dayn-màak
Dane (fem.)	คนเดนมาร์ก	khon dayn-màak
Danish (adj)	เดนมาร์ก	dayn-màak
Ireland	ประเทศไอร์แลนด์	bprà-thâyt ai-laen
Irish (masc.)	คนไอริช	khon ai-rít
Irish (fem.)	คนไอริช	khon ai-rít
Irish (adj)	ไอร์แลนด์	ai-laen

Iceland	ประเทศไอซ์แลนด์	bprà-thâyt ai-laen
Icelander (masc.)	คนไอซ์แลนด์	khon ai-laen
Icelander (fem.)	คนไอซ์แลนด์	khon ai-laen
Icelandic (adj)	ไอซ์แลนด์	ai-laen

Spain	ประเทศสเปน	bprà-thâyt sà-bpayn
Spaniard (masc.)	คนสเปน	khon sà-bpayn
Spaniard (fem.)	คนสเปน	khon sà-bpayn
Spanish (adj)	สเปน	sà-bpayn

Italy	ประเทศอิตาลี	bprà-thâyt i-dtaa-lee
Italian (masc.)	คนอิตาเลียน	khon i-dtaa-lian
Italian (fem.)	คนอิตาเลียน	khon i-dtaa-lian
Italian (adj)	อิตาลี	i-dtaa-lee

Cyprus	ประเทศไซปรัส	bprà-thâyt sai-bpràt
Cypriot (masc.)	คนไซปรัส	khon sai-bpràt
Cypriot (fem.)	คนไซปรัส	khon sai-bpràt
Cypriot (adj)	ไซปรัส	sai-bpràt

Malta	ประเทศมอลตา	bprà-thâyt mon-dtaa
Maltese (masc.)	คนมอลตา	khon mon-dtaa
Maltese (fem.)	คนมอลตา	khon mon-dtaa
Maltese (adj)	มอลตา	mon-dtâa

Norway	ประเทศนอร์เวย์	bprà-thâyt nor-way
Norwegian (masc.)	คนนอร์เวย์	khon nor-way
Norwegian (fem.)	คนนอร์เวย์	khon nor-way
Norwegian (adj)	นอร์เวย	nor-way

Portugal	ประเทศโปรตุเกส	bprà-thâyt bproh-dtù-gàyt
Portuguese (masc.)	คนโปรตุเกส	khon bproh-dtù-gàyt
Portuguese (fem.)	คนโปรตุเกส	khon bproh-dtù-gàyt
Portuguese (adj)	โปรตุเกส	bproh-dtù-gàyt

Finland	ประเทศฟินแลนด์	bprà-thâyt fin-laen
Finn (masc.)	คนฟินแลนด์	khon fin-laen
Finn (fem.)	คนฟินแลนด์	khon fin-laen
Finnish (adj)	ฟินแลนด์	fin-laen

France	ประเทศฝรั่งเศส	bprà-thâyt fà-ràng-sàyt
French (masc.)	คนฝรั่งเศส	khon fà-ràng-sàyt
French (fem.)	คนฝรั่งเศส	khon fà-ràng-sàyt
French (adj)	ฝรั่งเศส	fà-ràng-sàyt

Sweden	ประเทศสวีเดน	bprà-thâyt sà-wĕe-dayn
Swede (masc.)	คนสวีเดน	khon sà-wĕe-dayn
Swede (fem.)	คนสวีเดน	khon sà-wĕe-dayn
Swedish (adj)	สวีเดน	sà-wĕe-dayn

Switzerland	ประเทศสวิตเซอร์แลนด์	bprà-thâyt sà-wìt-sêr-laen
Swiss (masc.)	คนสวิส	khon sà-wìt
Swiss (fem.)	คนสวิส	khon sà-wìt
Swiss (adj)	สวิส	sà-wìt
Scotland	ประเทศสก็อตแลนด์	bprà-thâyt sà-gòt-laen
Scottish (masc.)	คนสก็อต	khon sà-gòt

| Scottish (fem.) | คนสก็อต | khon sà-gòt |
| Scottish (adj) | สก็อตแลนด์ | sà-gòt-laen |

Vatican City	นครรัฐวาติกัน	ná-khon rát waa-dtì-gan
Liechtenstein	ประเทศลิกเตนสไตน์	bprà-thâyt lík-tay-ná-sà-dtai
Luxembourg	ประเทศลักเซมเบิร์ก	bprà-thâyt lák-saym-bèrk
Monaco	ประเทศโมนาโก	bprà-thâyt moh-naa-goh

235. Central and Eastern Europe

Albania	ประเทศแอลเบเนีย	bprà-thâyt aen-bay-nia
Albanian (masc.)	คนแอลเบเนีย	khon aen-bay-nia
Albanian (fem.)	คนแอลเบเนีย	khon aen-bay-nia
Albanian (adj)	แอลเบเนีย	aen-bay-nia

Bulgaria	ประเทศบัลแกเรีย	bprà-thâyt ban-gae-ria
Bulgarian (masc.)	คนบัลแกเรีย	khon ban-gae-ria
Bulgarian (fem.)	คนบัลแกเรีย	khon ban-gae-ria
Bulgarian (adj)	บัลแกเรีย	ban-gae-ria

Hungary	ประเทศฮังการี	bprà-thâyt hang-gaa-ree
Hungarian (masc.)	คนฮังการี	khon hang-gaa-ree
Hungarian (fem.)	คนฮังการี	khon hang-gaa-ree
Hungarian (adj)	ฮังการี	hang-gaa-ree

Latvia	ประเทศลัตเวีย	bprà-thâyt lát-wia
Latvian (masc.)	คนลัตเวีย	khon lát-wia
Latvian (fem.)	คนลัตเวีย	khon lát-wia
Latvian (adj)	ลัตเวีย	lát-wia

Lithuania	ประเทศลิทัวเนีย	bprà-thâyt lí-thua-nia
Lithuanian (masc.)	คนลิทัวเนีย	khon lí-thua-nia
Lithuanian (fem.)	คนลิทัวเนีย	khon lí-thua-nia
Lithuanian (adj)	ลิทัวเนีย	lí-thua-nia

Poland	ประเทศโปแลนด์	bprà-thâyt bpoh-laen
Pole (masc.)	คนโปแลนด์	khon bpoh-laen
Pole (fem.)	คนโปแลนด์	khon bpoh-laen
Polish (adj)	โปแลนด์	bpoh-laen

Romania	ประเทศโรมาเนีย	bprà-thâyt roh-maa-nia
Romanian (masc.)	คนโรมาเนีย	khon roh-maa-nia
Romanian (fem.)	คนโรมาเนีย	khon roh-maa-nia
Romanian (adj)	โรมาเนีย	roh-maa-nia

Serbia	ประเทศเซอร์เบีย	bprà-thâyt sêr-bia
Serbian (masc.)	คนเซอร์เบีย	khon sêr-bia
Serbian (fem.)	คนเซอร์เบีย	khon sêr-bia
Serbian (adj)	เซอร์เบีย	sêr-bia

Slovakia	ประเทศสโลวาเกีย	bprà-thâyt sà-loh-waa-gia
Slovak (masc.)	คนสโลวาเกีย	khon sà-loh-waa-gia
Slovak (fem.)	คนสโลวาเกีย	khon sà-loh-waa-gia
Slovak (adj)	สโลวาเกีย	sà-loh-waa-gia

Croatia	ประเทศโครเอเชีย	bprà-thâyt khroh-ay-chia
Croatian (masc.)	คนโครเอเชีย	khon khroh-ay-chia
Croatian (fem.)	คนโครเอเชีย	khon khroh-ay-chia
Croatian (adj)	โครเอเชีย	khroh-ay-chia

Czech Republic	ประเทศเช็กเกีย	bprà-thâyt chék-gia
Czech (masc.)	คนเช็ก	khon chék
Czech (fem.)	คนเช็ก	khon chék
Czech (adj)	เช็กเกีย	chék-gia

Estonia	ประเทศเอสโตเนีย	bprà-thâyt àyt-dtoh-nia
Estonian (masc.)	คนเอสโตเนีย	khon àyt-dtoh-nia
Estonian (fem.)	คนเอสโตเนีย	khon àyt-dtoh-nia
Estonian (adj)	เอสโตเนีย	àyt-dtoh-nia

Bosnia and Herzegovina	ประเทศบอสเนีย และเฮอร์เซโกวีนา	bprà-thâyt bòt-nia láe her-say-goh-wí-naa
North Macedonia	ประเทศมาซิโดเนีย	bprà-thâyt maa-sí-doh-nia
Slovenia	ประเทศสโลวีเนีย	bprà-thâyt sà-loh-wee-nia
Montenegro	ประเทศมอนเตเนโกร	bprà-thâyt mon-dtay-nay-groh

236. Former USSR countries

Azerbaijan	ประเทศอาเซอร์ไบจาน	bprà-thâyt aa-sêr-bai-jaan
Azerbaijani (masc.)	คนอาเซอร์ไบจาน	khon aa-sêr-bai-jaan
Azerbaijani (fem.)	คนอาเซอร์ไบจาน	khon aa-sêr-bai-jaan
Azerbaijani, Azeri (adj)	อาเซอร์ไบจาน	aa-sêr-bai-jaan

Armenia	ประเทศอาร์เมเนีย	bprà-thâyt aa-may-nia
Armenian (masc.)	คนอาร์เมเนีย	khon aa-may-nia
Armenian (fem.)	คนอาร์เมเนีย	khon aa-may-nia
Armenian (adj)	อาร์เมเนีย	aa-may-nia

Belarus	ประเทศเบลารุส	bprà-thâyt blao-rút
Belarusian (masc.)	คนเบลารุส	khon blao-rút
Belarusian (fem.)	คนเบลารุส	khon blao-rút
Belarusian (adj)	เบลารุส	blao-rút

Georgia	ประเทศจอร์เจีย	bprà-thâyt jor-jia
Georgian (masc.)	คนจอร์เจีย	khon jor-jia
Georgian (fem.)	คนจอร์เจีย	khon jor-jia
Georgian (adj)	จอร์เจีย	jor-jia

Kazakhstan	ประเทศคาซัคสถาน	bprà-thâyt khaa-sák-sà-thǎan
Kazakh (masc.)	คนคาซัคสถาน	khon khaa-sák-sà-thǎan
Kazakh (fem.)	คนคาซัคสถาน	khon khaa-sák-sà-thǎan
Kazakh (adj)	คาซัคสถาน	khaa-sák-sà-thǎan

Kirghizia	ประเทศคีรกีซสถาน	bprà-thâyt khee-gèet-à-thǎan
Kirghiz (masc.)	คนคีรกีซสถาน	khon khee-gèet-sà-thǎan
Kirghiz (fem.)	คนคีรกีซสถาน	khon khee-gèet-sà-thǎan
Kirghiz (adj)	คีรกีซสถาน	khee-gèet-sà-thǎan

Moldova, Moldavia	ประเทศมอลโดวา	bprà-thâyt mon-doh-waa
Moldavian (masc.)	คนมอลโดวา	khon mon-doh-waa
Moldavian (fem.)	คนมอลโดวา	khon mon-doh-waa
Moldavian (adj)	มอลโดวา	mon-doh-waa

Russia	ประเทศรัสเซีย	bprà-thâyt rát-sia
Russian (masc.)	คนรัสเซีย	khon rát-sia
Russian (fem.)	คนรัสเซีย	khon rát-sia
Russian (adj)	รัสเซีย	rát-sia

Tajikistan	ประเทศทาจิกิสถาน	bprà-thâyt thaa-jì-gìt-thǎan
Tajik (masc.)	คนทาจิกิสถาน	khon thaa-jì-gìt-thǎan
Tajik (fem.)	คนทาจิกิสถาน	khon thaa-jì-gìt-thǎan
Tajik (adj)	ทาจิกิสถาน	thaa-jì-gìt-thǎan

Turkmenistan	ประเทศเติรกเมนิสถาน	bprà-thâyt dtèrk-may-nít-thǎan
Turkmen (masc.)	คนเติร์กเมนิสถาน	khon dtèrk-may-nít-thǎan
Turkmen (fem.)	คนเติรกเมนิสถาน	khon dtèrk-may-nít-thǎan
Turkmenian (adj)	เติรกเมนิสถาน	dtèrk-may-nít-thǎan

Uzbekistan	ประเทศอุซเบกิสถาน	bprà-thâyt ùt-bay-gìt-thǎan
Uzbek (masc.)	คนอุซเบกิสถาน	khon ùt-bay-gìt-thǎan
Uzbek (fem.)	คนอุซเบกิสถาน	khon ùt-bay-gìt-thǎan
Uzbek (adj)	อุซเบกิสถาน	ùt-bay-gìt-thǎan

Ukraine	ประเทศยูเครน	bprà-thâyt yoo-khrayn
Ukrainian (masc.)	คนยูเครน	khon yoo-khrayn
Ukrainian (fem.)	คนยูเครน	khon yoo-khrayn
Ukrainian (adj)	ยูเครน	yoo-khrayn

237. Asia

| Asia | เอเชีย | ay-chia |
| Asian (adj) | เอเชีย | ay-chia |

Vietnam	ประเทศเวียดนาม	bprà-thâyt wîat-naam
Vietnamese (masc.)	คนเวียดนาม	khon wîat-naam
Vietnamese (fem.)	คนเวียดนาม	khon wîat-naam
Vietnamese (adj)	เวียดนาม	wîat-naam

India	ประเทศอินเดีย	bprà-thâyt in-dia
Indian (masc.)	คนอินเดีย	khon in-dia
Indian (fem.)	คนอินเดีย	khon in-dia
Indian (adj)	อินเดีย	in-dia

Israel	ประเทศอิสราเอล	bprà-thâyt ìt-sà-rǎa-ayn
Israeli (masc.)	คนอิสราเอล	khon ìt-sà-rǎa-ayn
Israeli (fem.)	คนอิสราเอล	khon ìt-sà-rǎa-ayn
Israeli (adj)	อิสราเอล	ìt-sà-rǎa-ayn

Jew (n)	คนยิว	khon yiw
Jewess (n)	คนยิว	khon yiw
Jewish (adj)	ยิว	yiw

Indonesia	ประเทศอินโดนีเซีย	bprà-thâyt in-doh-nee-sia
Jordan	ประเทศจอร์แดน	bprà-thâyt jor-daen
Iraq	ประเทศอิรัก	bprà-thâyt i-rák
Iran	ประเทศอิหราน	bprà-thâyt i-ràan
Cambodia	ประเทศกัมพูชา	bprà-thâyt gam-phoo-chaa
Kuwait	ประเทศคูเวต	bprà-thâyt khoo-wâyt
Laos	ประเทศลาว	bprà-thâyt laao
Myanmar	ประเทศเมียนมาร์	bprà-thâyt mian-maa
Nepal	ประเทศเนปาล	bprà-thâyt nay-bpaan
United Arab Emirates	สหรัฐอาหรับเอมิเรตส์	sà-hà-rát aa-ràp ay-mí-râyt
Syria	ประเทศซีเรีย	bprà-thâyt see-ria
Palestine	ปาเลสไตน์	bpaa-lâyt-dtai
South Korea	เกาหลีใต้	gao-lěe dtâi
North Korea	เกาหลีเหนือ	gao-lěe něua

238. North America

United States of America	สหรัฐอเมริกา	sà-hà-rát a-may-rí-gaa
American (masc.)	คนอเมริกา	khon a-may-rí-gaa
American (fem.)	คนอเมริกา	khon a-may-rí-gaa
American (adj)	อเมริกา	a-may-rí-gaa
Canada	ประเทศแคนาดา	bprà-thâyt khae-naa-daa
Canadian (masc.)	คนแคนาดา	khon khae-naa-daa
Canadian (fem.)	คนแคนาดา	khon khae-naa-daa
Canadian (adj)	แคนาดา	khae-naa-daa
Mexico	ประเทศเม็กซิโก	bprà-thâyt mék-sí-goh
Mexican (masc.)	คนเม็กซิโก	khon mék-sí-goh
Mexican (fem.)	คนเม็กซิโก	khon mék-sí-goh
Mexican (adj)	เม็กซิโก	mék-sí-goh

239. Central and South America

Argentina	ประเทศอาร์เจนตินา	bprà-thâyt aa-jayn-dtì-naa
Argentinian (masc.)	คนอาร์เจนตินา	khon aa-jayn-dtì-naa
Argentinian (fem.)	คนอาร์เจนตินา	khon aa-jayn-dtì-naa
Argentinian (adj)	อาร์เจนตินา	aa-jayn-dtì-naa
Brazil	ประเทศบราซิล	bprà-thâyt braa-sin
Brazilian (masc.)	คนบราซิล	khon braa-sin
Brazilian (fem.)	คนบราซิล	khon braa-sin
Brazilian (adj)	บราซิล	braa-sin
Colombia	ประเทศโคลัมเบีย	bprà-thâyt khoh-lam-bia
Colombian (masc.)	คนโคลัมเบีย	khon khoh-lam-bia
Colombian (fem.)	คนโคลัมเบีย	khon khoh-lam-bia
Colombian (adj)	โคลัมเบีย	khoh-lam-bia
Cuba	ประเทศคิวบา	bprà-thâyt khiw-baa

Cuban (masc.)	คนคิวบา	khon khiw-baa
Cuban (fem.)	คนคิวบา	khon khiw-baa
Cuban (adj)	คิวบา	khiw-baa

Chile	ประเทศชิลี	bprà-thâyt chí-lee
Chilean (masc.)	คนชิลี	khon chí-lee
Chilean (fem.)	คนชิลี	khon chí-lee
Chilean (adj)	ชิลี	chí-lee

Bolivia	ประเทศโบลิเวีย	bprà-thâyt boh-lí-wia
Venezuela	ประเทศเวเนซุเอลา	bprà-thâyt way-nay-sú-ay-laa
Paraguay	ประเทศปารากวัย	bprà-thâyt bpaa-raa-gwai
Peru	ประเทศเปรู	bprà-thâyt bpay-roo
Suriname	ประเทศซูรินาม	bprà-thâyt soo-rí-naam
Uruguay	ประเทศอุรุกวัย	bprà-thâyt u-rúk-wai
Ecuador	ประเทศเอกวาดอร์	bprà-thâyt ay-gwaa-dor

The Bahamas	ประเทศบาฮามาส	bprà-thâyt baa-haa-mâat
Haiti	ประเทศเฮติ	bprà-thâyt hay-dtì
Dominican Republic	สาธารณรัฐโดมินิกัน	săa-thaa-rá-ná rát doh-mí-ní-gan
Panama	ประเทศปานามา	bprà-thâyt bpaa-naa-maa
Jamaica	ประเทศจาเมกา	bprà-thâyt jaa-may-gaa

240. Africa

Egypt	ประเทศอียิปต์	bprà-thâyt bprà-thâyt ee-yíp
Egyptian (masc.)	คนอียิปต์	khon ee-yíp
Egyptian (fem.)	คนอียิปต์	khon ee-yíp
Egyptian (adj)	อียิปต์	ee-yíp

Morocco	ประเทศมอร็อคโค	bprà-thâyt mor-rók-khoh
Moroccan (masc.)	คนมอร็อคโค	khon mor-rók-khoh
Moroccan (fem.)	คนมอร็อคโค	khon mor-rók-khoh
Moroccan (adj)	มอร็อคโค	mor-rók-khoh

Tunisia	ประเทศตูนิเซีย	bprà-thâyt dtoo-ní-sia
Tunisian (masc.)	คนตูนิเซีย	khon dtoo-ní-sia
Tunisian (fem.)	คนตูนิเซีย	khon dtoo-ní-sia
Tunisian (adj)	ตูนิเซีย	dtoo-ní-sia

Ghana	ประเทศกานา	bprà-thâyt gaa-naa
Zanzibar	ประเทศแซนซิบาร์	bprà-thâyt saen-sí-baa
Kenya	ประเทศเคนยา	bprà-thâyt khayn-yâa
Libya	ประเทศลิเบีย	bprà-thâyt lí-bia
Madagascar	ประเทศมาดากัสการ์	bprà-thâyt maa-daa-gàt-gaa

Namibia	ประเทศนามิเบีย	bprà-thâyt naa-mí-bia
Senegal	ประเทศเซเนกัล	bprà-thâyt say-nay-gan
Tanzania	ประเทศแทนซาเนีย	bprà-thâyt thaen-saa-nia
South Africa	ประเทศแอฟริกาใต้	bprà-thâyt àef-rí-gaa dtâi
African (masc.)	คนแอฟริกา	khon àef-rí-gaa
African (fem.)	คนแอฟริกา	khon àef-rí-gaa
African (adj)	แอฟริกา	àef-rí-gaa

241. Australia. Oceania

Australia	ประเทศออสเตรเลีย	bprà-thâyt òt-dtray-lia
Australian (masc.)	คนออสเตรเลีย	khon òt-dtray-lia
Australian (fem.)	คนออสเตรเลีย	khon òt-dtray-lia
Australian (adj)	ออสเตรเลีย	òrt-dtray-lia
New Zealand	ประเทศนิวซีแลนด์	bprà-thâyt niw-see-laen
New Zealander (masc.)	คนนิวซีแลนด์	khon niw-see-laen
New Zealander (fem.)	คนนิวซีแลนด์	khon niw-see-laen
New Zealand (as adj)	นิวซีแลนด์	niw-see-laen
Tasmania	ประเทศแทสเมเนีย	bprà-thâyt thâet-may-nia
French Polynesia	เฟรนช์โปลินีเซีย	frayn-bpoh-lí-nee-sia

242. Cities

Amsterdam	อัมสเตอร์ดัม	am-sà-dtêr-dam
Ankara	อังคารา	ang-khaa-raa
Athens	เอเธนส์	ay-thayn
Baghdad	แบกแดด	bàek-dàet
Bangkok	กรุงเทพฯ	grung thâyp
Barcelona	บาร์เซโลนา	baa-say-loh-naa
Beijing	ปักกิ่ง	bpàk-gìng
Beirut	เบรุต	bay-rút
Berlin	เบอร์ลิน	ber-lin
Mumbai (Bombay)	มุมไบ	mum-bai
Bonn	บอนน์	bon
Bordeaux	บอร์โด	bor doh
Bratislava	บราติสลาวา	braa-dtìt-laa-waa
Brussels	บรัสเซล	bràt-sayn
Bucharest	บูคาเรสต์	boo-khaa-râyt
Budapest	บูดาเปส	boo-daa-bpàyt
Cairo	ไคโร	khai-roh
Kolkata (Calcutta)	คัลคัตตา	khan-khát-dtaa
Chicago	ชิคาโก	chí-khaa-goh
Copenhagen	โคเปนเฮเกน	khoh-bpayn-hay-gayn
Dar-es-Salaam	ดาร์เอสซาลาม	daa àyt saa laam
Delhi	เดลี	day-lee
Dubai	ดูไบ	doo-bai
Dublin	ดับลิน	dàp-lin
Düsseldorf	ดุสเซลดอร์ฟ	dùt-sayn-dòf
Florence	ฟลอเรนซ์	flor-rayn
Frankfurt	แฟรงค์เฟิร์ท	fraeng-fêrt
Geneva	เจนีวา	jay-nee-waa
The Hague	เดอะเฮก	dùh hêyk
Hamburg	แฮมเบิร์ก	haem-bèrk

Hanoi	ฮานอย	haa-noi
Havana	ฮาวานา	haa waa-naa
Helsinki	เฮลซิงกิ	hayn-sing-gì
Hiroshima	ฮิโรชิมา	hí-roh-chí-mâa
Hong Kong	ฮองกง	hôrng-gong

Istanbul	อิสตันบูล	ìt-dtan-boon
Jerusalem	เยรูซาเลม	yay-roo-saa-laym
Kyiv	เคียฟ	khîaf
Kuala Lumpur	กัวลาลัมเปอร์	gua-laa lam-bper
Lisbon	ลิสบอน	lít-bon
London	ลอนดอน	lon-don
Los Angeles	ลอสแองเจลิส	lôt-aeng-jay-lít
Lyons	ลียง	lee-yong

Madrid	มาดริด	maa-drìt
Marseille	มารกเซย	màak-soie
Mexico City	เม็กซิโกซิตี้	mék-sí-goh sí-dtêe
Miami	ไมอามี่	mai-aa-mêe
Montreal	มอนทรีออล	mon-three-on
Moscow	มอสโกว	mor-sà-goh
Munich	มิวนิค	miw-ník

Nairobi	ไนโรบี	nai-roh-bee
Naples	เนเปิลส์	nay-bpern
New York	นิวยอร์ค	niw-yôk
Nice	นิช	nít
Oslo	ออสโล	òrt-loh
Ottawa	อ็อตตาวา	òt-dtaa-waa

Paris	ปารีส	bpaa-rêet
Prague	ปราก	bpràak
Rio de Janeiro	ริโอเอจาเนโร	rí-oh-ay jaa-nay-roh
Rome	โรม	rohm

Saint Petersburg	เซนต์ปิเตอร์สเบิร์ก	sayn bpì-dtèrt-bèrk
Seoul	โซล	sohn
Shanghai	เซี่ยงไฮ้	sîang-hái
Singapore	สิงคโปร์	sïng-khá-bpoh
Stockholm	สต็อกโฮล์ม	sà-dtòk-hohm
Sydney	ซิดนีย์	sít-nee

Taipei	ไทเป	thai-bpay
Tokyo	โตเกียว	dtoh-gieow
Toronto	โตรอนโต	dtoh-ron-dtoh
Venice	เวนิส	way-nít
Vienna	เวียนนา	wian-naa
Warsaw	วอร์ซอว	wor-sor
Washington	วอชิงตัน	wor ching dtan

243. Politics. Government. Part 1

| politics | การเมือง | gaan meuang |
| political (adj) | ทางการเมือง | thang gaan meuang |

politician	นักการเมือง	nák gaan meuang
state (country)	รัฐ	rát
citizen	พลเมือง	phon-lá-meuang
citizenship	สัญชาติ	săn-châat

national emblem	ตราประจำชาติ	dtraa bprà-jam châat
national anthem	เพลงชาติ	phlayng châat

government	รัฐบาล	rát-thà-baan
head of state	ผู้นำประเทศ	phôo nam bprà-thâyt
parliament	รัฐสภา	rát-thà-sà-phaa
party	พรรคการเมือง	phák gaan meuang

capitalism	ทุนนิยม	thun ní-yom
capitalist (adj)	แบบทุนนิยม	bàep thun ní-yom

socialism	สังคมนิยม	săng-khom ní-yom
socialist (adj)	แบบสังคมนิยม	bàep săng-khom ní-yom

communism	ลัทธิคอมมิวนิสต์	lát-thí khom-miw-nít
communist (adj)	แบบคอมมิวนิสต์	bàep khom-miw-nít
communist (n)	คนคอมมิวนิสต	khon khom-miw-nít

democracy	ประชาธิปไตย	bprà-chaa-thíp-bpà-dtai
democrat	ผู้นิยมประชาธิปไตย	phôo ní-yom bprà-chaa-típ-bpà-dtai
democratic (adj)	แบบประชาธิปไตย	bàep bprà-chaa-thíp-bpà-dtai
Democratic party	พรรคประชาธิปัตย์	phák bprà-chaa-tí-bpàt

liberal (n)	ผู้เอียงเสรีนิยม	phôo iang săy-ree ní-yom
Liberal (adj)	แบบเสรีนิยม	bàep săy-ree ní-yom

conservative (n)	ผู้เอียงอนุรักษ์นิยม	phôo iang a-nú rák ní-yom
conservative (adj)	แบบอนุรักษ์นิยม	bàep a-nú rák ní-yom

republic (n)	สาธารณรัฐ	săa-thaa-rá-ná rát
republican (n)	รีพับลิกัน	ree pháp lí gan
Republican party	พรรครีพับลิกัน	phák ree-pháp-lí-gan

elections	การเลือกตั้ง	gaan lêuak dtâng
to elect (vt)	เลือก	lêuak
elector, voter	ผู้ออกเสียงลงคะแนน	phôo òrk sĭang long khá-naen
election campaign	การรณรงค์หาเสียง	gaan ron-ná-rorng hăa sĭang

voting (n)	การออกเสียงลงคะแนน	gaan òrk sĭang long khá-naen
to vote (vi)	ลงคะแนน	long khá-naen
suffrage, right to vote	สิทธิในการเลือกตั้ง	sìt-thí nai gaan lêuak dtâng

candidate	ผู้สมัคร	phôo sà-màk
to run for (~ President)	ลงสมัคร	long sà-màk
campaign	การรณรงค์	gaan ron-ná-rorng
opposition (as adj)	ฝ่ายค้าน	fàai kháan
opposition (n)	ฝ่ายค้าน	fàai kháan
visit	การเยือน	gaan yeuan
official visit	การเยือนอย่างเป็นทางการ	gaan yeuan yàang bpen thaang gaan

international (adj)	แบบสากล	bàep săa-gon
negotiations	การเจรจา	gaan jayn-rá-jaa
to negotiate (vi)	เจรจา	jayn-rá-jaa

244. Politics. Government. Part 2

society	สังคม	săng-khom
constitution	รัฐธรรมนูญ	rát-thà-tham-má-noon
power (political control)	อำนาจ	am-nâat
corruption	การทุจริตคอรัปชั่น	gaan thút-jà-rìt khor-ráp-chân

| law (justice) | กฎหมาย | gòt măai |
| legal (legitimate) | ทางกฎหมาย | thaang gòt măai |

| justice (fairness) | ความยุติธรรม | khwaam yút-dtì-tham |
| just (fair) | เป็นธรรม | bpen tham |

committee	คณะกรรมการ	khá-ná gam-má-gaan
bill (draft law)	ราง	râang
budget	งบประมาณ	ngóp bprà-maan
policy	นโยบาย	ná-yoh-baai
reform	ปฏิรูป	bpà-dtì rôop
radical (adj)	รุนแรง	run raeng

power (strength, force)	กำลัง	gam-lang
powerful (adj)	ทรงพลัง	song phá-lang
supporter	ผู้สนับสนุน	phôo sà-nàp-sà-nŭn
influence	อิทธิพล	ìt-thí pon

regime (e.g. military ~)	ระบอบการปกครอง	rá-bòrp gaan bpòk khrorng
conflict	ความขัดแยง	khwaam khàt yáeng
conspiracy (plot)	การคบคิด	gaan khóp khít
provocation	การยั่วยุ	gaan yûa yú

to overthrow (regime, etc.)	ล้มล้าง	lóm láang
overthrow (of a government)	การลม	gaan lóm
revolution	ปฏิวัติ	bpà-dtì-wát

coup d'état	รัฐประหาร	rát-thà-bprà-hăan
military coup	การยึดอำนาจ	gaan yéut am-nâat
	ดวยกำลังทหาร	dûay gam-lang thá-hăan

crisis	วิกฤติ	wí-grìt
economic recession	ภาวะเศรษฐกิจถดถอย	phaa-wá sàyt-thà-gìt thòt thŏi
demonstrator (protester)	ผู้ประทวง	phôo bprà-thúang
demonstration	การประทวง	gaan bprà-thúang
martial law	กฎอัยการศึก	gòt ai-yá-gaan sèuk
military base	ฐานทัพ	thăan tháp

| stability | ความมั่นคง | khwaam mân-khong |
| stable (adj) | มั่นคง | mân khong |

| exploitation | การขูดรีด | gaan khòot rêet |
| to exploit (workers) | ขูดรีด | khòot rêet |

racism	ดูถินิยมเชื้อชาติ	khá-dtì ní-yom chéua châat
racist	ผู้เหยียดผิว	phôo yìat phǐw
fascism	ลัทธิฟาสซิสต์	lát-thí fâat-sít
fascist	ผู้นิยมลัทธิฟาสซิสต์	phôo ní-yom lát-thí fâat-sít

245. Countries. Miscellaneous

foreigner	คนต่างชาติ	khon dtàang châat
foreign (adj)	ต่างชาติ	dtàang châat
abroad (in a foreign country)	ต่างประเทศ	dtàang bprà-thâyt

emigrant	ผู้อพยพ	phôo òp-phá-yóp
emigration	การอพยพ	gaan òp-phá-yóp
to emigrate (vi)	อพยพ	òp-phá-yóp

the West	ตะวันตก	dtà-wan dtòk
the East	ตะวันออก	dtà-wan òrk
the Far East	ตะวันออกไกล	dtà-wan òrk glai

civilization	อารยธรรม	aa-rá-yá-tham
humanity (mankind)	มนุษยชาติ	má-nút-sà-yá-châat
the world (earth)	โลก	lôhk

| peace | ความสงบสุข | khwaam sà-ngòp-sùk |
| worldwide (adj) | ทั่วโลก | thûa lôhk |

homeland	บ้านเกิด	bâan gèrt
people (population)	ประชาชน	bprà-chaa chon
population	ประชากร	bprà-chaa gon
people (a lot of ~)	ประชาชน	bprà-chaa chon

| nation (people) | ชาติ | châat |
| generation | รุ่น | rûn |

territory (area)	อาณาเขต	aa-naa khàyt
region	ภูมิภาค	phoo-mí-phâak
state (part of a country)	รัฐ	rát

tradition	ธรรมเนียม	tham-niam
custom (tradition)	ประเพณี	bprà-phay-nee
ecology	นิเวศวิทยา	ní-wâyt wít-thá-yaa

| Indian (Native American) | อินเดียนแดง | in-dian daeng |
| Gypsy (masc.) | คนยิปซี | khon yíp-see |

| Gypsy (fem.) | คนยิปซี | khon yíp-see |
| Gypsy (adj) | ยิปซี | yíp see |

| empire | จักรวรรดิ | jàk-grà-wàt |
| colony | อาณานิคม | aa-naa ní-khom |

slavery	การใช้แรงงานทาส	gaan chái raeng ngaan thâat
invasion	การบุกรุก	gaan bùk rúk
famine	ความอดอยาก	khwaam òt yàak

246. Major religious groups. Confessions

| religion | ศาสนา | sàat-sà-năa |
| religious (adj) | ศาสนา | sàat-sà-năa |

faith, belief	ศรัทธา	sàt-thaa
to believe (in God)	นับถือ	náp thĕu
believer	ผู้ศรัทธา	phôo sàt-thaa

atheism	อเทวนิยม	a-thay-wá ní-yom
atheist	ผู้เชื่อว่า	phôo chêua wâa
	ไม่มีพระเจ้า	mâi mee phrá jâo

Christianity	ศาสนาคริสต์	sàat-sà-năa khrít
Christian (n)	ผู้นับถือ	phôo náp thĕu
	ศาสนาคริสต์	sàat-sà-năa khrít
Christian (adj)	ศาสนาคริสต์	sàat-sà-năa khrít

Catholicism	ศาสนาคาธอลิก	sàat-sà-năa khaa-thor-lík
Catholic (n)	ผู้นับถือ	phôo náp thĕu
	ศาสนาคาธอลิก	sàat-sà-năa khaa-thor-lík
Catholic (adj)	คาธอลิก	khaa-thor-lík

Protestantism	ศาสนา	sàat-sà-năa
	โปรแตสแตนท์	bproh-dtàet-dtaen
Protestant Church	โบสถ์นิกาย	bòht ní-gaai
	โปรแตสแตนท์	bproh-dtàet-dtaen
Protestant (n)	ผู้นับถือศาสนา	phôo náp thĕu sàat-sà-năa
	โปรแตสแตนท์	bproh-dtàet-dtaen

Orthodoxy	ศาสนาออร์ทอดอกซ์	sàat-sà-năa or-thor-dòrk
Orthodox Church	โบสถ์ศาสนาออร์ทอดอกซ์	bòht sàat-sà-năa or-thor-dòrk
Orthodox (n)	ผู้นับถือ	phôo náp thĕu
	ศาสนาออร์ทอดอกซ์	sàat-sà-năa or-thor-dòrk

Presbyterianism	นิกายเพรสไบทีเรียน	ní-gaai phrayt-bai-thee-rian
Presbyterian Church	โบสถ์นิกาย	bòht ní-gaai
	เพรสไบทีเรียน	phrayt-bai-thee-rian
Presbyterian (n)	ผู้นับถือนิกาย	phôo náp thĕu ní-gaai
	เพรสไบทีเรียน	phrayt bai thee rian

Lutheranism	นิกายลูเทอแรน	ní-gaai loo-thay-a-răen
Lutheran (n)	ผู้นับถือนิกาย	phôo náp thĕu ní-gaai
	ลูเทอแรน	loo-thay-a-răen

Baptist Church	นิกายแบ๊บติสท์	ní-gaai báep-dtìt
Baptist (n)	ผู้นับถือนิกาย	phôo náp thĕu ní-gaai
	แบบติสท	báep-dtìt

Anglican Church	โบสถ์นิกายแองกลิกัน	bòht ní-gaai ae-ngók-lí-gan
Anglican (n)	ผู้นับถือนิกาย	phôo náp thĕu ní-gaai
	แองกลิกัน	ae ngók lí gan
Mormonism	นิกายมอร์มอน	ní-gaai mor-mon
Mormon (n)	ผู้นับถือนิกาย	phôo náp thĕu ní-gaai
	มอรมอน	mor-mon

| Judaism | ศาสนายิว | sàat-sà-năa yiw |
| Jew (n) | คนยิว | khon yiw |

Buddhism	ศาสนาพุธ	sàat-sà-năa phút
Buddhist (n)	ผู้นับถือ	phôo náp thěu
	ศาสนาพุธ	sàat-sà-năa phút

Hinduism	ศาสนาฮินดู	sàat-sà-năa hin-doo
Hindu (n)	ผู้นับถือ	phôo náp thěu
	ศาสนาฮินดู	sàat-sà-năa hin-doo

Islam	ศาสนาอิสลาม	sàat-sà-năa ìt-sà-laam
Muslim (n)	ผู้นับถือ	phôo náp thěu
	ศาสนาอิสลาม	sàat-sà-năa ìt-sà-laam
Muslim (adj)	มุสลิม	mút-sà-lim

Shiah Islam	ศาสนา	sàat-sà-năa
	อิสลามนิกายชีอะฮ์	ìt-sà-laam ní-gaai shi-à
Shiite (n)	ผู้นับถือนิกายชีอะฮ์	phôo náp thěu ní-gaai shi-à

Sunni Islam	ศาสนา	sàat-sà-năa
	อิสลามนิกายซุนนี	ìt-sà-laam ní-gaai sun-nee
Sunnite (n)	ผู้นับถือนิกาย	phôo náp thěu ní-gaai
	ซุนนี	sun-nee

247. Religions. Priests

| priest | นักบวช | nák bùat |
| the Pope | พระสันตะปาปา | phrá săn-dtà-bpaa-bpaa |

monk, friar	พระ	phrá
nun	แม่ชี	mâe chee
pastor	ศาสนาจารย์	sàat-sà-năa-jaan

abbot	เจ้าอาวาส	jâo aa-wâat
vicar (parish priest)	เจาอาวาส	jâo aa-wâat
bishop	มุขนายก	múk naa-yók
cardinal	พระคาร์ดินัล	phrá khaa-dì-nan

preacher	นักเทศน์	nák thâyt
preaching	การเทศนา	gaan thâyt-sà-năa
parishioners	ลูกวัด	lôok wát

believer	ผู้ศรัทธา	phôo sàt-thaa
atheist	ผู้เชื่อว่า	phôo chêua wâa
	ไม่มีพระเจ้า	mâi mee phrá jâo

248. Faith. Christianity. Islam

Adam	อาดัม	aa-dam
Eve	เอวา	ay-waa
God	พระเจ้า	phrá jâo

| the Lord | พระเจ้า | phrá jâo |
| the Almighty | พระผู้เป็นเจ้า | phrá phôo bpen jâo |

sin	บาป	bàap
to sin (vi)	ทำบาป	tham bàap
sinner (masc.)	คนบาป	khon bàap
sinner (fem.)	คนบาป	khon bàap

| hell | นรก | ná-rók |
| paradise | สวรรค์ | sà-wăn |

| Jesus | พระเยซู | phrá yay-soo |
| Jesus Christ | พระเยซูคริสต์ | phrá yay-soo khrít |

the Holy Spirit	พระจิต	phrá jìt
the Saviour	พระผู้ไถ	phrá phôo thài
the Virgin Mary	พระนางมารีย์	phrá naang maa ree
	พรหมจารี	phrom-má-jaa-ree

the Devil	มาร	maan
devil's (adj)	ของมาร	khŏrng maan
Satan	ซาตาน	saa-dtaan
satanic (adj)	ซาตาน	saa-dtaan

angel	เทวทูต	thay-wá-thôot
guardian angel	เทวดาผู้	thay-wá-daa phôo
	คุมครอง	khúm khrorng
angelic (adj)	ของเทวดา	khŏrng thay-wá-daa

apostle	สาวก	săa-wók
archangel	หัวหน้าทูตสวรรค์	hŭa nâa thôot sà-wăn
the Antichrist	ศัตรูของพระคริสต์	sàt-dtroo khŏrng phrá khrít

Church	โบสถ์	bòht
Bible	คัมภีร์ไบเบิ้ล	kham-phee bai-bêrn
biblical (adj)	ไบเบิ้ล	bai-bêrn

Old Testament	พันธสัญญาเดิม	phan-thá-săn-yaa derm
New Testament	พันธสัญญาใหม	phan-thá-săn-yaa mài
Gospel	พระวรสาร	phrá won săan
Holy Scripture	พระคัมภีร์ไบเบิล	phrá kham-phee bai-bern
Heaven	สวรรค์	sà-wăn

Commandment	บัญญัติ	ban-yàt
prophet	ผู้เผยพระวจนะ	phôo phŏie phrá wá-jà-ná
prophecy	คำพยากรณ์	kham phá-yaa-gon

Allah	อัลลอฮ์	an-lor
Mohammed	พระมูฮัมหมัด	phrá moo ham màt
the Koran	อัลกุรอาน	an gù-rá-aan

mosque	สุเหร่า	sù-rào
mullah	มุลละ	mun lá
prayer	บทสวดมนต์	bòt sùat mon
to pray (vi, vt)	สวด	sùat
pilgrimage	การจาริกแสวงบุญ	gaan jaa-rík sà-wăeng bun

pilgrim	ผู้แสวงบุญ	phôo sà-wǎeng bun
Mecca	มักกะฮ	mák-gà
church	โบสถ์	bòht
temple	วิหาร	wí-hǎan
cathedral	มหาวิหาร	má-hǎa wí-hǎan
Gothic (adj)	แบบโกธิก	bàep goh-thík
synagogue	โบสถ์ของศาสนายิว	bòht khǒrng sàat-sà-nǎa yiw
mosque	สุเหรา	sù-rào
chapel	ห้องสวดมนต์	hôrng sùat mon
abbey	วัด	wát
convent	สำนักแม่ชี	sǎm-nák mâe chee
monastery	อาราม	aa raam
bell (church ~s)	ระฆัง	rá-khang
bell tower	หอระฆัง	hǒr rá-khang
to ring (ab. bells)	ตีระฆัง	dtee rá-khang
cross	ไม้กางเขน	mái gaang khǎyn
cupola (roof)	หลังคาทรงโดม	lǎng kaa song dohm
icon	รูปเคารพ	rôop kpao-róp
soul	วิญญาณ	win-yaan
fate (destiny)	ชะตากรรม	chá-dtaa gam
evil (n)	ความชั่วราย	khwaam chûa ráai
good (n)	ความดี	khwaam dee
vampire	ผีดูดเลือด	phěe dòot lêuat
witch (evil ~)	แมมด	mâe mót
demon	ปีศาจ	bpee-sàat
spirit	ผี	phěe
redemption (giving us ~)	การไถ่ถอน	gaan thài thǒrn
to redeem (vt)	ไถถอน	thài thǒrn
church service	พิธีมิสซา	phí-tee mít-saa
to say mass	ประกอบพิธี	bprà-gòp phí-thee
	ศีลมหาสนิท	sěen má-hǎa sà-nìt
confession	การสารภาพ	gaan sǎa-rá-phâap
to confess (vi)	สารภาพ	sǎa-rá-phâap
saint (n)	นักบุญ	nák bun
sacred (holy)	ศักดิ์สิทธิ์	sàk-gà-dì sìt
holy water	น้ำมนต์	nám mon
ritual (n)	พิธีกรรม	phí-thee gam
ritual (adj)	แบบพิธีกรรม	bpaep phí-thee gam
sacrifice	การบูชายัญ	gaan boo-chaa yan
superstition	ความเชื่องมงาย	khwaam chêua ngom-ngaai
superstitious (adj)	เชื่อมงาย	chêua ngom-ngaai
afterlife	ชีวิตหลังความตาย	chee-wít lǎng khwaam dtaai
eternal life	ชีวิตอันเป็นนิรันดร์	chee-wít an bpen ní-ran

MISCELLANEOUS

249. Various useful words

English	Thai	Transliteration
background (green ~)	ฉากหลัง	chàak lǎng
balance (of the situation)	สมดุล	sà-má-dun
barrier (obstacle)	สิ่งกีดขวาง	sìng gèet-khwǎang
base (basis)	ฐาน	thǎan
beginning	จุดเริ่มต้น	jùt rêrm-dtôn
category	หมวดหมู่	mùat mòo
cause (reason)	สาเหตุ	sǎa-hàyt
choice	ตัวเลือก	dtua lêuak
coincidence	ความบังเอิญ	khwaam bang-ern
comfortable (~ chair)	สะดวกสบาย	sà-dùak sà-baai
comparison	การเปรียบเทียบ	gaan bprìap thîap
compensation	การชดเชย	gaan chót-choie
degree (extent, amount)	ระดับ	rá-dàp
development	การพัฒนา	gaan phát-thá-naa
difference	ความแตกต่าง	khwaam dtàek dtàang
effect (e.g. of drugs)	ผลกระทบ	phǒn grà-thóp
effort (exertion)	ความพยายาม	khwaam phá-yaa-yaam
element	องค์ประกอบ	ong bprà-gòrp
end (finish)	จบ	jòp
example (illustration)	ตัวอย่าง	dtua yàang
fact	ข้อเท็จจริง	khôr thét jing
frequent (adj)	ถี่	thèe
growth (development)	การเติบโต	gaan dtèrp dtoh
help	ความช่วยเหลือ	khwaam chûay lěua
ideal	อุดมคติ	u-dom khá-dtì
kind (sort, type)	ประเภท	bprà-phâyt
labyrinth	เขาวงกต	khǎo-wong-gòt
mistake, error	ข้อผิดพลาด	khôr phìt phlâat
moment	ช่วงเวลา	chûang way-laa
object (thing)	สิ่งของ	sìng khǒrng
obstacle	อุปสรรค	u-bpà-sàk
original (original copy)	ต้นฉบับ	dtôn chà-bàp
part (~ of sth)	ส่วน	sùan
particle, small part	อนุภาค	a-nú phâak
pause (break)	การหยุดพัก	gaan yùt phák
position	ตำแหน่ง	dtam-nàeng
principle	หลักการ	làk gaan
problem	ปัญหา	bpan-hǎa
process	กระบวนการ	grà-buan gaan

progress	ความก้าวหน้า	khwaam gâao nâa
property (quality)	คุณสมบัติ	khun-ná-sŏm-bàt
reaction	ปฏิกิริยา	bpà-dtì gì-rí-yaa
risk	ความเสี่ยง	khwaam sìang

secret	ความลับ	khwaam láp
series	ลำดับ	lam-dàp
shape (outer form)	รูปร่าง	rôop râang
situation	สถานการณ์	sà-thăan gaan
solution	ทางแก	thaang gâe

standard (adj)	เป็นมาตรฐาน	bpen mâat-dtrà-thăan
standard (level of quality)	มาตรฐาน	mâat-dtrà-thăan
stop (pause)	การหยุด	gaan yùt
style	สไตล	sà-dtai

system	ระบบ	rá-bòp
table (chart)	ตาราง	dtaa-raang
tempo, rate	จังหวะ	jang wà
term (word, expression)	คำ	kham
thing (object, item)	สิ่ง	sìng

truth (e.g. moment of ~)	ความจริง	khwaam jing
turn (please wait your ~)	ตา	dtaa
type (sort, kind)	ประเภท	bprà-phâyt
urgent (adj)	เร่งด่วน	râyng dùan
urgently	อย่างเร่งด่วน	yàang râyng dùan

utility (usefulness)	ความมีประโยชน์	khwaam mee bprà-yòht
variant (alternative)	ขอ	khôr
way (means, method)	วิธีทาง	wí-thĕe thaang
zone	โซน	sohn

250. Modifiers. Adjectives. Part 1

additional (adj)	เพิ่มเติม	phêrm dterm
ancient (~ civilization)	โบราณ	boh-raan
artificial (adj)	เทียม	thiam
back, rear (adj)	หลัง	lăng
bad (adj)	แย	yâe

beautiful (~ palace)	สวย	sŭay
beautiful (person)	สวย	sŭay
big (in size)	ใหญ่	yài
bitter (taste)	ขม	khŏm
blind (sightless)	ตาบอด	dtaa bòrt

calm, quiet (adj)	สงบ	sà-ngòp
careless (negligent)	ประมาท	bprà-màat
caring (~ father)	ที่ห่วงใย	thêe hùang yai
central (adj)	กลาง	glaang

| cheap (low-priced) | ถูก | thòok |
| cheerful (adj) | รื่นเริง | rêun rerng |

children's (adj)	ของเด็ก	khǒrng dèk
civil (~ law)	พลเรือน	phon-lá-reuan
clandestine (secret)	ลับ	láp

clean (free from dirt)	สะอาด	sà-àat
clear (explanation, etc.)	ชัดเจน	chát jayn
clever (intelligent)	ฉลาด	chà-làat
close (near in space)	ใกล้	glâi
closed (adj)	ปิด	bpìt

cloudless (sky)	ไร้เมฆ	rái mâyk
cold (drink, weather)	เย็น	yen
compatible (adj)	เข้ากันได้	khâo gan dâai
contented (satisfied)	มีความสุข	mee khwaam sùk
continuous (uninterrupted)	ต่อเนื่อง	dtòr nêuang

cool (weather)	เย็น	yen
dangerous (adj)	อันตราย	an-dtà-raai
dark (room)	มืด	mêut
dead (not alive)	ตาย	dtaai
dense (fog, smoke)	หนาแน่น	nǎa nâen

destitute (extremely poor)	ยากจน	yâak jon
different (not the same)	ต่างกัน	dtàang gan
difficult (decision)	ยาก	yâak
difficult (problem, task)	ยาก	yâak
dim, faint (light)	สลัว	sà-lǔa

dirty (not clean)	สกปรก	sòk-gà-bpròk
distant (in space)	หางไกล	hàang glai
dry (clothes, etc.)	แห้ง	hâeng
easy (not difficult)	ง่าย	ngâai

empty (glass, room)	ว่าง	wâang
even (e.g. ~ surface)	เรียบ	rîap
exact (amount)	ถูกต้อง	thòok dtôrng
excellent (adj)	ยอดเยี่ยม	yôrt yîam
excessive (adj)	เกินขีด	gern khèet

expensive (adj)	แพง	phaeng
exterior (adj)	ภายนอก	phaai nôrk
far (the ~ East)	ไกล	glai
fast (quick)	เร็ว	reo
fatty (food)	มันๆ	man man

fertile (land, soil)	อุดมสมบูรณ์	ù-dom sǒm-boon
flat (~ panel display)	แบน	baen
foreign (adj)	ต่างชาติ	dtàang châat
fragile (china, glass)	เปราะบาง	bpròr baang

free (at no cost)	ฟรี	free
free (unrestricted)	ไม่จำกัด	mâi jam-gàt
fresh (~ water)	จืด	jèut
fresh (e.g. ~ bread)	สด	sòt
frozen (food)	แช่แข็ง	châe khǎeng
full (completely filled)	เต็ม	dtem

gloomy (house, forecast)	มืดมัว	mêut mua
good (book, etc.)	ดี	dee
good, kind (kindhearted)	ดี	dee
grateful (adj)	สำนึกในบุญคุณ	săm-néuk nai bun khun
happy (adj)	มีความสุข	mee khwaam sùk
hard (not soft)	แข็ง	khăeng
heavy (in weight)	หนัก	nàk
hostile (adj)	เป็นศัตรู	bpen sàt-dtroo
hot (adj)	ร้อน	rórn
huge (adj)	ใหญ่	yài
humid (adj)	ชื้น	chéun
hungry (adj)	หิว	hĭw
ill (sick, unwell)	ป่วย	bpùay
immobile (adj)	ไม่ขยับ	mâi khà-yàp
important (adj)	สำคัญ	săm-khan
impossible (adj)	เป็นไปไม่ได้	bpen bpai mâi dâai
incomprehensible	เข้าใจไม่ได้	khâo jai mâi dâai
indispensable (adj)	จำเป็น	jam bpen
inexperienced (adj)	ขาดประสบการณ์	khàat bprà-sòp gaan
insignificant (adj)	ไม่สำคัญ	mâi săm-khan
interior (adj)	ภายใน	phaai nai
joint (~ decision)	รวมกัน	rûam gan
last (e.g. ~ week)	กลาย	glaai
last (final)	ท้ายสุด	tháai sùt
left (e.g. ~ side)	ซ้าย	sáai
legal (legitimate)	ทางกฎหมาย	thaang gòt măai
light (in weight)	เบา	bao
light (pale color)	อ่อน	òrn
limited (adj)	จำกัด	jam-gàt
liquid (fluid)	เหลว	lĕo
long (e.g. ~ hair)	ยาว	yaao
loud (voice, etc.)	ดัง	dang
low (voice)	ต่ำ	dtàm

251. Modifiers. Adjectives. Part 2

main (principal)	หลัก	làk
matt, matte	ด้าน	dâan
meticulous (job)	พิถีพิถัน	phí-thĕe-phí-thăn
mysterious (adj)	ลึกลับ	léuk láp
narrow (street, etc.)	แคบ	khâep
native (~ country)	ดั้งเดิม	dâng derm
nearby (adj)	ใกล้	glâi
needed (necessary)	จำเป็น	jam bpen
negative (~ response)	แง่ลบ	ngâe lóp
neighbouring (adj)	เพื่อนบ้าน	phêuan bâan
nervous (adj)	กระวนกระวาย	grà won grà waai

new (adj)	ใหม่	mài
next (e.g. ~ week)	ถัดไป	thàt bpai
nice (agreeable)	ดี	dee
pleasant (voice)	ดี	dee
normal (adj)	ปกติ	bpòk-gà-dtì
not big (adj)	ไม่ใหญ่	mâi yài
not difficult (adj)	ไม่ยาก	mâi yâak
obligatory (adj)	จำเป็น	jam bpen
old (house)	เก่า	gào
open (adj)	เปิด	bpèrt
opposite (adj)	ตรงข้าม	dtrorng khâam
ordinary (usual)	ปกติ	bpòk-gà-dtì
original (unusual)	ดั้งเดิม	dâng derm
past (recent)	ที่ผ่านมา	thêe phàan maa
permanent (adj)	ถาวร	thǎa-won
personal (adj)	ส่วนตัว	sùan dtua
polite (adj)	สุภาพ	sù-phâap
poor (not rich)	จน	jon
possible (adj)	เป็นไปได้	bpen bpai dâai
present (current)	ปัจจุบัน	bpàt-jù-ban
previous (adj)	ก่อนหน้า	gòrn nâa
principal (main)	หลัก	làk
private (~ jet)	ส่วนบุคคล	sùan bùk-khon
probable (adj)	เป็นไปได้	bpen bpai dâai
prolonged (e.g. ~ applause)	ยาวนาน	yaao naan
public (open to all)	สาธารณะ	sǎa-thaa-rá-ná
punctual (person)	ตรงเวลา	dtrorng way-laa
quiet (tranquil)	เงียบ	ngîap
rare (adj)	หายาก	hǎa yâak
raw (uncooked)	ดิบ	dìp
right (not left)	ขวา	khwǎa
right, correct (adj)	ถูก	thòok
ripe (fruit)	สุก	sùk
risky (adj)	เสี่ยง	sìang
sad (~ look)	เศร้า	sâo
sad (depressing)	เศร้า	sâo
safe (not dangerous)	ปลอดภัย	bplòrt phai
salty (food)	เค็ม	khem
satisfied (customer)	พอใจ	phor jai
second hand (adj)	มือสอง	meu sǒrng
shallow (water)	ตื้น	dtêun
sharp (blade, etc.)	คม	khom
short (in length)	สั้น	sân
short, short-lived (adj)	มีอายุสั้น	mee aa-yú sân
short-sighted (adj)	สายตาสั้น	sǎai dtaa sân
significant (notable)	สำคัญ	sǎm-khan

| similar (adj) | คุล้ายคลึง | khláai khleung |
| simple (easy) | ง่าย | ngâai |

skinny	ผอม	phŏrm
small (in size)	เล็ก	lék
smooth (surface)	เนียน	nian
soft (~ toys)	นิ่ม	nîm
solid (~ wall)	แข็ง	khăeng

sour (flavour, taste)	เปรี้ยว	bprîeow
spacious (house, etc.)	กว้างขวาง	gwâang khwăang
special (adj)	พิเศษ	phí-sàyt
straight (line, road)	ตรง	dtrorng
strong (person)	แข็งแกร่ง	khăeng gràeng

stupid (foolish)	โง่	ngôh
suitable (e.g. ~ for drinking)	ที่เหมาะสม	thêe mòr sŏm
sunny (day)	แดดแรง	dàet raeng
superb, perfect (adj)	ยอดเยี่ยม	yôrt yîam
swarthy (dark-skinned)	คล้ำ	khlám

sweet (sugary)	หวาน	wăan
tanned (adj)	ผิวดำแดง	phĭw dam daeng
tasty (delicious)	อร่อย	à-ròi
tender (affectionate)	อ่อนโยน	òn yohn

the highest (adj)	สูงสุด	sŏong sùt
the most important	ที่สำคัญที่สุด	thêe săm-khan thêe sùt
the nearest	ใกล้ที่สุด	glâi thêe sùt
the same, equal (adj)	เหมือนกัน	mĕuan gan

thick (e.g. ~ fog)	หนา	năa
thick (wall, slice)	หนา	năa
thin (person)	ผอม	phŏrm
tight (~ shoes)	คับ	kháp
tired (exhausted)	เหนื่อย	nèuay

tiring (adj)	น่าเหนื่อยหน่าย	nâa nèuay nàai
transparent (adj)	ใส	săi
unclear (adj)	ไม่ชัดเจน	mâi chát jayn
unique (exceptional)	อย่างเดียว	yàang dieow
various (adj)	หลาย	lăai

warm (moderately hot)	อุ่น	ùn
wet (e.g. ~ clothes)	เปียก	bpìak
whole (entire, complete)	ทั้งหมด	tháng mòt
wide (e.g. ~ road)	กว้าง	gwâang
young (adj)	หนุ่ม	nùm

MAIN 500 VERBS

252. Verbs A-C

to accompany (vt)	ร่วมไปด้วย	rûam bpai dûay
to accuse (vt)	กลาวหา	glàao hăa
to acknowledge (admit)	ยอมรับ	yorm ráp
to act (take action)	ปฏิบัติ	bpà-dtì-bàt
to add (supplement)	เพิ่ม	phêrm
to address (speak to)	พูดกับ	phôot gàp
to admire (vi)	ชมเชย	chom choie
to advertise (vt)	โฆษณา	khôht-sà-naa
to advise (vt)	แนะนำ	náe nam
to affirm (assert)	ยืนยัน	yeun yan
to agree (say yes)	เห็นด้วย	hĕn dûay
to aim (to point a weapon)	เล็ง	leng
to allow (sb to do sth)	อนุญาตให้	a-nú-yâat hâi
to amputate (vt)	ตัดอวัยวะ	dtàt a-wai-wá
to answer (vi, vt)	ตอบ	dtòrp
to apologize (vi)	ขอโทษ	khŏr thôht
to appear (come into view)	ปรากฏ	bpraa-gòt
to applaud (vi, vt)	ปรบมือ	bpròp meu
to appoint (assign)	มอบหมาย	môrp măai
to approach (come closer)	เข้าใกล้	khâo glâi
to arrive (ab. train)	มาถึง	maa thĕung
to ask (~ sb to do sth)	ขอ	khŏr
to aspire to …	ปรารถนา	bpràat-thà-năa
to assist (help)	ช่วย	chûay
to attack (mil.)	โจมตี	johm dtee
to attain (objectives)	บรรลุ	ban-lú
to avenge (get revenge)	แก้แค้น	gâe kháen
to avoid (danger, task)	หลีกเลี่ยง	lèek lîang
to award (give a medal to)	มอบรางวัล	môrp raang-wan
to battle (vi)	สู้รบ	sôo róp
to be (vi)	เป็น	bpen
to be a cause of …	เป็นสาเหตุ…	bpen săa-hàyt…
to be afraid	กลัว	glua
to be angry (with …)	โกรธ	gròht
to be at war	ทำสงคราม	tham sŏng-khraam
to be based (on …)	อิง	ing
to be bored	เบื่อ	bèua

233

to be convinced	ถูกโน้มน้าว	thook nóhm náao
to be enough	พอเพียง	phor phiang
to be envious	อิจฉา	ìt-chǎa
to be indignant	ขุนเคือง	khùn kheuang
to be interested in ...	สนใจ	sŏn jai
to be lost in thought	มัวแต่ครุ่นคิด	mua dtàe khrûn-khít
to be lying (~ on the table)	อยู่	yòo
to be needed	เป็นที่ต้องการ	bpen thêe dtôrng gaan
to be perplexed (puzzled)	สับสน	sàp sŏn
to be preserved	ได้รับการรักษา	dâai ráp gaan rák-sǎa
to be required	มีความจำเป็น	mee khwaam jam bpen
to be surprised	ประหลาดใจ	bprà-làat jai
to be worried	กังวล	gang-won
to beat (to hit)	ตี	dtee
to become (e.g. ~ old)	กลายเป็น	glaai bpen
to behave (vi)	ประพฤติตัว	bprà-phréut dtua
to believe (think)	คิด	khít
to belong to ...	เป็นของของ...	bpen khǒrng khǒrng...
to berth (moor)	จอดเรือ	jòrt reua
to blind (other drivers)	ทำให้มองไม่เห็น	tam hâi morng mâi hěn
to blow (wind)	เป่า	bpào
to blush (vi)	หน้าแดง	nâa daeng
to boast (vi)	อวด	ùat
to borrow (money)	ขอยืม	khŏr yeum
to break (branch, toy, etc.)	ทำพัง	tham phang
to breathe (vi)	หายใจ	hǎai jai
to bring (sth)	นำมา	nam maa
to burn (paper, logs)	เผา	phǎo
to buy (purchase)	ซื้อ	séu
to call (~ for help)	เรียก	rîak
to call (yell for sb)	เรียก	rîak
to calm down (vt)	ทำให้...สงบ	tham hâi...sà-ngòp
can (v aux)	สามารถ	sǎa-mâat
to cancel (call off)	ยกเลิก	yók lêrk
to cast off (of a boat or ship)	ถอดออก	thòrt òrk
to catch (e.g. ~ a ball)	รับ	ráp
to change (~ one's opinion)	เปลี่ยน	bplìan
to change (exchange)	แลกเปลี่ยน	lâek bplìan
to charm (vt)	หว่านเสน่ห์	wàan sà-nàay
to choose (select)	เลือก	lêuak
to chop off (with an axe)	ตัดออก	dtàt òrk
to clean (e.g. kettle from scale)	ทำความสะอาด	tham khwaam sà-àat
to clean (shoes, etc.)	ทำความสะอาด	tham khwaam sà-àat
to clean up (tidy)	จัดระเบียบ	jàt rá-bìap
to close (vt)	ปิด	bpìt

to comb one's hair	หวีผม	wěe phǒm
to come down (the stairs)	ลง	long
to come out (book)	ออกวางจำหน่าย	òrk waang jam-nàai
to compare (vt)	เปรียบเทียบ	bprìap thîap
to compensate (vt)	ชดเชย	chót-choie

to compete (vi)	แข่งขัน	khàeng khǎn
to compile (~ a list)	รวบรวม	rûap ruam
to complain (vi, vt)	บ่น	bòn
to complicate (vt)	ทำให้...ซับซ้อน	tham hâi...sáp són

to compose (music, etc.)	แต่ง	dtàeng
to compromise (reputation)	ทำให้...เสียเกียรติ	tham hâi...sǐa gìat
to concentrate (vi)	ตั้งสมาธิ	dtâng sà-maa-thí
to confess (criminal)	สารภาพ	sǎa-rá-phâap

to confuse (mix up)	สับสน	sàp sǒn
to congratulate (vt)	แสดงความยินดี	sà-daeng khwaam yin dee
to consult (doctor, expert)	ปรึกษา	bprèuk-sǎa
to continue (~ to do sth)	ดำเนินการต่อ	dam-nern gaan dtòr

to control (vt)	ควบคุม	khûap khum
to convince (vt)	โน้มน้าว	nóhm náao
to cooperate (vi)	ร่วมมือ	rûam meu
to coordinate (vt)	ประสานงาน	bprà-sǎan ngaan

to correct (an error)	แก้ไข	gâe khǎi
to cost (vt)	มีราคา	mee raa-khaa
to count (money, etc.)	นับ	náp
to count on ...	พึ่งพา	phêung phaa

to crack (ceiling, wall)	แตก	dtàek
to create (vt)	สร้าง	sâang
to crush, to squash (~ a bug)	บี้	bêe
to cry (weep)	ร้องไห้	rórng hâi
to cut off (with a knife)	ตัดออก	dtàt òrk

253. Verbs D-G

to dare (~ to do sth)	กล้า	glâa
to date from ...	มาตั้งแต่...	maa dtâng dtàe...
to deceive (vi, vt)	หลอก	lòrk
to decide (~ to do sth)	ตัดสินใจ	dtàt sǐn jai

to decorate (tree, street)	ตกแต่ง	dtòk dtàeng
to dedicate (book, etc.)	อุทิศ	u thít
to defend (a country, etc.)	ปกป้อง	bpòk bpôrng
to defend oneself	ปกป้อง	bpòk bpôrng

to demand (request firmly)	เรียกร้อง	rîak rórng
to denounce (vt)	ประณาม	bprà-naam
to deny (vt)	ปฏิเสธ	bpà-dtì-sàyt
to depend on ...	พึ่งพา...	phêung phaa...
to deprive (vt)	ตัด	dtàt

to deserve (vt)	สมควรได้รับ	sŏm khuan dâai ráp
to design (machine, etc.)	ออกแบบ	òrk bàep
to desire (want, wish)	ปรารถนา	bpràat-thà-năa
to despise (vt)	รังเกียจ	rang gìat

to destroy (documents, etc.)	ทำลาย	tham laai
to differ (from sth)	แตกต่าง	dtàek dtàang
to dig (tunnel, etc.)	ขุด	khùt
to direct (point the way)	บอกทาง	bòrk thaang

to disappear (vi)	หายไป	hăai bpai
to discover (new land, etc.)	คนพบ	khón phóp
to discuss (vt)	หารือ	hăa-reu
to distribute (leaflets, etc.)	แจกจ่าย	jàek jàai

to disturb (vt)	รบกวน	róp guan
to dive (vi)	ดำ	dam
to divide (math)	หาร	hăan
to do (vt)	ทำ	tham

to do the laundry	ซักผ้า	sák phâa
to double (increase)	เพิ่มเป็นสองเท่า	phêrm bpen sŏrng thâo
to doubt (have doubts)	สงสัย	sŏng-săi
to draw a conclusion	สรุป	sà-rùp

to dream (daydream)	ฝัน	făn
to dream (in sleep)	ฝัน	făn
to drink (vi, vt)	ดื่ม	dèum
to drive a car	ขับรถ	khàp rót
to drive away (scare away)	ไล่ไป	lâi bpai

to drop (let fall)	ทำให้...ตก	tham hâi...dtòk
to drown (ab. person)	จมน้ำ	jom náam
to dry (clothes, hair)	ทำให้...แห้ง	tham hâi...hâeng
to eat (vi, vt)	กิน	gin

to eavesdrop (vi)	ลอบฟัง	lôrp fang
to emit (diffuse - odor, etc.)	ปล่อย	bplòi
to enjoy oneself	มีความสุข	mee khwaam sùk
to enter (on the list)	เขียน...ใส่	khĭan...sài

to enter (room, house, etc.)	เข้า	khâo
to entertain (amuse)	ทำให้รื่นเริง	thám hâi rêun rerng
to equip (fit out)	ติด	dtìt
to examine (proposal)	ตรวจสอบ	dtrùat sòrp

to exchange (sth)	แลกเปลี่ยน	lâek bplìan
to excuse (forgive)	ให้อภัย	hâi a-phai
to exist (vi)	มีอยู่	mee yòo
to expect (anticipate)	คาดหวัง	khâat wăng

to expect (foresee)	คาดหวัง	khâat wăng
to expel (from school, etc.)	ไล่ออก	lâi òrk
to explain (vt)	อธิบาย	à-thí-baai
to express (vt)	แสดงออก	sà-daeng òrk
to extinguish (a fire)	ดับ	dàp

to fall in love (with …)	ตกหลุมรัก	dtòk lǔm rák
to fancy (vt)	ชอบ	chôrp
to feed (provide food)	ให้อาหาร	hâi aa-hǎan

to fight (against the enemy)	สู้	sôo
to fight (vi)	สู้	sôo
to fill (glass, bottle)	เติมให้เต็ม	dterm hâi dtem
to find (~ lost items)	ค้นหา	khón hǎa

to finish (vt)	จบ	jòp
to fish (angle)	จับปลา	jàp bplaa
to fit (ab. dress, etc.)	เหมาะ	mò
to flatter (vt)	ชม	chom

to fly (bird, plane)	บิน	bin
to follow … (come after)	ไปตาม…	bpai dtaam…
to forbid (vt)	ห้าม	hâam
to force (compel)	บังคับ	bang-kháp

to forget (vi, vt)	ลืม	leum
to forgive (pardon)	ยกโทษให้	yók thôht hâi
to form (constitute)	ก่อตั้ง	gòr dtâng
to get dirty (vi)	สกปรก	sòk-gà-bpròk

to get infected (with …)	ติดเชื้อ	dtìt chéua
to get irritated	หงุดหงิด	ngùt-ngìt
to get married	แต่งงาน	dtàeng ngaan
to get rid of …	กำจัด…	gam-jàt…

to get tired	เหนื่อย	nèuay
to get up (arise from bed)	ลุกขึ้น	lúk khêun
to give (vt)	ให้	hâi
to give a bath (to bath)	อาบน้ำให้	àap náam hâi

to give a hug, to hug (vt)	กอด	gòrt
to give in (yield to)	ยอม	yorm
to glimpse (vt)	เหลือบมอง	lèuap morng
to go (by car, etc.)	ไป	bpai

to go (on foot)	ไป	bpai
to go for a swim	ว่ายน้ำ	wâai náam
to go out (for dinner, etc.)	ออกไป	òrk bpai
to go to bed (go to sleep)	ไปนอน	bpai norn

to greet (vt)	ทักทาย	thák thaai
to grow (plants)	ปลูก	bplòok
to guarantee (vt)	รับประกัน	ráp bprà-gan
to guess (the answer)	คาดเดา	khâat dao

254. Verbs H-M

to hand out (distribute)	แจกจ่าย	jàek jàai
to hang (curtains, etc.)	แขวน	khwǎen
to have (vt)	มี	mee

| to have a bath | อาบน้ำ | àap náam |
| to have a try | ลอง | lorng |

to have breakfast	ทานอาหารเช้า	thaan aa-hăan cháo
to have dinner	ทานอาหารเย็น	thaan aa-hăan yen
to have lunch	ทานอาหารเที่ยง	thaan aa-hăan thîang
to head (group, etc.)	นำ	nam
to hear (vt)	ได้ยิน	dâai yin

to heat (vt)	อุ่นให้ร้อน	ùn hâi rórn
to help (vt)	ช่วย	chûay
to hide (vt)	ซ่อน	sôrn
to hire (e.g. ~ a boat)	จ้าง	jâang
to hire (staff)	จ้าง	jâang

to hope (vi, vt)	หวัง	wăng
to hunt (for food, sport)	ล่าหา	lâa hăa
to hurry (vi)	รีบ	rêep
to imagine (to picture)	มีจินตนาการ	mee jin-dtà-naa gaan
to imitate (vt)	เลียนแบบ	lian bàep

to implore (vt)	ขอร้อง	khŏr rórng
to import (vt)	นำเข้า	nam khâo
to increase (vi)	เพิ่ม	phêrm
to increase (vt)	เพิ่ม	phêrm
to infect (vt)	ทำให้ติดเชื้อ	tham hâi dtìt chéua

to influence (vt)	มีอิทธิพล	mee ìt-thí phon
to inform (e.g. ~ the police about …)	แจ้ง	jâeng
to inform (vt)	แจ้ง	jâeng
to inherit (vt)	รับมรดก	ráp mor-rá-dòrk
to inquire (about …)	สอบถาม	sòrp thăam

to insert (put in)	สอดใส่	sòrt sài
to insinuate (imply)	พูดเป็นนัย	phôot bpen nai
to insist (vi, vt)	ยืนยัน	yeun yan
to inspire (vt)	บันดาลใจ	ban-daan jai
to instruct (teach)	สอน	sŏrn

to insult (offend)	ดูถูก	doo thòok
to interest (vt)	ทำให้...สนใจ	tham hâi...sŏn jai
to intervene (vi)	แทรกแซง	sâek saeng
to introduce (sb to sb)	แนะนำ	náe nam

to invent (machine, etc.)	ประดิษฐ์	bprà-dìt
to invite (vt)	เชิญ	chern
to iron (clothes)	รีด	rêet
to irritate (annoy)	ทำให้...รำคาญ	tham hâi...ram-khaan
to isolate (vt)	แยก	yâek

to join (political party, etc.)	เข้าร่วมใน	khâo rûam nai
to joke (be kidding)	ลอเล่น	lór lên
to keep (old letters, etc.)	เก็บ	gèp
to keep silent, to hush	นิ่งเงียบ	nîng ngîap
to kill (vt)	ฆ่า	khâa

to knock (on the door)	เคาะ	khór
to know (sb)	รู้จัก	róo jàk
to know (sth)	รู้	róo
to laugh (vi)	หัวเราะ	hŭa rór
to launch (start up)	เปิด	bpèrt
to leave (~ for Mexico)	ออกเดินทาง	òrk dern thaang
to leave (forget sth)	ลืม	leum
to leave (spouse)	หย่า	yàa
to liberate (city, etc.)	ปลดปล่อย	bplòt bplòi
to lie (~ on the floor)	นอน	norn
to lie (tell untruth)	โกหก	goh-hòk
to light (campfire, etc.)	จุดไฟ	jùt fai
to light up (illuminate)	ทำให้สว่าง	tham hâi sà-wàang
to limit (vt)	จำกัด	jam-gàt
to listen (vi)	ฟัง	fang
to live (~ in France)	อยู่อาศัย	yòo aa-săi
to live (exist)	มีชีวิต	mee chee-wít
to load (gun)	ใส่กระสุน	sài grà-sŭn
to load (vehicle, etc.)	ขนของ	khŏn khŏrng
to look (I'm just ~ing)	มองดู	morng doo
to look for ... (search)	หา	hăa
to look like (resemble)	เหมือน	mĕuan
to lose (umbrella, etc.)	ทำหาย	tham hăai
to love (e.g. ~ dancing)	ชอบ	chôrp
to love (sb)	รัก	rák
to lower (blind, head)	ลด	lót
to make (~ dinner)	ทำ	tham
to make a mistake	ทำผิดพลาด	tham phìt phlâat
to make angry	ทำให้...โกรธ	tham hâi...gròht
to make easier	ทำให้...ง่ายขึ้น	tham hâi...ngâai khêun
to make multiple copies	ถ่ายสำเนาหลายฉบับ	thàai săm-nao lăai chà-bàp
to make the acquaintance	ทำความรู้จัก	tham khwaam róo jàk
to make use (of ...)	ใช้	chái
to manage, to run	จัดการ	jàt gaan
to mark (make a mark)	ทำเครื่องหมาย	tham khrêuang măai
to mean (signify)	บ่งบอก	bòng bòrk
to memorize (vt)	จดจำ	jòt jam
to mention (talk about)	กล่าวถึง	glàao thĕung
to miss (school, etc.)	พลาด	phlâat
to mix (combine, blend)	ผสม	phà-sŏm
to mock (make fun of)	เยาะเย้ย	yór-yóie
to move (to shift)	ย้าย	yáai
to multiply (math)	คูณ	khoon
must (v aux)	ต้อง	dtôrng

255. Verbs N-R

to name, to call (vt)	เรียก	rîak
to negotiate (vi)	เจรจา	jayn-rá-jaa
to note (write down)	จดโน้ต	jòt nóht
to notice (see)	สังเกต	săng-gàyt
to obey (vi, vt)	เชื่อฟัง	chêua fang
to object (vi, vt)	คาน	kháan
to observe (see)	สังเกตการณ์	săng-gàyt gaan
to offend (vt)	ลวงเกิน	lûang gern
to omit (word, phrase)	เว้น	wén
to open (vt)	เปิด	bpèrt
to order (in restaurant)	สั่งอาหาร	sàng aa-hăan
to order (mil.)	สั่งการ	sàng gaan
to organize (concert, party)	จัด	jàt
to overestimate (vt)	ตีค่าสูงเกิน	dtee khâa sŏong gern
to own (possess)	เป็นเจ้าของ	bpen jâo khŏrng
to participate (vi)	มีส่วนรวม	mee sùan rûam
to pass through (by car, etc.)	ผ่าน	phàan
to pay (vi, vt)	จ่าย	jàai
to peep, to spy on	แอบดู	àep doo
to penetrate (vt)	แทรกซึม	sâek seum
to permit (vt)	อนุญาต	a-nú-yâat
to pick (flowers)	เก็บ	gèp
to place (put, set)	วาง	waang
to plan (~ to do sth)	วางแผน	waang phăen
to play (actor)	เล่นบท	lên bòt
to play (children)	เล่น	lên
to point (~ the way)	ชี้	chée
to pour (liquid)	ริน	rin
to pray (vi, vt)	ภาวนา	phaa-wá-naa
to prefer (vt)	ชอบ	chôrp
to prepare (~ a plan)	เตรียม	dtriam
to present (sb to sb)	แนะนำ	náe nam
to preserve (peace, life)	รักษา	rák-săa
to prevail (vt)	ชนะ	chá-ná
to progress (move forward)	คืบหน้า	khêup nâa
to promise (vt)	สัญญา	săn-yaa
to pronounce (vt)	ออกเสียง	òrk sĭang
to propose (vt)	เสนอ	sà-nĕr
to protect (e.g. ~ nature)	ปกป้อง	bpòk bpôrng
to protest (vi)	ประท้วง	bprà-thúang
to prove (vt)	พิสูจน์	phí-sòot
to provoke (vt)	ยั่วยุ	yûa yú
to pull (~ the rope)	ดึง	deung
to punish (vt)	ลงโทษ	long thôht

to push (~ the door)	ผลัก	phlàk
to put away (vt)	เก็บที่	gèp thêe
to put in order	จัดเรียง	jàt riang
to put, to place	วาง	waang

to quote (cite)	อ้างอิง	âang ing
to reach (arrive at)	ไปถึง	bpai thěung
to read (vi, vt)	อ่าน	àan
to realize (a dream)	ทำให้...เป็นจริง	tham hâi...bpen jing
to recognize (identify sb)	จดจำ	jòt jam

to recommend (vt)	แนะนำ	náe nam
to recover (~ from flu)	ฟื้นตัว	féun dtua
to redo (do again)	ทำซ้ำ	tham sám
to reduce (speed, etc.)	ลด	lót

to refuse (~ sb)	ปฏิเสธ	bpà-dtì-sàyt
to regret (be sorry)	เสียใจ	sĭa jai
to reinforce (vt)	เสริม	sěrm
to remember (Do you ~ me?)	จำ	jam

to remember (I can't ~ her name)	จำ	jam
to remind of ...	นึกถึง	néuk thěung
to remove (~ a stain)	ลางออก	láang òrk
to remove (~ an obstacle)	กำจัด	gam-jàt

to rent (sth from sb)	เช่า	châo
to repair (mend)	ซอม	sôrm
to repeat (say again)	พูดซ้ำ	phôot sám
to report (make a report)	รายงาน	raai ngaan

to reproach (vt)	ตำหนิ	dtam-nì
to reserve, to book	จอง	jorng
to restrain (hold back)	ยับยั้ง	yáp yáng
to return (come back)	กลับ	glàp

to risk, to take a risk	เสี่ยง	sìang
to rub out (erase)	ขัดออก	khàt òrk
to run (move fast)	วิ่ง	wîng
to rush (hurry sb)	รีบ	rêep

256. Verbs S-W

to satisfy (please)	ทำให้...พอใจ	tham hâi...phor jai
to save (rescue)	ช่วยชีวิต	chûay chee-wít
to say (~ thank you)	พูด	phôot
to scold (vt)	ด่ว่า	dù wâa

to scratch (with claws)	ข่วน	khùan
to select (to pick)	เลือก	lêuak
to sell (goods)	ขาย	khǎai
to send (a letter)	ส่ง	sòng
to send back (vt)	ส่งคืน	sòng kheun

to sense (~ danger)	รับรู้	ráp róo
to sentence (vt)	พิพากษา	phí-phâak-săa
to serve (in restaurant)	เซิร์ฟ	sêrf
to settle (a conflict)	ยุติ,	yút-dtì
to shake (vt)	เขย่า	khà-yào
to shave (vi)	โกน	gohn
to shine (gleam)	ส่องแสง	sòrng săeng
to shiver (with cold)	หนาวสั่น	năao sàn
to shoot (vi)	ยิง	ying
to shout (vi)	ตะโกน	dtà-gohn
to show (to display)	แสดง	sà-daeng
to shudder (vi)	สั่น	sàn
to sigh (vi)	ถอนหายใจ	thŏrn hăai-jai
to sign (document)	ลงนาม	long naam
to signify (mean)	บงบอก	bòng bòrk
to simplify (vt)	ทำให้ง่ายขึ้น,	tham hâi ngâai khêun
to sin (vi)	ทำบาป	tham bàap
to sit (be sitting)	นั่ง	nâng
to sit down (vi)	นั่ง	nâng
to smell (emit an odor)	มีกลิ่น	mee glìn
to smell (inhale the odor)	ดมกลิ่น	dom glìn
to smile (vi)	ยิ้ม	yím
to snap (vi, ab. rope)	ขาด	khàat
to solve (problem)	แก้ไข	gâe khăi
to sow (seed, crop)	หว่าน	wàan
to spill (liquid)	ทำให้...หก	tham hâi...hòk
to spill out, scatter (flour, etc.)	หก	hòk
to spit (vi)	ถุย	thŭi
to stand (toothache, cold)	ทน	thon
to start (begin)	เริ่ม	rêrm
to steal (money, etc.)	ขโมย	khà-moi
to stop (for pause, etc.)	หยุด	yùt
to stop (please ~ calling me)	หยุด	yùt
to stop talking	หยุดพูด	yùt phôot
to stroke (caress)	ลูบ	lôop
to study (vt)	เรียน	rian
to suffer (feel pain)	ทรมาน	thor-rá-maan
to support (cause, idea)	สนับสนุน	sà-nàp-sà-nŭn
to suppose (assume)	สมมุติ	sŏm mút
to surface (ab. submarine)	ขึ้นมาที่ผิวน้ำ	khêun maa thêe phĭw náam
to surprise (amaze)	ทำให้...ประหลาดใจ	tham hâi...bprà-làat jai
to suspect (vt)	สงสัย	sŏng-săi
to swim (vi)	ว่ายน้ำ	wâai náam
to take (get hold of)	เอา	ao
to take a rest	พัก	phák

to take away (e.g. about waiter)	เอาไป	ao bpai
to take off (aeroplane)	บินขึ้น	bin khêun
to take off (painting, curtains, etc.)	เอาออก	ao òrk
to take pictures	ถ่ายภาพ	thàai phâap
to talk to ...	คุยกับ	khui gàp
to teach (give lessons)	สอน	sŏrn
to tear off, to rip off (vt)	ฉีก	chèek
to tell (story, joke)	เล่า	lâo
to thank (vt)	แสดงความขอบคุณ	sà-daeng khwaam khòrp kun
to think (believe)	เชื่อ	chêua
to think (vi, vt)	คิด	khít
to threaten (vt)	ขู่	khòo
to throw (stone, etc.)	ขว้าง	khwâang
to tie to ...	ผูกกับ...	phòok gàp...
to tie up (prisoner)	มัด	mát
to tire (make tired)	ทำให้...เหนื่อย	tham hâi...nèuay
to touch (one's arm, etc.)	สัมผัส	sǎm-phàt
to tower (over ...)	ทำให้...สูงเหนือ	tham hâi...sǒong nĕua
to train (animals)	ฝึก	fèuk
to train (sb)	ฝึก	fèuk
to train (vi)	ฝึก	fèuk
to transform (vt)	เปลี่ยนแปลง	bplìan bplaeng
to translate (vt)	แปล	bplae
to treat (illness)	รักษา	rák-sǎa
to trust (vt)	เชื่อ	chêua
to try (attempt)	พยายาม	phá-yaa-yaam
to turn (e.g., ~ left)	เลี้ยว	líeow
to turn away (vi)	ม้วนหน้า	múan nâa
to turn off (the light)	ปิด	bpìt
to turn on (computer, etc.)	เปิด	bpèrt
to turn over (stone, etc.)	พลิก	phlík
to underestimate (vt)	ดูถูก	doo thòok
to underline (vt)	ขีดเส้นใต้	khèet sên dtâi
to understand (vt)	เข้าใจ	khâo jai
to undertake (vt)	ดำเนินการ	dam-nern gaan
to unite (vt)	ทำให้...รวมกัน	tham hâi...ruam gan
to untie (vt)	แก้มัด	gâe mát
to use (phrase, word)	ใช้	chái
to vaccinate (vt)	ฉีดวัคซีน	chèet wák-seen
to vote (vi)	ลงคะแนน	long khá-naen
to wait (vt)	รอ	ror
to wake (sb)	ปลุกให้ตื่น	bplùk hâi dtèun
to want (wish, desire)	ต้องการ	dtôrng gaan
to warn (of a danger)	เตือน	dteuan

to wash (clean)	ล้าง	láang
to water (plants)	รดน้ำ	rót náam
to wave (the hand)	โบกมือ	bòhk meu
to weigh (have weight)	มีน้ำหนัก	mee nám nàk
to work (vi)	ทำงาน	tham ngaan
to worry (make anxious)	ทำให้...เป็นห่วง	tham hâi...bpen hùang
to worry (vi)	เป็นห่วง	bpen hùang
to wrap (parcel, etc.)	ห่อ	hòr
to wrestle (sport)	มวยปล้ำ	muay bplâm
to write (vt)	เขียน	khĭan
to write down	จด	jòt